Send for Freddie

The Story of Monty's Chief of Staff
Major-General Sir Francis de Guingand
KBE, CB, DSO

CHARLES RICHARDSON

WILLIAM KIMBER · LONDON

First published in 1987 by
WILLIAM KIMBER & CO. LIMITED
100 Jermyn Street, London, SW1Y 6EE

ISBN 0–7183–0641–4

Photoset by Grove Graphics, Tring, Hertfordshire
and printed in Great Britain by
Adlard & Son Ltd The Garden City Press,
Letchworth, Herts. SG6 1JS

*Dedicated to those comrades,
known and unknown, who
served Montgomery well*

Contents

List of Illustrations

Author's Note

'Freddie' de Guingand had a host of friends in many walks of life: I was fortunate to be one of them. We first met as fellow instructors at the Middle East Staff College, Haifa Palestine in 1940. Later, when he joined Auchinleck's Eighth Army Headquarters in August 1942, he found me there already as GSO I (Plans); thereafter I served with him until the end of the Sicily campaign. I rejoined him in April 1944 as his Brigadier (Plans) at the headquarters of 21st Army Group, and maintained contact with him after the war. In 1947 he asked me to join him in Johannesburg, but I decided to continue serving in the Army.

His enigmatic relationship with Montgomery has always puzzled and at times dismayed the small band of friends who were aware of it, particularly those who had had personal experience of his outstanding services to Montgomery as Chief of Staff. This aspect of his life and the versatility and success of his post-war career prompted me to write this book.

I was encouraged to proceed by Sir Denis Hamilton, and by his son Nigel, author of *Monty*, Vols I to III, which contain much material about Freddie de Guingand. Those volumes provided me with a historical thread to guide my recollections through the critical years of Freddie's war service: this has proved invaluable. Sir Denis arranged for me to have prior access to the relevant Montgomery archives at the Imperial War Museum, including Montgomery's letters to Freddie from 1934 to 1969, and Nigel Hamilton handed over to me voluminous unpublished transcripts which were the raw material used by Freddie in parts of his four published books. The Dwight D. Eisenhower Library in the USA provided me with copies of Freddie's correspondence with Eisenhower and Bedell Smith, and I had much assistance from the late General Sir Frank Simpson and Lady Simpson. To all the above I record my thanks.

Sir Edgar Williams, Montgomery's Intelligence Chief, with whom I served in the war, gained a comprehensive and intimate knowledge of both Freddie and Montgomery; generous with his help, he read and commented on the typescript. A draft has also been read by 'Johnny' Henderson (J. R. Henderson CVO MBE), who as ADC to Montgomery witnessed the development of his master's personal relationship with Freddie in the war, and maintained his friendship with both of them in the post-war years. Of a different generation, my friend Sir Michael Gow also read the typescript, and gave me many helpful comments.

Mr David Willers, London Director of the South Africa Foundation, very kindly read an early draft of Chapter 14: 'The Future of Africa'.

Viscount Montgomery gave his immediate consent to my request to quote his father's writings and I am most grateful to him.

I should like to thank also the members of Freddie de Guingand's family who have given me such willing help and cooperation in the researches I have undertaken: Mrs M. P. Frere, Freddie's sister; Freddie's daughter Marylou (Mrs. J. C. Henderson) and her husband; her mother Arlie, now Lady Sackville; Mrs R. M. R. Forster, and Mrs Angela de Guingand.

Finally, there are many friends, acquaintances, and colleagues of Freddie who have been immensely helpful with their recollections and advice. To all those listed below I record my appreciation and gratitude.

Mr John Adler
Mr David Andrews
Brigadier E. F. E. Armstrong
Mrs Barlow
Lt-General Sir Roger Bower
Air Chief Marshal Sir Harry Broadhurst
Field Marshal the Lord Carver
The Rt Hon the Lord Cayzer
The Rt Hon the Lord Chalfont
Mrs Cobb

Brigadier G. H. Cree
Sir Robert Crichton-Brown
Brigadier J. M. Cubiss
Brigadier P. Cuddon
Edwin R. Culver III
Mrs H. Cunningham-Reid
Mrs P. J. Curlewis
Major-General Sir Charles Dalton
Lt Colonel C. P. Dawnay
Lt Colonel Carlo d'Este

Mr John Devlin
Major-General Sir Gerald
  Duke
Major-General Sir Charles
  Dunphie
Mrs Lavinia Greacen
General Sir John Hackett
Mr E. Harwood
Mrs Brian Hawkins
Lady Henderson
The Rt Hon the Lord Home
  of the Hirsel
Sir David Hunt
Elsa Hurchler
General Sir William Jackson
Brigadier J. R. B. Knox
Sir Harry Llewellyn
Mr Brian Maples
Sir William Mather
The Hon David Montagu
Brigadier E. C. W. Myers
Mr Paul Odgers

Major-General M. ST J.
  Oswald
Lady Pelly
The Rt Hon the Lord
  Pritchard
The Rt Hon the Lord Plowden
Major General G. P. B.
  Roberts
Dr Anton Rupert
Professor Eric Samuel
Major General E. K. G.
  Sixsmith
Father Alberic Stacpoole
Lt-Colonel David Stirling
The Rev Canon Strangeways
Conrad Swan Esq, York
  Herald of Arms
Brigadier G. Taylor
Mr Malcolm Thompson
Air Commodore E. W.
  Towsey
David J. Willers

I must record my thanks to the staffs of those institutions who have been very helpful in providing relevant material: the Directors and staff of the Imperial War Museum, the Liddell Hart Centre at King's College London, the Public Record Office, the Librarians of the Ministry of Defence, the Staff College Camberley, and the Royal Military Academy Sandhurst. Also Major-General H. M. Tillotson (Colonel, the Prince of Wales Own Regiment of Yorkshire) and the Regimental Secretary: the Headmasters of St Benedict's School, Ampleforth College and Wellington College, Directors of the Rothman's International Group and Tube Investments: General Sir David Mostyn, Military Secretary (Army) Ministry of Defence, and his staff.

My thanks are also due to Messrs David Higham Associates for permission to quote from the published works of Freddie de Guingand and from *Middle East 1940-1942: A Study in Air Power* by P. Guedalla, to the Controller of Her Majesty's Stationery Office from *British Intelligence in the Second World War* and to Mr Stephen Bedell Smith for permission to quote his uncle's letter to Field Marshal Smuts.

CHAPTER ONE

Le Comte de Guingand

If there was ever a prototype of a British major-general, Francis Wilfred de Guingand never resembled it; nor would he have wished to do so. He and his background were most unusual.

He was born at 19 Heathfield Road, Acton, London W4 on 28th February 1900, and was the eldest son in a Roman Catholic family comprising an elder sister, Marie Pauline and two brothers John Emile and Edward Paul. His father, Francis Julius, was by descent French, and son of Emile de Guingand, born in 1828, and Pauline le Chertier. After the overthrow of Louis Philippe in 1848, Emile had left France and had become a French master at Wellington College. Thus Francis Julius came to be born in England. He married an Englishwoman, Monica Priestman, from a Yorkshire family, orginally sheep farmers in the Dales and later bankers at Richmond; so, the future major-general was the offspring of a Yorkshire mother and a French father.

The French side of the family had come originally from Guingamp near St Malo in Brittany, a region of tough, independent fishermen and sailors who still speak a variant of the ancient British tongue allied to Welsh and Cornish, and are said to resemble the Celtic peoples in their physical and moral characteristics. The region, once known as 'Britannia Minor' as a result of colonisation in the sixth century, was eventually brought under the French monarchy by the marriage of Anne Duchess of Brittany with Louis XII, King of France, in 1498. The Duchess seized the opportunity to bring some of her poor relations to the court at Paris, and one of them was de la Romble de Guingand, who prospered in royal service and on retirement became Comte de Saint-Mathieu, named after the place in the Haute-Vienne near Limoges, to which the family had moved. When the French revolution erupted, this de Guingand ancestor again moved with his family to Brussels, and later to Bourges where for ten years he was mayor.

15

Even after many centuries, the French cousins looked upon Francis Julius in England as the head of the de Guingand family, and referred to him as 'Monsieur le Comte'. But 'Monsieur le Comte', born in England, chose at the age of twenty-one to become English and became very proud of the fact. Although indistinguishable from an Englishman, he was still linked to France by the family business: the importation of briar pipes in the rough from St Claude in the Jura, and their assembly and finishing at the de Guingand factory in Mansell Street, Barking.

The family business flourished and the de Guingands were always comfortably off, living in their large house near Gunnersbury Park, where Marie Pauline the first child was born in 1898. She and Francis, the eldest brother, became particularly close friends. All four children with mother and father, who were devoted to each other, led a secure, happy life. They were looked after by a nanny of whom they were very fond. The Park, which was well maintained, with a park-keeper in uniform and top hat, included a tennis club, and Lord Rothschild who lived nearby was often to be seen on his way to the City with two dalmatians running behind his coach. After tea in the nursery nanny would make the children tidy and send them downstairs where their English mother would read to them, often from Rudyard Kipling. The French grandparents lived nearby, and the two eldest children, Marie and Francis, were frequently sent round to them to converse in French, which Francis did not enjoy. He never acquired a French accent; nor did he do well at his piano lessons, despite his mother's musical talent: his teacher said he had great ability but seldom practised. His sister used to produce a *Nursery Magazine*, for which young Francis wrote an adventure story; at the exciting climax would appear the words 'to be continued in our next', but regrettably this seldom happened.

However he was obviously a clever little boy with a strong personality which sometimes caused friction with his equally strong-minded father, who in the French tradition was very much the head of the family.

Although both mother and father were Roman Catholics, and his mother's family included many nuns and priests, the de Guingands as a whole were not ardent devotees of their faith. Freddie is remembered play-acting at conducting Mass in the nursery with an old pair of bloomers cut up to make a vestment – arms through leg holes. Even at that early stage, his sense of humour was well developed. In his subsequent career this was to make him an attractive figure with devoted friends in many walks of life from President Eisenhower to a five-year old niece, who remembers sitting on his knee while he typed out a letter to Peter, her bantam cock.

But even his devoted mother, a Yorkshire woman immensely keen on betting at the races would never have backed him to become in Britain's darkest hour the indispensable partner of a strange wilful boy, from County Donegal, called Bernard Law Montgomery.

Francis entered St Benedict's School as a day boy in 1909. It was a small boarding school with a few day boys, run largely by Benedictine monks of Ealing Priory who had come from Downside Abbey in Somerset at the turn of the century. There, he passed all his examinations with the minimum of effort and left for Ampleforth in 1915 together with Oswald Vanheems, a boy of Dutch extraction. They remained inseparable throughout their wartime school days, comically earning reputations as 'those Germans' because of their names and their slightly foreign sophistication. This sophistication in young Francis' personality, derived possibly from the aristocratic forbears in his French ancestry, was to prove a considerable asset in his subsequent career.

A prominent and enjoyable feature of the boys' lives at this period was sailing. Father Francis, with Breton blood in his veins, was a capable and enthusiastic yachtsman: in 1921 he was to be elected Vice-Commodore of the Royal Corinthian Yacht Club. His yacht, normally based at Burnham-on-Crouch, was often in French or Spanish waters and, in the school holidays he would set the boys a challenge to join him in a foreign port; he would give them a sum of money just sufficient for the whole party. It was then that Francis, the eldest brother, took charge, directing the examination of maps and time-tables, pronouncing on a variety of competing plans and settling his brothers' claims on the common purse. To his younger brothers he was a natural leader. With a love of the sea deeply felt by father and son, it was decided that Francis' career was to be in the Royal Navy.

His father went to France from time to time on business and was in Paris when the First World War ended: in 1919 the year of the Treaty of Versailles, he strongly condemned the punitive treatment of the Germans, and commented that the outcome would be another German war in twenty-five years' time. Francis aged nineteen remarked: 'That will give me my chance.'

When the time came for Francis to be medically examined for entry into the Royal Navy he was found to be colour-blind and was immediately turned down. This disaster, totally unexpected, extinguished the long-established hopes of father and son, and caused great misery to both. For days, father was irritable, while his silent son sought solace in the garden with the dogs for which, throughout his life he had an exceptional fondness. As an alternative option, entry to a university where, to judge from his subsequent career he would have prospered, was not considered. As a second best, Francis chose the Army, and in 1918 passed fifteenth into the Royal Military College, Sandhurst, as a prize cadet. His father declined to avail himself of the bursary; Francis commented that he would not mind having the money himself, but this suggestion was not pursued.

At Sandhurst his French name immediately earned him the soubriquet 'Freddie', derived from the popular cartoon, then current, of 'Freddie the Frog'. Thereafter he was Freddie to all and sundry.

Although as a boy of five he had spent some time with his French grandmother, he still spoke French badly and with an appalling accent. Once boasting to the family: '*Moi, je suis le Comte de Guingand*', his father countered '*Et tu parles français comme un cochon*'.

Like Gentleman Cadet Montgomery at Sandhurst thirteen years before him, Freddie did not greatly exert himself intellectually. Having passed in fifteenth, his subsequent places in the Order of Merit varied from 146 to 33 to 110. His main interests were concentrated on racing and gambling, pursuits which greatly appealed to his mother, and were discouraged by his father. Although he gambled at cards, on horses and later on the stockmarket on every possible occasion in peace and war, success was rare.

In appearance he was dark-haired, of medium height and with a pale skin; he had a broad brow, a gap in his front teeth, and he wore a small dark moustache; but the striking feature was his bright humorous eyes. When wearing a *casquette* in France he could be mistaken for a Frenchman. Although not of athletic build, he soon became a very good golfer and squash player, and a useful horseman, and rugger player.

With a Yorkshire mother, and four years at Ampleforth College, York, behind him, it was no surprise that he opted to join the West Yorkshire Regiment, with which he was familiar as the regiment had sponsored the Officers' Training Corps at his school.

He was commissioned in 1919 and joined the second battalion in India. A contemporary remembers that it was customary in the regiment at that time to put young officers into a sort of 'purdah'. Freddie considered this perverse. His period of service there was not a success, partly because he suffered from gallstones, an affliction which was to recur during some of the most critical periods of his future career, and partly because many of his seniors, a tough product of the last war, some of them not gifted with great intelligence, were uncongenial. Although clever and sophisticated, Freddie was always sensitive to the judgement of his superiors. In those early years of his service, there were some brother officers who thought him conceited and pretentious, perhaps because of his keen mind or because he liked occasionally to refer to his French ancestor 'Le Comte de Guingand'. But he soon overcame this youthful foible, and later in life played down his distinguished French ancestry.

There is no doubt that during this period Freddie was bored. This is hardly surprising. The North West Frontier of India with no operations in train at that period must have been very much a sideshow. Freddie, in bad health, was situated far from the bright lights, the girls and the yachts, which with golf had been his principal interests in England and France. It was later that he developed in Africa his great enthusiasms for big game shooting and fishing. It is not surprising that in these circumstances the accusation of 'bookishness' was levied by some officers against the young subaltern, an accusation which in some regiments at that time could be fatal.

In 1922 when defence expenditure had to be reduced under 'the Geddes Axe', the name de Guingand was one of two submitted to higher authority for possible redundancy. However this was not to happen; fate intervened and Freddie, very ill with fever and gall-stones, was invalided home with a prognosis from the Army doctors that his life expectancy was six months. A second opinion however, sought in Harley Street, was reassuring.

After a period of convalescence, he was posted at the age of twenty-two to the second battalion of his regiment in Southern Ireland at Cork, the very centre of the republican unrest. Only a year before, the Irish Free State had been established by treaty, but 'the Troubles', kept the battalion actively engaged, and were to continue thereafter for more than sixty years. Many years before, Thackeray had written of Cork: 'The citizens are the most book-loving men I ever met . . . I listened to two boys almost in rags talking about one of the Ptolemys.' Whether the book-loving Freddie could have found the atmosphere of Cork sympathetic must be doubted, since social contacts with the local inhabitants were severely restricted. No one knew who might be murdered next.

It was here in Cork that Freddie first met Brevet-Major B. L. Montgomery DSO, whose reputation, despite an unpromising start at school and Sandhurst now stood high as a successful infantryman and staff officer. Twenty-five years later Freddie, after four years as Montgomery's Chief of Staff wrote:

> It was in Southern Ireland as a second-lieutenant that I first heard of him. He was Brigade Major of the brigade to which my battalion belonged. I doubt whether he remembered me, but I still remember him well in that capacity. He always possessed that ability to get himself across. We certainly all thought he was a most efficient and experienced Staff Officer.[1]

Montgomery did not remember him: this is hardly suprising as the brigade, the largest in Ireland, comprised seven battalions, and counter-insurgency activity was intense. Freddie nevertheless enjoyed this phase. When off duty, horse-racing and shooting were readily available and his health had improved. Soon he was to serve his future master professionally and get to know him more intimately.

Lieutenant de Guingand's next move was to the regimental depot at York where he was put in charge of the training of NCO's. The headquarters of the 49th (West Riding) Division of the Territorial

Army was also located there, and Major B. L. Montgomery was the GSO 2 of that division. Montgomery as a bachelor lived in the same Mess as Freddie.

> I quickly spotted him as a very intelligent young officer and made use of him and his training cadre to help me with the TA Division by giving demonstrations of platoon tactics. His life in those days revolved round wine, women and gambling – in all of which he excelled.[2]

Freddie was then aged twenty-four and Montgomery thirty-seven.

'We became great friends,' Montgomery wrote forty years later. 'We played a lot of golf together, and bridge most evenings in the Mess.'[3] Freddie, also good at squash, entered the Army championships, and found he was to take on Edward, Prince of Wales. Freddie's friends found that for once his habitual self-confidence was abated, and the crowd of spectators at the match obviously impaired his game. During this formative period he learnt a great deal from Montgomery. He admired his professionalism and his passionate dedication to the Army, and he smiled at his oddities. He also observed his skill as a trainer and the way in which he so strikingly put across his tactical ideas. Sitting up at night with the young officers Montgomery would tell them about World War I; he introduced a wonderfully refreshing atmosphere in the Mess, and devoted hours of his time to coaching young officers in the subjects which later they would have to take in the Staff College exam.

Montgomery 'saw (Freddie's) potentialities (and) urged him . . . to begin a serious study of his profession and to read widely, because he was too young then to take the exam'.[4] From this we must suppose that Freddie aged twenty-four, with his many demanding hobbies, had not in Montgomery's view developed a serious approach to his profession. But Montgomery's glittering eye was upon him.

As to women, Montgomery declared at that time that matrimony and the military life did not go well together; he argued that a young officer to be successful must spend so much time in getting to know his soldiers and studying his profession that a wife would receive inadequate attention. But Freddie who 'excelled with women' did not concur, and had a succession of girlfriends; but was always discreet in the French manner. They admired his humour, his savoir-faire, and his friendly temperament which flourished in the presence of pretty women. Yet, despite a teenage romance with a girl who was very fond of him and, in his twenties, an engagement terminated by overseas service, he did not marry until the age of forty-two after many years of absence from England. Some said that his attitude was that matrimony was the one activity in which one should not gamble: one should wait for a 'dead cert'.

The Regimental Journal of the West Yorkshire Regiment at this period mentions the arrival at their depot of the highly efficient de Guingand with his fertile brain, and records his successes at golf. But more seriously, an unusual contribution to the training of recruits which was much appreciated, was his production of lectures illustrated with amateur lantern slides presenting the 'Evolution of War' from pre-historic days. These were evidently in the form of humorous cartoons, and the Journal records in 1924:

> All ranks have been vastly entertained by our local Tom Webster [a well-known cartoonist]. This highly efficient officer has wasted a great deal of his valuable time for the gratification of a numerous and enthusiastic audience . . . there seems no limit to his powers of production and . . . we hope they will help us to get through many a long winter evening.[5]

By August 1925 Freddie had completed his full tour at the Depot and his departure was recorded in these words:

> We shall miss our little Tom Webster very much at the Depot. All who have joined during the last few years will remember with pleasure their last fortnight at the Depot when they learnt something of the lighter but none the less instructive side of soldiering. We wish 'Whiz-Bang' as much success with the Battalion as he had at the Depot.

The nickname 'Whiz-Bang' seems to have been derived from the unsuccessful attempts of Ampleforth schoolboys to cope with 'de Guingand'; this became Dee-Ging-Gang, from which it was but a short step to Ding-Bang and thence Whiz-Bang. The name was not inappropriate for a young man with a remarkably quick brain. The Whiz-Bang shell of World War 1 was such that the sound of its flight was heard only an instant, if at all, before the sound of its explosion.

In April 1926 the sophisticated Captain de Guingand took an unusual step: he applied to serve with the King's African Rifles in Nyasaland, an unlikely territory in which to find wine, women and gambling. His sample of life under the British 'Raj' on the NW Frontier of India had not appealed to him. As a teenager the Comte de Guingand had known the bright lights of Le Touquet and the South of France, keenly accompanying his mother to the local casino (where his elder sister fell asleep at the table), but there had as yet been no contact with Africa, which was to be the scene of later triumphs, and was to engage his passions until his life's end. Perhaps the decision was made to test his dreams, and to replenish his bank account, which it was rumoured had been seriously diminished by gambling.

CHAPTER TWO

Whiz-Bang in Africa

Many young officers at that period were seeking adventure overseas to escape from the humdrum of regimental life in the United Kingdom. Freddie was lucky to have found in the regiment some particularly congenial and generous friends, Lt-Colonel and Mrs Brian Hawkins. Anne Hawkins was French, and they had a house at Le Touquet to which young Freddie was frequently invited. There, his keenness for golf and his passion for gambling could be well satisfied. Even his French, still abominable, could be exercised.

Brian Hawkins, with a DSO from the First World War, had volunteered to serve with the King's African Rifles in Nyasaland, and he fired Freddie with his own enthusiasm: 'You try Africa,' he said to Freddie. 'You'll love it.' Freddie fell for it, and had five happy, exciting years, first as Adjutant to Hawkins commanding the 1st Battalion KAR, and finally as Officer Commanding Troops, Nyasaland. In boyhood days he had been entranced with Africa, and after listening spellbound to a friend's stories of big game hunting, he had been enthralled with Rider Haggard's *King Solomon's Mines* and had adopted Alan Quartermaine as his hero.

Nyasaland – Malawi as it is today – had been opened up by Europeans after Livingstone had reached Lake Nyasa in 1859, and was administered in 1926 by a British Governor assisted by Residents in the Districts. The Church of Scotland had established a mission at Blantyre in 1876, and shortly afterwards the African Lakes Company had set up a trading station. In 1889 the British Government had made treaties of protection with the local chiefs, and two years later the Central African Protectorate had been declared. The country had initially been developed with large European estates growing tobacco, tea, cotton and maize; this had been followed by a rapidly increasing number of peasant farms. In 1907 the name British Central Africa was changed to Nyasaland, which after independence in 1964 became Malawi.

The King's African Rifles, founded in 1904, was a first class colonial force with officers seconded from the British Army. It operated in the colonial territories of East Africa, and was funded by the Colonial Office in Whitehall.

In the Regimental Journal, Freddie wrote of 'halcyon days when drinking from the cup that Africa alone can offer'. The combination of magnificent scenery, superb in its unspoilt wildness, with Hawkins's tough imaginative training and wonderful opportunities for fishing and unlimited shooting of every sort of game, from duck to elephant, had a powerful appeal, and exerted a lasting influence on the young 'Comte de Guingand', for whom perhaps the 'bright lights' and the casino had momentarily began to pall. He became very adept as a shot and was a keen and skilful fisherman.

Hawkins who had served for many years in Africa was an excellent commanding officer, and his battalion in 1926 gained many successes. Like his adjutant he enjoyed life to the full; but by personality and character he could cope with any crisis and see it through to the end. He had a remarkable influence on his African troops; his influence on Freddie must have been immensely beneficial: the pair were particularly well-matched.

It was in Nyasaland that Hawkins and his Adjutant heard in 1927 that Montgomery had married a widow, Mrs Elizabeth Carver. They immediately cabled to their old friend, teasing him about his pronouncements on marriage in the Army and asking which was it to be, 'the soldier or the husband?'

The life they led in the KAR must have appealed greatly to an active adventurous young man. They lived at 3,000 feet under the shadow of Mount Zomba; their houses were scattered in park-like country, watered with mountain streams which kept their gardens green throughout the year. Oranges, pineapples, peaches, strawberries and delightful native fruits could easily be grown. From the Mess they could see across the plains to another great mountain range rising to 10,000 feet, and across Lake Chilwa, forty miles long, to the hills on the Portuguese border.

After the end of company and battalion training, came the Battalion March lasting several weeks. On one occasion they started by marching eighty-three miles in four days to the southern end of Lake Nyasa; there they embarked on a Government steamer, which in three days took them 250 miles up the lake, anchoring each night in a quiet bay where the men, five hundred of them, disembarked and cooked their food. Freddie himself had developed an interest in cooking: having ordered cookery books and utensils from Paris and London, he was always ready to produce French dishes of great sophistication.

Continuing the march the battalion reached its destination 250 miles away in eight days. Then during the following seven days, progress was under active service conditions by day and night, battling against an 'enemy' provided initially by the police and later by one of their own companies. There were no maps, and no one had seen the country before, but they advanced ten to fifteen miles a day over two intervening mountain ranges before a great escarpment was reached. Then the forest began to give way to huge open rolling downs cut up by deep ravines; they halted at a plateau at 6,000 feet, uninhabited except by game, and there they had two days' rest, awakened each day by the rising of the sun over the lake, 5,000 feet below.

The officers then went shooting from dawn to dusk, bringing back good supplies of meat for all. After a further ten days' marching, and the construction of a bridge over a river, there was another halt for rest and shooting. Then they marched back to barracks; in eight weeks they had covered 517 miles on foot and 380 miles by steamer.

Almost all the officers of the battalion were keen on shooting. The ivory from elephant produced a useful supplement for a junior officer's pay, often as much as £200 per year, equivalent to £4000 today. Conservation of wild life was an idea hardly known in those days, but Freddie in later life was to become a keen supporter of the World Wild Life Fund.

Leave was generous and on a typical shooting expedition, recorded in his diary, Freddie and two others set off in November when the long burnt grass had given place to new young grass dearly loved by the game. Although a series of storms had cooled the district considerably, water was still scarce and the game tended to be localised round the water holes.

They left in a lorry provided by a local contractor – fourteen persons all told with guns, kit, rations and petrol for 500 miles. Their immediate destination was 200 miles away. At a halt for lunch under a large shady tree they saw the great lake to the east, with grassy plateaux and great rocky hills in the foreground. Then passing through a delightful spot at 5,000 feet with beautiful country surounding it, they dropped down to a lower level. Freddie wrote up his diary by the light of a wonderful African moon, the night being perfect and pleasantly cool.

They called next morning on the Acting Resident whom they found charming and helpful. He had procured thirty porters and two hunters for them as well as up-to-date information about game.

On their way to their next stop, they called in on the White Fathers at Likuni Mission. Freddie commented in his diary: 'Poor fellows, they get a year's leave after their first ten years and then come back to die. One father returning to Canada after fifteen years, found himself completely ''at sea'', and realising he now belonged to Africa, returned within the month.' The White Fathers were recognised as the best missionaries there. 'They make the native realise that he must work and be loyal to his master first, instead of packing his head with religious ideas which he has no hope of understanding, and treating him as a brother and an equal, as some of the Missions do.' Such was Freddie's verdict on the Bantu African at the age of twenty-six.

The next evening, they were entertained by the headman to an unusual village dance. As Freddie watched, a bright moon shone down, and with three tall orderlies standing behind their chairs guarding their *buanas* (masters), childhood memories of *King Solomon's Mines* were stirred again. The dance portrayed a hunt with game, with representations of buffalo and eland etc arranged by two men, while the remainder of the performers baited them with spears and uttered dreadful screams. This entertainment was attended by the pregnant women of the village, who hoped thereby that their sons would be great and fearless hunters.

There followed many exciting days shooting sable, buck lion and elephant. Freddie, writing up his diary and already rejoicing in the use of words, commented: 'We have only been away in the ''blue'' for just under a week, yet how soon one loses interest in the outside world – coal strikes, tailors' bills, Cambridgeshire winners – these once important items seem gradually to become absorbed into the haze of another world.'[1]

Although big game hunting and fishing figured so largely in his life, there were other more serious activities. Freddie gained particular distinction from an expedition which he and another junior officer successfully carried out with the object of surveying a route to connect Northern Nyasaland with NE Rhodesia. This was the type of project that he always dreamt about – an independent command of several months' duration. No wonder that the lure of Africa remained with Freddie all his life.

Long afterwards some of his admirers suspected that Freddie's emotional attachment to Africa had been too extreme. One night in a safari camp, a close war-time friend, Geoffrey Keating, given to clowning, stole away from the convivial group around the camp fire after dinner and produced a convincing reproduction of a hyena's howl. 'Isn't that a marvellous sound?' said the enchanted Freddie, only to be disillusioned as the clown returned.

It can be seen from the diary in which he recorded his adventures that he was beginning to develop an easy, lucid style which, some years later, was to serve him well under more rigorous conditions, including the drafting of reports for a Secretary of State and writing controversial papers on strategy for Commanders-in-Chief.

By 1931 Freddie had left Africa, and was back in Strensall near York. What had those five years in Africa taught him and to what extent had his experiences been relevant to the great responsibilities which lay ahead? Despite his health problems which had been remedied but by no means eliminated, he had shown himself to be remarkably active. He was very successful with his African soldiers; within the traditional disciplined framework of the British Army it was not unusual for a highly intelligent officer to engender great affection and respect from primitive, uneducated men of another race. This he did, and they still remembered him thirty years later. His *joie de vivre* and humour combined with his love of sporting activity endeared him to them and to his fellow officers. But most of all he matured and found his feet. But like many young officers of that period he would have sought to maintain his amateur status, denying any suggestion that he was intent on becoming a dedicated professional soldier. Nevertheless those five years were to a limited degree an effective preparation for the future war, which even then he must have sensed was inevitable.

Once back in England there was an unavoidable reaction. 1931 was a year of the great depression and its effects in the country extended to the Army. The anticlimax was severe. After some leave and six weeks' duty at Strensall, Freddie found he had little work to do. After those years in the King's African Rifles, where at the end of his tour he had borne exceptionally heavy responsibilities for his age, this phase of marking time in England with little to do was too much for a man who loved adventure, enjoyed intellectual stimulus and thrived on challenge.

Years later Freddie wrote:

> I formed up at the orderly room one day to see my colonel. He was of the old type, had served with the Egyptian Army for some years and was very fond of his port. I explained to him that I was bored stiff and would like to be given some work to do. This request nearly finished my colonel who went purple in the face, and turning to his adjutant who shared the same office, said: 'God Almighty, to think that I should live to see the day that an officer of the Prince of Wales' Own [Regiment of Yorkshire] should ask for work.[2]

Nevertheless Freddie formally applied to resign and was given leave pending retirement. The incident, not unique, demonstrated his impatience when confronted with a job that offered no challenge. Looking for employment, he was invited to subscribe some of his small capital to a madcap scheme to make a film about Livingstone in Africa, for which he was to be a consultant. Fortunately, however, his commanding officer persuaded him to change his mind and be posted to Egypt where the overseas battalion was commanded by a very efficient colonel who was an excellent trainer. Freddie got on well with the new colonel, Harold Franklyn by name, and later became his adjutant. According to the Commander-in-Chief, Burnett Stuart, the battalion became the best trained unit in Egypt. Franklyn, who had come to them from the Green Howards (and eventually became Commander-in-Chief Home Forces) was resented by some of the West Yorkshire officers, but thanks to a lively lot of subalterns, led by Whiz-Bang the Adjutant, he was accepted as a new broom well worth following. The methods of training were imaginative; platoons and sections carried out a type of initiative training in the Sinai Desert, testing endurance, leadership and stamina. Some men of the Intelligence section were even trained to operate on camels.

At Moascar in the Suez Canal Zone, although there was no big game to be shot, the Adjutant continued to mix pleasure with business. He became the champion jockey of the regiment and, looking for adventure as usual, he went on a trip at Christmas across Sinai to Jerusalem and Amman, where as yet no road had been built by the Suez Canal Company. Freddie was the organiser of the party, consisting of the Colonel and five officers. In a light-hearted account written in March 1933[3] he describes, typically laughing at himself, how at the outset his car while being rafted across the Canal at Fayid plunged overboard. Only the bonnet was visible, but with the help of fifty Egyptians the Buick was hauled out. Immediately the sump and petrol tank were drained and the distributor cleaned; then the draining of the cylinders was entrusted to an Egyptian who inserted a piece of tube down each plug-hole and sucked out all the water and oil for a reward of one piastre per suck. The car was then primed with petrol and, after a short push, she started and ran perfectly for the next thousand miles.

Later they passed 'the spotless hull of the *Empress of Britain* passing through the Great Bitter Lake on her journey round the world – a lovely sight'.[4] After a night spent in the desert in a zareba formed of their cars, they motored on towards Jerusalem and spent the night at a Police Post where all the hospitality of the traditional inn-keeper was displayed by the police sergeant. They dined on 'Mock turtle soup, Homard à l'Americaine, savoury and dessert'. Here we see the *chef* and *bonviveur*. They then moved on to Beersheba and after a glorious drive through the hills of Judea reached the King David Hotel in Jerusalem. Moving on fast next day on the wonderful roads in Palestine they visisted Jerash, the beautiful Roman city built in AD50, and so to Amman in Transjordan. Soon they were back in Moascar after an eight-day holiday which had obviously been a great success. 'We were sorry to get back,' wrote Freddie. 'The wilderness has a charm all of its own, and makes one long to return and explore its remoter regions.'

At that time Lt-Colonel Montgomery with his wife was also stationed at Alexandria in Egypt commanding the 1st Battalion of the Royal Warwickshire Regiment. With typical single-mindedness he was conducting the training of his battalion introducing novel ideas with great imagination, and his incisive personality, tactical skill and immense confidence were atracting much attention. On an important exercise in 1933 he was made acting commander of the brigade, and Captain de Guingand was selected by the General to be Montgomery's Brigade Major for the exercise. Montgomery was already a great exponent of the night attack and, impetuously, was about to launch an approach march by night without accurate information as to the location of the enemy. Freddie with great perseverence was able to dissuade him until information of the enemy's dispositions could be acquired from an RAF reconnaissance plane which, by personal initiative, he had succeeded in requisitioning. Then some of the intelligence section of the West Yorkshire battalion mounted on camels borrowed for the exercise with Freddie's assistance, navigated the brigade faultlessly to its correct destination and Montgomery's victory was complete. He gave credit to the Intelligence Section and he never forgot his acting Brigade Major's fertile mind: only a year later he took steps to advance his career. Neither of them could have visualised that only nine years later and fifty miles to the west they would be engaged in real battles on a scale fifty times as great.

By the year 1934, Lt-Colonel Montgomery had become chief instructor at the Staff College Quetta in Baluchistan, and Freddie also at Quetta was still Adjutant of the same battalion, but was fervently hoping to get command of a KAR battalion; had he done so his career could well have ended in oblivion. But he was far from fit and on one occasion fell down in a dead faint in the orderly room. This did not deter him from going on a shooting expedition with a friend to Sind, where duck were plentiful. They obtained an enormous bag, which would not have survived the heat of the return journey to Quetta.

'Let's give them all to the British Military Hospital,' said Freddie. This was done anonymously, but the Commanding Officer, despite the illegibility of Freddie's signature in the Rest House where they had stayed, followed them up with a grateful letter.

He had sat once for the Staff College examination: a friend close by had been amused to hear him obtain permission to wear a cricket cap throughout the session; this was to obviate his habit when concentrating of twisting his forelock almost to destruction. He had entered his name very late for the examination and was debarred by age from sitting a second time to improve his results, which were not good largely owing to his handwriting; this, which had been beautifully formed at St Benedict's School, had sadly degenerated; in the service of his fast brain processes, it had become a cryptic shorthand.

Freddie disclosed his disappointment to his friend Montgomery who 'knowing his worth' as he reminisced years later, 'decided to go into battle on his behalf and wrote personally to the Chief of the General Staff at Delhi and asked him to nominate Freddie for the Staff College – which he did.'[5]

Freddie, who until the last moment had wavered between returning to the KAR or entering the Staff College, decided to forego the lure of Africa, and Montgomery wrote to him that all would be well. He appreciated that Montgomery had accepted him into that small coterie of officers considered likely to be of use to the Army – in Montgomery's phrase, 'proper chaps'. Freddie, anything but naive, must have realised that he was hitching his wagon to a star. The glad tidings were as follows:[6]

Staff College

Quetta

30.7.34

My dear Freddie,

Thank you for your letter. I heard from the D.S.D. [Director of Staff Duties] some days ago. His letter was dated 27th June and I gathered from it that as far as he was concerned all would be well. I did not tell you as accidents sometimes happen.

I am not used to backing the wrong horse when it comes to asking favours of people in high places; it would result only in one's own undoing. You ought to do very well at Camberley. I know many of the instructors there, and some of them very well; one of them – Nye – is in my Regt. I will write and commend you to them in due course.

We are coming to your dance on 14th August, and are dining first with the Army Comdr.

Yours ever

B. L. Montgomery

Montgomery's theme about 'backing the wrong horse . . . would result in one's own undoing' would not have appeared untypical to Freddie, but when brought up again twelve years later in 1946 it was to have sinister implications. However in 1934 it was fortunate for his *protégé* that Montgomery took this initiative. Taken by anyone else, it might have been regarded as unacceptable. For a colonel belonging to one regiment to write to a senior general, however friendly, at Army Headquarters requesting a nomination for a captain in a another regiment, who had been so distracted from his profession as to forego a second chance of qualifying, might in those punctilious days have savoured of impertinence. Doubtless Montgomery's reputation was powerful enough even then to brush protocol aside. It was at this time that at one of his lectures at the Quetta Staff College he startled his listeners with the statement: – 'And when I am Commander-in-Chief of the Allied Armies in the next war, ...'. It would be only eight years later that, entirely by coincidence, he would take over *in situ* the same Freddie, now a brigadier, and discover that as Army Commander and Chief of Staff they were to form a highly successful partnership.

But this eventuality would never have occurred to Freddie as he, like many others, was not yet a truly dedicated soldier. In peacetime in the nineteen thirties, the life of a junior officer, particularly in the United Kingdom, could be dull and provide little incentive. Training was restricted in scope, and often unimaginative in form. Owing to the current system of promotion, soon to be reformed by Hore-Belisha, officers could spend up to twenty years waiting for their majority. Pay, except for those fortunate to be serving overseas on local rates, was far from generous, and was not calculated to satisfy those who sought the good things of life. In 1933 Freddie, with his family connections, had been offered a job in the steel industry by a friend, Sir Geoffrey Burton. Fortunately, after toying with the idea he had turned it down, saying: 'There will be a war in seven years'. Soon the reality of war was to produce in Whiz-Bang a startling transformation.

CHAPTER THREE

Playboy Student

From 1934 onwards the combined influence of a far-sighted commanding officer and Montgomery, the mentor, brought a change in
Freddie's development. The Fates were beginning to work, though
not always in an obvious fashion. At the Staff College Camberley,
into which with his Montgomery-sponsored nomination Freddie
entered in 1935, he still showed few outward signs of the professional
soldier he was to become in war. Contemporaries remember him
forging easily through the syndicate exercises, which many found
demanding, with little obvious application and sometimes scant
respect. One such exercise based on an imaginary conflict with the
Turkish Army was designed to test the students' ability to build up
an enemy's order of battle[1] from fragmentary intelligence reports.
Freddie completed this in record time, and immediately drove off to
the bright lights of London.

He enjoyed the liveliness of one of the instructors, Lt-Colonel E.
E. Dorman-Smith, a future comrade-in-arms, and particularly admired
the personality and wisdom of another, Lt-Colonel W. Slim, the
future field-marshal. Increasingly, the fertility and quickness of
Freddie's brain were matched by a great capacity to communicate,
and this made him a dominant figure in discussion. But these
qualities had to fight for prominence with the siren calls of the bridge
table, sometimes diversified by chemin de fer, the golf course,
frequent parties in the London night clubs, and as always the race
course. On an important exercise in Wales, when he should have
been engaged in tactical appreciation from a hilltop, he was found
listening to the Derby on his portable radio. As a bachelor he was
recognised as the life and soul of any party. His small sports car
would start eastwards along the A30 to London at the earliest
possible moment, and when next morning his fellow students
assembled punctually at 8.55 am preparatory to their studies, a pale-

faced captain still in a dinner jacket would sometimes rush in with murmured apologies and a shamefaced grin.

His private life lacked organisation, and more than once he left his uniform in strange places. On one occasion, his particular girlfriend of that period packed his jacket in a couturier's flower-decked box with the sleeves stuffed with tissue paper drenched with scent, and had it delivered to the Staff College, where his friends insisted on a public disclosure of the contents. Fortunately Freddie, throughout his life, could always laugh at himself.

After the Staff College, Freddie rejoined in 1936 the second battalion of the West Yorkshire's for a spell of regimental duty, as was the routine in those days. On arrival he was very properly put in charge of training in order to pass on and exploit the ideas and techniques he had learnt. The role of the unit had recently been changed to a machine-gun battalion, and in that situation Freddie's contribution was outstanding. He became conspicuous as a leader in all the discussions on tactical use of the weapon, new to the battalion, and on the experimentation which followed. A contemporary remembered that he 'brought a breath of fresh air' into the conduct of training and was particularly successful with the training of officers. Soon he was to command a company of the newly organised machine-gun battalion.

In 1936 he was reported on by the General Officer Commanding as 'this brilliant young officer'. Why '*young?*' said Freddie to a friend, 'I'm thirty-six.' He was quite right. But it would take a war to prove his point; in five years' time Michael Carver, a future field-marshal, whom he in his turn would teach at another Staff College, would be commanding an armoured brigade at the age of twenty-nine.

Freddie left the battalion in 1937 for his first staff job, Brigade Major at the Small Arms School, Netheravon. The Regimental Journal reported 'His services to us since he left the Staff College a year ago have been invaluable, and we are glad to hear that his new job will enable him to pay us fairly frequent visits'. However in the pecking order of staff appointments, his new job at the Small Arms School could not have ranked very highly. An officer with the highest ambitions would have hoped to become a Brigade Major of an active brigade – the post which Freddie had filled, but only temporarily, for Montgomery's exercise in Egypt.

At Netheravon Freddie, now recognised as ambitious, and with a sharp inquisitive mind which always sought to explore levels above the prescribed routine of his appointment, decided to visit his French and German counterparts, despite the threatening international situation. After overcoming considerable opposition in the War Office where there were political anxieties lest a reciprocal visit would be demanded, he was allowed to do so, but had to bear most of the cost himself. With a friend, he spent two days in Paris, where as usual he sampled and enjoyed the good things of life, and then went on to Mourmelon, the French equivalent of Netheravon, near Châlons-sur-Marne. The outward appearance of the French Small Arms School was depressing: untidy huts, decaying roads and a general air of dilapidation. Freddie was taken on a tour of the devastated areas of the last war, where his hosts repeatedly stressed that the next war must not be fought on French soil. However they were very kind and frank; but he left convinced that there were big deficiences in funds and equipment and that much remained to be done to create a modern army.

He moved on to the German Infantry School via Berlin, where the British Military Attaché warned him that any telephone conversation might be 'bugged' and that any confidential documents he had brought might be interfered with. Freddie, a future Director of Military Intelligence, set up a trap in his hotel bedroom and found that his papers, carefully listed, had indeed been disturbed.

The School at Dobrietz was very different to Mourmelon. It was smart and lavishly equipped, and he was greatly impressed with the tone and sense of discipline. Freddie found their weapons and training methods were superior to those of the British Army, and that everything was being done without financial restrictions. He was struck by the high priority given to defence against low-flying aircraft – a lesson learnt from the Spanish Civil War. The Commandant made disparaging remarks about the French, and hinted (as indeed was Hitler's hope) that the Germans and British should cooperate together. Before leaving Germany, Freddie was able to witness the celebrations in the Wilhelmstrasse, Berlin, marking the fourth anniversary of Hitler's election as Chancellor. He was amazed at the Teutonic hysteria, and left with no illusions about the power of the Nazi military machine and the unpreparedness of the British Army to face the major continental war which now seemed imminent.

In June 1939 after nearly two years as Brigade Major at the Small Arms School, Freddie with one or two others was interviewed by Mr Hore-Belisha, the Secretary of State for War, for appointment as his Military Assistant. After a discussion about the West Yorkshire Regiment, the Small Arms School and the training of officers, Freddie was selected; three weeks were to pass before he was informed.

Mr Hore-Belisha, an unusual politician aged forty-three, is said to have made his choice because, of those he interviewed he found that Freddie was less like a regular officer than any he had ever met. This could not have applied to his appearance which no doubt for a critical interview would have been extremely smart; more probably it referred to the breadth of outlook, *savoir faire* and tactful eloquence of this unusually sophisticated young major.

A Military Assistant to a high Government official, be he a general or a minister, has to combine the capabilities of ADC, personal secretary, progress chaser, diplomat, psychiatrist, confidant and loyal champion of his master; if to these he can on appropriate occasions produce the qualities of a court jester his success should be assured. By now Freddie had developed such talents to a marked degree.

In 1939 with Hitler's intentions now crystal clear, the role demanded instant comprehension, exceptional intelligence, great industry and unusual foresight. It required also an understanding of the interplay of the political and military worlds, and some appreciation of the right balance when these conflicted. It was part of Freddie's duties to attend defence debates in the House of Commons, and he witnessed many of the most critical scenes leading up to the declaration of war. The experience gained by him in this appointment, in which urgent military matters at the highest governmental level passed daily through his hands, contributed greatly to his professional development. Thereafter, he was never deterred from engaging in matters of high policy when, on the military stage, they unavoidably presented themselves.

The stress of business was acute, and he referred years later to his first two weeks as a nightmare. Not only were the resources of the country being belatedly reorganised and mobilised for a war which the Government at last had recognised was unavoidable, but the Secretary of State, an ambitious and patriotic man, was determined to drive through a series of reforms which were long overdue. He was frustrated by bureaucratic delays and on many occasions Freddie, already a skilled communicator, had to use his tact and diplomacy to damp down the military opposition generated by the impatience of his youthful master.

Amongst the ministers of Chamberlain's government, most of them elderly and old-fashioned, Hore-Belisha was atypical. His brilliant analytical mind, reflected in the pursuit of the extensive reforms he introduced so expeditiously, his effective use of Public Relations which shocked and irked some of his colleagues, and the somewhat flamboyant lifestyle of a rich Jew – all generated envy or opposition in many quarters, but not in the mind of his Military Assistant, whose intelligence, despite the lack of a university train- ing, was equally acute, and whose slightly foreign sophistication and well-developed taste in claret matched those of his master. Freddie wrote in 1946: 'Hore-Belisha I found a most colourful character; initially I did not take to him much, but later I developed a great affection and regard for my new master.'[2]

In the dark days of 1939 they soon developed an easy and effective relationship. Hore-Belisha's custom was to demand verbal briefings on even the most complicated topics emanating from the War Office or the Cabinet, and it was Freddie's duty to assimilate the latest relevant information, often in the early hours of the morning, and present a verbal synopsis to the Secretary of State while he was dressing at home. A contemporary remembers the Military Assis- tant being particularly agile in the bathroom recovering the cake of soap when it slipped from his master's fingers. Freddie was also responsible, alternately with the Minister's Principal Private Secretary, for taking the minutes of the Army Council, a taxing but highly educative process, particularly after the declaration of war on 3rd September 1939.

Towards the end of 1939, Freddie realised that his master was in for trouble but, when approached tactfully, Hore-Belisha would not believe him. Shortly afterwards, the Prime Minister told his

Secretary of State for War that he had his full confidence, and if he was dissatisfied with any of the senior generals, he could make changes. Hore-Belisha was delighted, and suggested that Freddie had been talking nonsense.

Nevertheless the Military Assistant, perceptive and diplomatic as always, had observed that the S of S and the CIGS, General Ironside, hardly ever spoke to each other, and he suggested he might try to do something about it. This was agreed, and by appointment he went to see the CIGS, a large, oppressive and daunting figure.

'I found him sitting at his desk with his diary open in which he recorded what happened at various interviews. He sat there like a great bull and glared at me.'[3] But even in those early days, this diplomatic sally by young Freddie into the stratospheric level of government achieved success, and the S of S and CIGS for a time met daily for a fireside chat.

Amongst many controversial topics that Hore-Belisha pursued was the subject of air support for the Army. In this Freddie became closely involved. It was a subject in its infancy, but one to which at a later date Freddie, by his pragmatic advocacy, was able to make a major contribution. After Munich, as aircraft of any type were extremely scarce, the RAF had embarked on an enormous effort to expand its resources. The Secretary of State for War took a personal interest in the air needs of the Army and found that a joint Committee of the War Office and the Air Ministry had achieved little progress. After the Wehrmacht's success in Poland, he pressed for increased Air Support for the Army and even hinted for the need of an Army Air Arm. The Army authorities, despite having been given on paper a major say in the type, design and numbers of the aircraft they required, had not as yet pursued the subject with vigour. However Freddie had obtained a report by one of the Air Ministry observers in Poland which stressed the successful use of German aircraft in intimate support of the German Army, and at a confrontation between Hore-Belisha and Kingsley Wood, the S of S for Air, the S of S for War pulled the rug from under his Cabinet colleague, using Freddie's Polish report, and thus was able to raise the whole subject to the Prime Minister's level. Eventually a useful agreement was reached by which control of the RAF Component with the BEF was to be improved, and some bomber squadrons were earmarked for their use; moreover the Army would in future have a say in the design and type of aircraft supporting them, and Army/Air training would be initiated while staff branches would be set up in both ministries to study air support for the Army. This was undoubtedly a considerable achievement, for which Freddie must receive a share of the credit.

Earlier he had been much involved with the negotiations carried out by the British Government with the object of inducing the USSR to join in an alliance with Britain and France against the Germans. There were strong forces in Britain which disliked the thought of a military alliance with the USSR, and it was hoped that this might prove unnecessary. The Russians doubtless were aware of this, and knew that many people in Britain hoped that a political line-up against Hitler might be enough to deter him. The Soviet Government for their part wanted to strengthen their security by absorbing the Baltic States and Western Poland; they wished to move into those neighbouring states when, in their opinion, indirect aggression had taken place. Britain felt that to agree to this would be fatal to the independence of those states. The second point of disagreement arose from Britain's refusal to give strong support in land and in air forces against German aggression. Britain could offer initially only economic aid and naval support.

All this political manoeuvring came to nothing, and it served to emphasise the fact that Britain's military resources were desperately inadequate. In respect of the Army, this was Hore-Belisha's main concern. Engaged in augmenting, reorganising and reequipping the Army with great urgency, he was also intent on backing his case with popular support. He liked to see things for himself, and Freddie accompanied him on many of his visits to units in the United Kingdom and to critical meetings in France. Later when the notorious pillboxes to extend the Maginot Line were being built, Freddie was at Hore-Belisha's side during the three months which finally culminated in the forced but unjustified resignation of the Secretary of State for War on 4th January 1940.

Referring in 1947 to the 'colossal sensation' of 1939, Freddie wrote:

'Hore-Belisha ousted by the Brass-Hats' was typical of the posters one saw. In my view this was nearer the truth than many believed. . . . A visit to the British Expeditionary Force in France in November [1939] produced the ammunition for which some were waiting.[4]

While it can be justly said that all the actions taken by Hore-Belisha were directed solely towards improving the security of the British Expeditionary Force, it is not difficult to identify some which motivated rancour in the minds of the senior generals. The manner in which the Secretary of State had juggled with the Army's top appointments, including the invention of 'Inspector General of Overseas Forces', an impossible role, with the incumbent located and thereby neutralised in Gibraltar, his brusque technique for dismissing the 'Old Guard' in the Army Council, his keenness to 'see for himself' in order to supplement the advice tendered to him through official channels which, although praiseworthy, inevitably crossed the wires, his habit of seeking direct contact with soldiers in order to popularise the image of the Army (and of the S of S), and his understandable tendency to ride roughshod over obstacles seemingly created by the professionals, all this generated dislike and opposition in the minds of his principal antagonists.

Freddie's opinion of Ironside the CIGS, and of Gort, the C-in-C of the British Expeditionary Force, who at that time were in the two most critical positions for securing the safety of the nation, was low; P. J. Grigg himself, the Permanent Under Secretary, who subsequently became an ardent supporter of Montgomery, wrote at a later date: 'Ironside has no doubt many qualities but precision of thought and an orderly mind are not among them. He has not much idea of running a large machine'.[5] Thus the young Military Assistant sitting in the corridors of power had an unique opportunity for observing the frictions in the nation's defence machinery at the very outset of war, and his sophisticated mind must have found ample opportunities for criticism in the situation where he had always wanted to be – at the centre. The Secretary of State formed the highest opinion of him and forecast that he would be of very great use in the Army. Freddie for his part, remained loyal to his political master until he died, and repaid his friendship with many acts of kindness. Years later with a typically imaginative gesture he invited him to observe the British Army crossing the Rhine preparatory to the defeat of Germany in 1945.

At the end of the Hore-Belisha affair, when the unhappy Secretary of State, contrary to the advice of Churchill and Beaverbrook, declined to accept the Prime Minister's offer of the Board of Trade, Freddie drove with him to the Palace, where his master handed in his seals of office. Freddie immediately went to see Ironside and asked if he could be relieved of his appointment. The CIGS asked him what he would like to do, and he replied that he wished to rejoin his regiment. The CIGS phoned through the necessary instructions and in due course Freddie received orders on 21st January 1940 to report to the Training Centre of the West Yorkshire Regiment where he was given leave. On 25th February that order was cancelled, and on the next day the Military Secretary told him he was to report to the new Middle East Staff College at Haifa to be an instructor. Although eminently suitable for this appointment, this news discouraged Freddie: first because the official view was that Italy might not yet come into the war, and secondly he feared he was being 'banished' because he knew too much about the infighting leading to Hore-Belisha's dismissal. No official record is available to support Freddie's suspicions. It is more likely that, as the new Staff College at Haifa was being urgently established, pressure was exerted to find a first class instructor and Freddie, unexpectedly out of a job, filled the bill admirably. In the event this move for Freddie was unpredictably to open prospects of unimagined service and distinction in what was to become at that time the only active theatre of war on land.

CHAPTER FOUR

Peerless Planner

At the Middle East Staff College, which had been set up in early 1940 at Telsch House, a requisitioned Jewish hotel in the Mount Carmel district of Haifa, Freddie, now a lieutenant-colonel, at once made a great impression.

I had been sent to Telsch House as an instructor after Dunkirk, and met him there for the first time; we occupied a little villa on Mount Carmel. I assumed his name was of Huguenot extraction and that he was the standard British regular officer; however, very soon I realised that he was strikingly different from any officer I had ever met. Forty years later I wrote: 'He brought to Telsch House a whiff of the clubland of St James where he would have been welcome as a *bon viveur* and gambler and hardly recognised as a soldier.'[1] At Haifa I soon found he was a most entertaining friend, and when off duty always ready for a lark. Very early one morning we jointly pulled out of bed our naval liaison officer, a gallant submarine commander, stripped off his pyjamas and plunged him into a cold bath to disperse his hang-over and prepare him for a shooting expedition, which Freddie had organised.

The first commandant of the College had been Brigadier A. Galloway, who had been succeeded by Dorman-Smith, now a brigadier and well known to Freddie from Camberley days; the Deputy Commandant was the amiable Colonel Tiarks of the 1st King's Dragoon Guards.

'Chink' Dorman-Smith as he was known (he had taught me tactics in 1928 as a newly-commissioned Sapper officer) was a highly intelligent and entertaining extrovert like Freddie, and they now became intimate friends. Freddie to Chink's mind was very French, both in his discreet pursuit of women and his subsequent pigeon-holing of them; he rarely fell in love, but now and again had fallen deeply for older and very glamorous women. Yet he had always managed to keep the friendship of his old girlfriends, as he was a good listener and very kind. Both he and Chink were attracted by

43

style, beauty and wit, and Freddie had an almost feminine interest in gossip and personalities, which often enlivened a whole evening when they dined *à deux* in Cairo. Chink assessed his friend as ambitious and very capable. 'He was amused by Freddie's fascination with clothes, perfumes and fashion, but also recognised his keen interest in power and the interplay between leaders.'[2]

Although Dorman-Smith had recently established a considerable reputation as Auchinleck's Director of Military Training in India, at Telsch House he left a great deal of the instructional work to Freddie, the senior instructor. In the innovative and theoretical atmosphere of the Haifa Staff College, the fertility of Dorman-Smith's mind, undisciplined by practical restraints, was not as irksome to Freddie as to those students who soon would come to the college straight from a desert battlefield; thus the personal friendship was maintained, and Dorman-Smith soon developed a genuine appreciation of Freddie's talents.

Many of those who passed through the college either as instructors or as students, two of whom after the war became field-marshals,[3] regarded Freddie as the professional leader and driving force of the establishment. Hot-foot from Whitehall, Freddie soon found that his fellow members of the directing staff, also recently arrived, were hard put to it to draw up and complete their indoor and outdoor exercises in time for the tight programme of the course. He himself was a fluent and witty lecturer who conveyed to the students his deeply studied professional advice without a hint of pomposity, and provided brilliant intellectual leadership to his junior colleagues.

A student of those days, who was a member of Freddie's syndicate of eight officers, recalled over forty years later his naturally kind and generous temperament which brought the best out of each of them and made the instruction so interesting and enjoyable. Moreover his outstanding ability enabled him to hold forth intelligently in a charming and outwardly relaxed manner on practically any aspect of the military scene. If the programmed subject tended to be boring and in the students' opinion had been adequately explored, Freddie would willingly agree to digress and tell them of his fascinating experiences of national and international affairs in the corridors of power. When, as was their wont, the Commandant or his Deputy looked in to see how they were progressing, the students helped

Freddie to change the subject instantly to coincide with the syllabus.

When off duty he exploited as always the opportunities, limited as they were, for sport by day and for social entertainment after dark. His contemporaries had happy memories of early morning chikor shoots on Mount Carmel, and hilarious suppers at the local night club, graced with the platonic attentions of attractive Jewish 'hostesses'.

As the senior instructor, Freddie was given the particular task of presenting every week a résumé of the world-wide military situation. Although in private life an ardent gambler usually for modest stakes, professionally he was always a firm realist. The military scene in 1940 gave little opportunity for optimism. One week he had to pronounce on the disastrous expedition to Norway and draw lessons from the faulty planning of that operation; not long afterwards when Germany attacked in the West in May, he delivered an outspoken address predicting that France would fall within three weeks.

The Commandant, Dorman-Smith, an optimistic Irishman whose military thinking after some years in India may have lacked Freddie's realism, was incensed, and ordered his friend off the platform. The culprit refused to move, saying that it was about time they all faced up to realities; he was then placed under arrest and escorted to his room. Emissaries were sent to persuade him to change his attitude, but he declined. Fortunately at the end of the day the Commandant relented, and released him from arrest. Thereafter the weekly talks were given by a different speaker, but Freddie's predictions proved nearly correct.

Beneath his natural ease of manner, there was concealed an unusual sensitivity; it was small wonder that after the fall of France, his father's country, which held for the son so many memories of joyous holidays in Cannes, Paris and Le Touquet, Freddie became greatly saddened. His syndicate was worried to see him so deeply depressed, and three of them persuaded him to accompany them in their car for a weekend in a hotel in Damascus, two hours' drive from Haifa. But Damascus, still under strong French influence, was a city of gloom and many places of entertainment were closed. Their task of reviving Freddie's spirits was hopeless, and sadly they motored back to Haifa with their instructor as subdued as ever.

Dorman-Smith was a man of high ambition and great courage, and not unnaturally was restive at Telsch House; he seized every opportunity to get nearer the battlefield. In his absence, Freddie, with Colonel Tiarks presiding benignly in the background, assumed increasing responsibilities; but he alike was keen to escape to a job more closely related to the war then in train against the Italians. There was a false start when, promoted to colonel, he was appointed as Commandant of a new School of Combined Operations; but later, strongly recommended by Dorman-Smith, he became at the beginning of December 1940 a member of the Joint Planning Staff at General Headquarters Middle East Command, working with a team which included Group Captain Claude Pelly, RAF. His colleagues soon recognised his intellectual talents and the independence of his outlook.

In Cairo, Freddie was appointed secretary to the Commanders-in-Chief Committee, the body which, guided by Churchill and the Chiefs of Staff in Whitehall, directed the prosecution of the war in the Middle East. As a member of the Inter-Service Joint Planning Staff, he had a multitude of critical strategic problems on which he was required to write advisory papers in collaboration with his colleagues for the consideration of the Commanders-in-Chief, namely Admiral A. B. Cunningham, General Wavell and Air Marshal Longmore.

Among the Army operational staff at GHQ there were many brilliant young officers who were to make their names later in the war. To them Freddie was 'The Oracle'; when in doubt over some question of strategy, the newcomer was told: 'Go and ask Freddie'. Those who followed this advice recalled many years later the friendly welcome they had received from that unusual officer, several years their senior, who treated them in every way as equals. Always approachable and ready to help 'the customer', he was in marked contrast to some of the elderly inhabitants of GHQ, who appeared to these youngsters to be fossilised.

The months of January and February 1941, by which time Freddie had settled in, were a crucial period of the war in the Middle East. Fighting solely against the Italians, British Forces had done well. By February 1941 Lieutenant-General Richard O'Connor had soundly defeated the Italian Forces on the Egyptian frontier with Libya, and Tobruk had been captured. The Joint Planners had convinced themselves that, after a pause of a week or two, an advance with adequate forces could be made to capture Tripoli, over a thousand miles from Cairo. They did not know then that on 6th February Hitler had summoned a General Erwin Rommel to the Berlin Chancellery and there given him command of a force of two divisions, the Afrika Korps, to stiffen their Italian allies. But intelligence from Ultra soon disclosed to Wavell that the two divisions were to be expected in Cyrenaica in April and May 1941.

A new strategic factor then arose; should Britain send aid to Greece now threatened by the Axis forces and what effect would this have on the North African theatre? Hence the first critical issue facing the Joint Planning Staff was the question of diverting resources from O'Connor's highly successful operations in Libya in order to support the Greeks, who were fighting gallantly against the Italians in Albania and expecting an imminent German attack.

Freddie with the planners listed the many disadvantages of such a course, which he regarded as overwhelming; but political factors, not for the first or last time dominated the debate in Whitehall, and the decision was taken by Churchill to launch the Greek expedition.

Freddie accompanied Eden, General Sir John Dill and General Wavell with Naval and Air Chiefs and their advisors to Greece, and was present at the critical conferences in Athens with Papagos and the King of Greece. After the decision to divert from North Africa to the Greek Army resources which Eden described as formidable, but which Freddie always regarded as inadequate, he was sent off to reconnoitre the Aliakmon Line, the position chosen for the ultimate defence of Greece. On that extensive journey he first survived an earthquake and then, armed with his Greek laissez-passer as a 'journalist', was arrested as a spy. From both experiences he recovered with his usual resilience; and when the tragic evacuation of the British forces took place, the operation, splendidly conducted by the Royal Navy, was effected in accordance with plans which the Joint Planning Staff had privately worked out at an early date contrary to Wavell's initial orders. Long after the war Freddie described the sequence of events as follows:[4]

> I was convinced that having captured Benghazi we could with the Navy's assistance, drive on and capture Tripoli and eventually join up with the loyal French troops in Tunisia. So I started producing plans for the evacuation from Greece which looked a certainty. However Wavell got to hear of this, and Arthur Smith his CGS gave me an order not to proceed with these plans. I was furious and went to see the other Commanders-in-Chief – Tedder and Cunningham, who agreed with me and gave me permission to produce plans on the Navy's and RAF's behalf.

The next morning I arrived at the banks of the Nile to catch a flying boat due to depart for Greece. On arrival I found Wavell waiting there. He called me over and asked me what I was doing and I explained and he permitted me to go. On arrival at Piraeus I let Wavell and Co depart and then got on with discussions with the RAF regarding plans of our evacuation. The RAF commander was Air Marshal D'Albiac. In the afternoon I received a telephone call from Wavell saying he wanted to see me the next afternoon at 3 p.m.

I arrived at the Hotel Grand Bretagne at the appointed hour and was led up to his suite. When I entered he greeted me with 'Hullo Freddie'. This was the first time he had addressed me by my christian name and he told me that the situation was very bad and that evacuation was quite on the cards. Knowing that I had been working on plans for such an eventuality, he gave me permission to discuss such plans with certain people such as General Wilson [commanding British Troops in Egypt] and the Base Commander. So I spent the rest of the day and most of the night briefing these various soldiers. The next morning I flew back to Cairo and informed my colleagues of the turn of events.

Freddie in writing of these matters with the benefit of hindsight in 1946[5] and again in 1964[6] was severely critical of Eden – who, he tartly observed, invariably removed his spectacles before being photographed – and he accused him of magnifying the scale of British assistance to the Greeks to bolster their resistance to the Germans. He criticised Wavell for not making a firmer stand against an operation which, though politically desirable should have been recognised as militarily unsound. In Freddie's recollection, the Planners were not asked to produce a paper on the feasibility of the project, but the Director of Military Intelligence, Brigadier Shearer, did so, emphasising the great dangers of the campaign in view of German resources and methods. The paper came back from Wavell with the note 'War is an option of difficulties: Wolfe. A.P.W.' Freddie and his Naval and Air colleagues, while admiring the spirit, questioned the judgement. It was said that Freddie responded with 'Only numbers can annihilate: Nelson.'

In his post-war book *Generals at War* Freddie contested Churchill's argument that the Greek expedition had helped the USSR by delaying the date of 'Barbarossa', the German attack on Russia. But historians may feel that the author was relying too much on his personal recollections of 1941, and that his critical statements published in a weighty volume were insufficiently supported by post-war research. President Eisenhower, who subsequently received a copy of the book in 1965, wrote to Freddie: 'I thought you were a little hard on Wavell . . . Twice at least he was given really impossible situations, and I have a suspicion that behind some of his instructions were political pressures that possibly his associates knew nothing about.' This indeed was true. The political pressure arose from the British Government's unqualified undertaking made in the spring of 1939 to assist in the defence of Greece. Although Churchill declared that he would base his decision on professional military advice, Eden his Foreign Secretary was adamant that military assistance should be sent.

When Freddie's views on the strategy of the Greek debacle were published in 1947 in *Operation Victory*, Churchill (who had received an inscribed copy) commented: 'There is more in this story than you know.'

But whatever the verdict of historians, Freddie's experiences at the age of forty-one were a most formative preparation for the key appointments that lay ahead. As a planner in Cairo to be deeply, even emotionally involved in arguing the strategical implications of the Greek expedition, then to be present at the crucial political conferences in Athens itself, then to carry out a personal reconnaissance of the Aliakmon defence line chosen off the map in Cairo, and finally to initiate plans for the evacuation, in his mind inevitable, and to see them brought urgently into use, these must have been educative experiences which few staff officers could hope for.

Soon he was to have more of them in the sands of the Western Desert. With the arrival of Rommel on the scene, British forces, which had captured Benghazi and reached Agheila, had been hurriedly forced back, to the neighbourhood of Tobruk.

Freddie, returning from Greece to Cairo, was ordered to go with the Air C-in-C Air Marshal Sir Arthur Tedder, to report on the situation facing the 'fortress' of Tobruk which Wavell felt must be held despite Rommel's successful attack on 31st March against the British forces greatly weakened by the diversions to Greece. Freddie's account written after the war gives an eye-witness impression of this crisis in the desert, the first of many.

That afternoon April 17th a meeting took place in Cairo at which the

Commander-in-Chief, Eden and Dill were present. The atmosphere was
certainly tense. The subject was Tobruk. I noticed Eden's fingers drumming
on the table; he looked nervous and a very different person to the Eden at
the Palace in Athens. After the problem had been discussed from each service
point of view, Wavell was asked to give his views. I admired him
tremendously at that moment. He had a very heavy load to carry but he
looked calm and collected, and said that in his view we must hold Tobruk,
and that he considered that this was possible. One could feel the sense of relief
that this decision produced, and the other Commanders-in-Chief agreed,
and it was decided to send Air Marshal Tedder and myself up the next day
to Tobruk to report on the situation and to discuss possible reinforcements
. . . The next day, April 18th, I left in Tedder's aircraft with the object of
reaching Tobruk. The situation was very fluid and information was scanty.
Enemy armoured patrols had been reported in the vicinity of the frontier
about Sollum. Just before take-off we received a message that we could land
at Sollum airfield, and so Tedder decided to do so and find out the latest form.
I had a liaison officer with me who was to be dropped there with some orders
from GHQ. They related to the line of action that should be taken on the
frontier; for communications appeared to have broken down between this
area and Headquarters of the Western Desert Force. Certain reinforcements
were on their way up from the Delta and it was important that they should
be stopped at the frontier and organised as a 'long-stop' in the Sollum area.
I should mention here that General Wavell had sent General O'Connor up
as a sort of advisor to General Neame [the new Commander of the Western
Desert Force] in view of his past experience in desert warfare.

We touched down at Sollum and found everything quite peaceful, but no
one seemed to know what was happening in the Tobruk direction. Tedder
therefore flew on to Gambut which was about midway between Sollum and
Tobruk. We found the RAF in process of evacuating the airfield. The
transport was moving off and bombs were being blown up. Here a car was
requisitioned and we drove to Tobruk, telling our pilot to try and make its
airfield if he got an all clear. We first called the RAF Control Headquarters
just outside the town, and they were more or less in ignorance of the general
situation. No one had heard where the Force Headquarters was now
situated, nor the whereabouts of Neame or O'Connor. We drove along the
road leading westward from Tobruk and a mile or two out we met a Garrison
Engineer who indicated a group of transport and tents which he said were
Force Headquarters. On reaching the area it was only to find that this was
'Rear HQ's' and they knew nothing much of what was happening. They
thought 'Main HQ's' were moving into Tobruk itself. The whole
atmosphere was typical of a situation of this sort. No one knew anything and

odd bodies of troops and vehicles were moving rather aimlessly about. The Australian Division was on its way into Tobruk, having marched a long distance from the Jebel. They looked very tired. The whole area was naked, and if the enemy had had the forces available to send to Tobruk I'm afraid there was nothing much to stop them. We could hear a battle raging to the south-west which turned out to be the fight at Mekili between the enemy and an Indian Motor Brigade and a sadly depleted British armoured division.

We drove back into Tobruk and soon found signs of a headquarters taking up a new location. Signal cables were being run out, motor transport arriving and sign boards being fixed up. We were told the BGS was inside a certain building, so we went in to hear the news and deliver our message. Here in one of the rooms we found Brigadier John Harding. He looked terribly tired but cheerful. We were told that news had just come in showing that both Generals Neame and O'Connor had been captured the day before. They had been ambushed in the Jebel country . . .

Later on we heard that our aircraft had managed to make Tobruk airfield and so drove out there to emplane for Cairo . . . We felt pretty wretched at leaving our friends to an uncertain fate, whilst we were on our way back to sleep in a comfortable bed in Cairo. On arrival back we went round to the AOC-in-C's house where General Wavell joined the party. The news of the capture of both Neame and O'Connor came as a real shock to the C-in-C, and I have never seen him so moved. He listened to my report, asked a few questions and then left to go back to his house.[7]

On that trip, as Freddie viewed the unending stretch of the single coast road linking Cairo and Tunis, and, to the south, the vast open spaces littered with the burnt-out vehicles of recent battles, he would have gained vivid confirmation of the singular environment of this desert battlefield. Throughout the long history of British arms, confined until then to major continental wars and minor colonial conflicts, such strange terrain had seldom been encountered. The desert was not a sand sea: everywhere there were small recognisable features, some associated with the Birs, the water systems of the Romans; and in the Jebel of Cyrenaica there were large areas of scrub-covered hills. Nevertheless the strategy to be attempted bore some resemblance to operations at sea. Mobility for the warrior on land, so circumscribed in the agricultural landscape of Europe, here in the desert was relatively easy, and on the southern flank, extending over a thousand miles to the Sahara, there were endless opportunities for outflanking movements provided adequate maintenance could be assured.

Thus the strategic pattern became one of bases, like secure anchorages, from which powerful mobile forces, the cruiser squadrons of the desert, could sally forth intent on defeating the enemy by concentrating superior force at a decisive point in time and space.

In these novel circumstances there was soon to be produced an abundance of theories on battlefield tactics, particularly under Auchinleck, who was shortly to appear on the scene supported by his intellectual mentor Dorman-Smith, already renowned for a prolif- eration of inventive solutions, as wild as they were impracticable. One such tentative solution was the 'Cowpat' scheme, under which a series of bases, protected by infantry, artillery and minefields, would be established one by one in front of our positions, from which strong armoured forces would sally forth to destroy the enemy. The fallacy of this theory was that the dispersion of forces which it demanded made them an easy prey to a concentrated thrust by the enemy, who often was superior in armour and mobility. Freddie, the realist, was to get involved in these brainstorming sessions, which he found totally unrewarding. For the British, lacking superiority in armour, it was inevitably a time for clutching at straws.

On 1st May 1941 the Greek campaign came to its foreseeable and tragic end. 'We lost most things other than our honour,' Freddie wrote in retrospect.

Crete was to be lost four weeks later. Freddie with the Joint Plan- ners had been involved in advising the Commanders-in-Chief on the policy for the defence of Crete, but they were not witnesses of the battle. Much earlier they had recognised the strategic importance of the island, particularly to the Royal Navy; but despite permission having been given by the Greeks to send British troops there as early as December 1940, little had been done before the campaign in Greece was launched to prepare adequate defences. By then it was too late and sufficient resources were no longer available.

To Freddie, still sleeping in his comfortable bed in Cairo and doubtless gambling late at night at the Mohammed Ali Club, the next few months, when British and Commonwealth troops, forced to retreat, were being killed with no apparent advantage to the com- mon cause, must have been tragic indeed. Unlike so many of the cheer-leaders who proliferated in the meeting places of Cairo, Freddie was not to be diverted from the harsh facts, and intellectually he was fast becoming a professional in the art of war. He could see all too clearly that unforgivable strategic mistakes were being made and that hundreds of lives were being cast away for nothing.

Meanwhile Churchill in London was demanding offensive action, with the result that Wavell's long-expected counter-attack in the Western Desert, 'Battleaxe', was launched on 15 June 1941. The object was to defeat the Axis forces under Rommel, who had recently arrived on the scene, before he could build up his resources. To support this intention, a convoy of tanks had daringly been sent by Churchill through the Mediterranean instead of by the long Cape route. Political pressure to exploit this initiative was very strong. The Joint Planning Staff drew attention to the poor prospects of success, but the die was cast.

In launching the offensive, little heed had been paid to the power of the German 88 mm gun combined with the brilliant tactics of Rommel. Compared to the German panzers, the British 'I' tank was slow and unsatisfactory. Moreover it was known by Shearer, the then Director of Military Intelligence, that Rommel would shortly receive as reinforcement the 15th Panzer Division, which Montgomery subsequently found was one of the most formidable, élite divisions of the German Army.

At this period the inefficiency of the British Intelligence organisation which Freddie in eight months' time was to take over as director, was serious; long afterwards when historians had studied the actions of both contestants it was tersely summed up as follows:

One reason for the failure [of 'Battleaxe'], the most important indeed, was the technical superiority of the German equipment, particularly armour and anti-tank guns. British intelligence had given no warning of this, and its extent was revealed for the first time during the British counter-attack. At the same time, intelligence performed poorly during the fighting. Although the GAF Enigma (Ultra) contained much tactical information it was often out of date by the time it was read at the Government Code and Cipher School. When it was sent out to the Middle East there was the same difficulty as before in getting the intelligence from Cairo to the British Forces, a difficulty which can easily be appreciated if it is remembered that the British commanders were sometimes as much out of touch with the whereabouts and movements of their own forces as with those of the enemy. . . .[8]

By contrast Rommel, in addition to his superiority in equipment, had at that time an intelligence organisation greatly superior to that of the British. We now know that: 'As a result of intercepting British signals, he was expecting the attack on the day it was delivered, and he was supplied with good information from W/T and captured documents throughout the battle . . .'[9]

On 28th May, Wavell himself had signalled to the CIGS eighteen days before the start of 'Battleaxe': 'I think it is right to inform you that the measure of success which will attend this operation is in my opinion doubtful . . .'[10] 'Nothing went right,' as Freddie wrote in 1964, 'and we returned to the defensive on 17th June having lost nearly a hundred tanks and suffered a thousand casualties.'[11] Churchill in London commented on the loyalty of Wavell in supporting the risks which the Cabinet had run in sending the tank convoy through the Mediterranean; nevertheless on 5th July Wavell was relieved of his command, and appointed Commander-in-Chief India.

An ironical commentator might observe that Freddie, the arch gambler in his private life, in his professional role carried cautious realism almost to extremes. This was no disadvantage when all too soon he was to find himself teamed up with Montgomery who, despite later American criticisms of over-caution, could be impetuous. Certainly it is the task of the operational planner to identify all the risks and attempt to weigh them in the balance; but Wavell found himself between the Scylla of political pressure and the Charybdis of military risk. In Europe the same problem would face Montgomery.

With the arrival of General Sir Claude Auchinleck, who himself was to be removed from command in less than a year, Freddie became more optimistic. He had criticised Wavell, who could not be described by even his greatest admirers as an extrovert publicist, for communicating only with the highest level of staff officers. In the corridors of GHQ, the C-in-C could frequently be seen totally ignoring a senior staff officer, of whose name after several months he appeared to be unaware. This was in glaring contrast to Freddie's own methods, by which a powerful link of friendship was established with his subordinates at the first opportunity. After the war he compared Wavell's apparent taciturnity to Montgomery's technique of taking immense pains not only to 'present' himself frequently to all his staff but to make himself known, often face to face, with a high proportion of the soldiers under his command. Montgomery kept a little book in which he wrote the personal details of officers whom he regarded as useful to the Army.

Auchinleck's arrival in Cairo coincided with a potential improvement in the military situation: reinforcements of troops and material were on the way. The Joint Planners emerged from their despondency, and in October they were given a novel and unforeseen task: on behalf of the Commanders-in-Chief to visit the subordinate commands in Syria, Palestine, Iraq and Iran to coordinate their plans. This was to be followed by a visit to India. Freddie, aged forty-one, was to be the leader, and he took with him his RAF colleague Group Captain Claude Pelly.

This was the sort of mission in which Freddie excelled. Ever since his private visits to the French and German Infantry training establishments in 1939, he had never hesitated to accept unusual responsibilities in those military spheres where diplomacy was an essential tool. In Baghdad they found harmony, and achieved success with the British Command, but felt quite rightly that they should assess with the Soviet representatives, expected shortly, the speed of a possible German advance into the Caucasus. They were firmly told by their British advisers that nothing would thereby be achieved; but they persisted only to be told by the Russians: 'We find it difficult to understand your requests; the Germans have not reached the Caucasus. If by any chance such an event did take place, and the Red Army could not stop them, how could you?'[12]

They flew on to Teheran where profitable talks were held with the British Minister; but after two days of gracious living which Freddie as always grasped with both hands, his sepoy driver collided with a tree, badly dislocating and damaging his passenger's arm. This was the first of many mishaps of increasing severity which, combined with his chronic physical weaknesses were to harm Freddie in the next three years. However, on this occasion during a week's leave in Poona, he was soon able to recover his poise.

By the autumn of 1941 the situation in the Middle East Command seemed to have markedly improved. The 'Crusader' offensive into Cyrenaica had been successful, and on the Eastern Front the USSR had prevented the Wehrmacht from reaching Moscow. The situation in Italy's East African Colonies had been resolved and Abyssinia had been liberated.

Freddie by now had been working with his colleagues of the Royal Navy and the Royal Air Force for several months; this was an effective preparation for the vast amphibious operations which, unknown to him, lay ahead. Moreover he had gained the friendship and confidence of the Commanders-in-Chief of the other two services, an advantage which likewise was to stand him in good stead in the days to come. His qualities had always been recognised by the uncommunicative Wavell and appreciated more enthusiastically by Auchinleck, to whose direct soldierly personality Freddie found it easier to respond. He had now moved into the 'top league': he possessed not only the full professional expertise of the 'Whitehall Warrior' and of the 'Gaberdine Swine' (as soldiers out in the Desert so kindly dubbed staff officers in Cairo) but was also becoming involved in the Desert War and the life of those who had 'sand in their shoes'. He was in fact on the threshold of his greatest wartime achievements.

Auchinleck, aware from Dorman-Smith of Freddie's great qualities, warmed to him and made use of his quick analytical brain in reviewing the operations which, after the great offensive 'Crusader' had unexpectedly foundered disastrously in the face of Rommel's attack. Lt-General Sir Alan Cunningham, the Army Commander who had failed, was relieved by Major-General Neil Ritchie who in turn was relieved by Auchinleck himself. It was a disastrous period for Eighth Army, which in January 1942 was forced back from Benghazi to Gazala, and for Auchinleck, who would soon turn to Freddie, the brilliant planner, to play a bigger part in the attempt to restore British fortunes in the Middle East.

CHAPTER FIVE

Intelligence Chief

Fortune smiled on Freddie when in February 1942 Auchinleck, on Dorman-Smith's recommendation, selected him, still a lieutenant-colonel aged forty-two in the Joint Planning Staff, to become Director of Military Intelligence, Middle East Command, with the rank of brigadier. After the war, Freddie repeatedly cited this as evidence of Auchinleck's failure to choose the right man for the job, but this must have been due to some distorted judgement induced either by excessive modesty or indifferent health. When he protested at the time that he knew nothing of intelligence, Auchinleck said that it was for that reason that he had chosen him, and that he would do it well.

It is true that Auchinleck, as a general rule, was not a good chooser: he had surrounded himself with some ineffective subordinates such as Major-General Dorman-Smith and Lt-General T. W. Corbett his DCGS. But even from a hasty assessment Freddie must have looked a potential winner for the post of DMI. He had always had an unusual gift of constructive imagination and this was combined with a good memory and one one of the sharpest brains amongst the intelligentsia of GHQ. On many occasions his colleagues and superiors must have seen Whiz-Bang's intellect brought into play with lightning rapidity and the result communicated to his listeners with humour and charm. If there were any advisors who thought that a Director of Intelligence must have had personal experience of intelligence techniques, they were wrong, for it was the Director's task, not to get bogged down in detail but to motivate his many subordinates, define broad objectives and supply a balanced judgement on the available evidence. All this Freddie could do extremely well. His critics could find only one fault: his great determination to beat the enemy sometimes made him too keen with operational suggestions on how to do it. In this he anticipated the days to come.

He was brought in at a difficult moment when his predecessor Shearer had been removed at short notice. 'John' Shearer (he was in fact Eric James) was a man of considerable ability. Born in 1892 he had been commissioned in the Indian Army and had fought in the First World War; he had gained a Military Cross and had held staff appointments in the War Office until 1929, when he had retired and become Joint Managing Director of Fortnum and Mason in London. He had left them to return to the Army on the outbreak of war in 1939, becoming head of Military Intelligence Middle East Command in 1940.

In early 1941 following the receipt of intelligence of the dispatch to Cyrenaica of the Afrika Korps under Rommel, Shearer had organised in Cairo a system by which appreciations of Rommel's intentions were made by a group of officers 'living in the enemy's shoes'. One such pronouncement by the imaginary German general 'X' was:

> As a striking force I have full confidence in my command. Subject to administrative preparations, I believe that the German Armoured Corps, after a week's training in desert warfare conditions, and unless the British substantially reinforce their present forces in Libya, could successfully undertake the reoccupation of Cyrenaica.[1]

Although Shearer knew little of Rommel's previous record, this turned out to be a remarkably perceptive and accurate forecast, but the significance of it did not immediately strike Wavell, who later was surprised at the masterly performance of the German Afrika Korps' commander.

In the summer of 1941, before the 'Battleaxe' operation, a Special Liaison Unit (SLU) had been sent out to Cairo in order to facilitate the rapid transmission from the United Kingdom of Ultra signals direct to Middle East Command; thereafter Auchinleck on his visits to the battle zone had always taken his SLU with him, so as to keep in continuous touch with the special intelligence reports. Churchill not infrequently used these to embarrass and to spur on his Commanders-in-Chief. Thus the head of Military Intelligence and his C-in-C were from then onwards given at frequent intervals accurate and reliable indications of enemy intentions, order of battle and supply situation.

Amongst the intelligence community at GHQ, Shearer had gained recognition as a skilful operator by using as a double agent the Gauleiter of Mannheim, a parachutist spy who, with his radio set and codes, had been captured in Palestine. A false scenario, that British preparations for operation 'Crusader', obvious from the air, were only a cover plan for the move of a large force northward to help the Soviet Union resist the German threat to their oilfields, had been successfully fed to Rommel, who accepted it. The intelligence staff would no doubt have briefed Freddie on this successful achievement of deception. Shearer was however very unsuccessful in developing good relationships with senior commanders, due to his lack of psychological insight and to his inability to admit that he was wrong. In December he had made a disastrously optimistic estimate over Rommel's reinforcements of tanks; he had been informed by Ultra of an Axis convoy of tanks of which forty-five in two ships were sunk; but twenty-three in another ship had been successfully landed in Tripoli, and twenty-two landed from a fourth ship in Benghazi despite the lack of unloading facilities and the blocking of the harbour, which Shearer's naval advisors had assured him would prevent unloading. These twenty-two tanks were just sufficient to enable Rommel to counter-attack, inflicting heavy tank casualties on the British armoured brigade and turning Auchinleck's 'Crusader' battle, still hanging in the balance, into a disaster.

For some time past, rightly or wrongly, Shearer's evaluation of enemy capabilities had been regarded in Whitehall as well as in Cairo as dangerously optimistic; this incident proved fatal to his reputation with senior commanders and he was summarily replaced. He retired from the Army and again pursued a successful career in business. His departure left the way open for Freddie, despite his lack of experience, to take on greatly enlarged responsibilities.

The intelligence organisation in Middle East Command had come into being in early 1940 with only one officer who had had a half share in a room and a half share in a clerk. Few regular officers had been available, and so the Chief, then a Deputy Director of Military Intelligence, had had to embark on an extensive programme of training, while simultaneously he was involved in operations. Much talent had been found amongst the non-regular officers, but they were handicapped by the lack of a military background, and many of them, once trained, had to be sent to other commands, with the result that turnover in the Headquarters had been excessive. Nevertheless a new organisation had been successfully developed to obtain intelligence from prisoners of war by novel sophisticated methods, and a comprehensive organisation for signals interception had been set up. Steps had been taken also to introduce measures for deceiving the enemy and these had been highly successful. The whole concept of security and its techniques had been developed, and finally a section of intelligence had been established to make detailed calculations of enemy shipping and transportation to deduce his maintenance capability by air, sea and land. It was this wide range of activities that now passed under Freddie's control as Director of Military Intelligence.

To my eyes he appeared to fit the role admirably. After Telsch House, I had found myself appointed chief of operations in the headquarters in Cairo of SOE, the 'Special Operations Executive', engaged in secret subversion and the support of Resistance Groups in enemy-occupied countries in the Balkans. Thus our paths did occasionally meet, and I observed that Freddie, with his comprehensive grasp of the military scene, his superb memory and his sophisticated powers of expression had now developed into a most authoritative figure.

He had by now established a very warm relationship with Auchinleck whom he much admired, and this was reciprocated. 'The Auk inspired tremendous loyalty and affection amongst those who served close to him,' he wrote after the war.[2] As DMI he had excellent opportunities to get to know the Commander-in-Chief, since he was frequently invited to accompany him on his visits to Eighth Army, as the Western Desert Force had now become. He was on such a visit to the Desert when Rommel attacked at Gazala, and again later during the chaotic times when Eighth Army was falling back to the Alamein area, having lost Tobruk. When called upon to take instructions from Auchinleck to Ritchie a pencilled note often appeared in the margin: 'De Guingand knows my views.'

As Director of Military Intelligence, a post which he occupied for only five months, Freddie was undoubtedly a great success. Auchinleck treated this newcomer to Intelligence very sympathetically, and the staff of the Directorate responded readily to Freddie's sharp intellect and winning ways. Early on, he spotted two exceptionally able young officers: Captain J. Ewart and Captain 'Bill' Williams,[3] both university dons. Later Bill Williams rose to positions of high responsibility under Montgomery. He was present in Cairo when Freddie took over and, many years later, painted a vivid picture of that scene in 1942:

> Colonel de Guingand had impressed the taciturn Wavell, whose replacement by the Auk in 1941 led to the inspired selection of de Guingand as Director of Military Intelligence early in 1942, at a time when that branch was under attack. He swiftly took grip. We had our camp beds in Freddie's office in Grey Pillars where every night he came in after midnight from the Mohammed Ali Club – or the Turf Club – for one of these briefing sessions before the Auk sent off his latest (and inevitably out of date) instruction. Freddie was a brilliant DMI in Cairo.[4]

Auchinleck tended to try out the merits or otherwise of plans submitted to him by means of a Brains Trust technique, a War Game with 'enemy' and 'own' troops to test new ideas. This method did not appeal to Freddie, particularly when, carrying the Brains Trust idea still further, he was pressed to use Shearer's 'German Cell' of a few officers, who would live in an enemy atmosphere and endeavour to read into the enemy's mind. This concept was backed by Dorman-Smith, and Freddie tactfully turned it down owing to the danger of creating two channels of advice, one of which was based on 'hunches'.

The C-in-C gave his new DMI the priority task of establishing confidence between the commanders and staffs in Eighth Army and Military Intelligence. In a matter of weeks the relationship was vastly improved. This was particularly important as the reputation of the Directorate had been sullied by the public criticism of Freddie's predecessor, who as DMI was *ipso facto* 'spokesman' to the Press. Williams, as an eye-witness of Freddie's performance in that role, commented thirty-eight years later:

> Freddie had always impressed the powerful body of able war correspondents, men like Alan Moorehead, Alex Clifford and Christopher Buckley, by his Press conferences. As professionals they recognised, as

Wavell had done, the qualities in Freddie of a very good reporter. Throughout the war he remained one of their favourites, for he had a singular capacity to tell them the truth in context, to define the strategic picture in imaginative terms.[5]

With access to all sources of intelligence, and responsible personally for briefing the C-in-C on the enemy situation, Freddie was present in GHQ at all the many crises of this disastrous period. He recalled in particular the conference in the War Room called at 9.30 pm on 14th June to decide whether despite Eighth Army's retreat, Tobruk should be held. The appreciation of Ritchie, the Army Commander, was read out. The DMI then stated his view that the enemy, unless struck by strong Allied armour and Air Forces, could penetrate the Tobruk defences. Auchinleck thanked him for his statement and said that although he appreciated the dangers, he felt an attempt should be made to hold the fortress. He then personally drafted an instruction to Ritchie. The conference did not end until midnight, when Freddie retired to bed relieved that at last a firm decision had been taken: such decisions were like 'gusts of fresh air in the fog of war'.[6]

After only a few days Rommel launched his attack against Tobruk: in Freddie's view the South African Division, which with other formations formed the garrison never had a chance. He was at the headquarters of Eighth Army on 21st June when news, which was to shake the Western world, came in – the fall of Tobruk. There followed the retreat to the Alamein position, a far from orderly operation, which he witnessed at close quarters. Fortunately the efforts of the Desert Air Force prevented the German Air Force from turning the retreat into a rout.

By the end of June, morale in Cairo was at a low ebb. Nevertheless, the Egyptians and their officials with whom Freddie, wearing his 'security' hat, had important business to transact, behaved well. Although there was a run on the banks there was little sign of civilian panic. However at 'Grey Pillars', GHQ, and at 'Red Pillars', the headquarters of the secret Special Operations Executive, there was a pervasive smell of disaster in the air. The chimneys of Red and Grey Pillars smoked visibly as top secret documents were hurriedly burnt; charred remains floated accusingly in the sultry air. Warships at Alexandria swiftly took evasive action, and women and children including the charming girls of SOE were sent in batches to Palestine for 'safety'.

In this situation, where the maintenance of morale was vital – the morale not only of Middle East Command and Eighth Army but of the polyglot city of Cairo – it was fortunate that Freddie had established such a dominant but friendly influence over the Press.

By early July, Eighth Army's situation had improved. Formations on arrival at the 'Alamein position', which was not more than a line on the map, had sorted themselves out, dug in, and established communications. Minor offensive operations were undertaken to deter Rommel from launching a further thrust to Cairo, for which as Ultra had disclosed, he did not as yet possess adequate supplies. Freddie like many others who were present at that time considered that these attacks, which have been glorified by some historians as the First Battle of Alamein, were a mistake. The troops and formations were either too tired or too green and were untrained to the Desert: and no exploitation on a large scale was possible. Large losses of tanks were sustained when attacking the 88 mm gun screens of the Afrika Korps. However, we now know from German sources that Rommel suffered critical losses from these attacks.

Freddie was invited by Auchinleck, who was still commanding Eighth Army to stay with him for ten days. The C-in-C, doubling the role of Army Commander with his responsibilities at GHQ Cairo, had appreciated that Brigadier Whiteley, the BGS (operations), who had borne much of the brunt of the repeated crises of the last eight months, needed a rest and a change; thus Freddie in Cairo received a signal to hand over his responsibilities to his deputy and leave immediately for HQ Eighth Army to become BGS (operations). But once again he was reluctant to accept this new challenge – this time with more justification, as he had never been in a unit in battle and had had little previous experience of staff work 'in the field'. Moreover he felt that by now he had mastered his job of intelligence. He protested personally to the Military Secretary who, sharing his views, discussed the appointment with Auchinleck. A peremptory signal followed, ordering Freddie to report to HQ Eighth Army immediately.

Thus his thoughts were compounded of great excitement and considerable anxiety. Although always ambitious, and keen to find himself at centres of power, he had private reservations as to his ability to perform as an executive staff officer in an unfamiliar battle environment, and at a level much above anything he had attempted before. Nor would he have been ignorant of the pressures being exerted by Churchill on his Commander-in-Chief and of the difficult relationship existing between the two men. This did not bode well for a successful conduct of operations at a time of great crisis.

However for him there was no choice so, reconciled to the new situation and longing to make the grade, he duly reported at Headquarters Eighth Army, located at a junction of dung-strewn camel tracks near Ruweisat Ridge. Much has been written of that long-established spot, so inappropriate for its purpose as the headquarters of an army, soon to be ridiculed by Churchill on his visit in August, and thereafter to be consigned to oblivion by Montgomery immediately on arrival. For Freddie it was in marked contrast to the urban ethos of 'Grey Pillars' and his sybaritic life in Cairo. He with Auchinleck, and Brigadier J. F. M. Whiteley, the BGS (operations) and the superfluous Dorman-Smith, busy as VCGS, had caravans; the other staff officers, myself and a few others, had an assortment of office trucks and slept in individual slit trenches, sometime roofed with a small tent. Communication with forward formations was by indistinct desert tracks requiring sometimes the use of a sun-compass. Water was scarce and rationed with severity. Every morning at reveille, Freddie would have seen miscellaneous figures ranging from corporal to colonel, standing stark naked in the much-worn sand and sponging themselves from head to foot.

To add to his troubles, Freddie was having one of his bouts of ill-health; and his friend Chink commented, tongue in cheek: 'Freddie is stretched out on a row of camp stools in my lorry office, clamouring for soft women, and doing himself no good by developing a fixation over the back-page girl of the *Egyptian Mail*. . . . He moans about being 42 and impotent . . .'[7]

Nevertheless he was to adapt himself to the new life very quickly. After all, disregarding enemy activity it was not so very different to

2nd Lieutenant Francis de Guingand, commissioned in the 2nd Battalion of the Prince of Wales's Own West Yorkshire Regiment in 1919.

Left: A trout stream in Malawi. It was in that country, then called Nyasaland, that Freddie, a young officer in the King's African Rifles, became a skilful fly-fisher and shot.

Below: In June 1939 Mr Hore-Belisha, the Secretary of State for War, selected Freddie to be his Military Assistant in the War Office.

'bushwhacking' in Nyasaland, and the Comte de Guingand, a figure that had so often been seen in a dinner jacket in French and Egyptian casinos, would soon adjust to these novel, harsh conditions.

CHAPTER SIX

Desert Warrior

Freddie was not surprised by the desperate situation which confronted him when he arrived in late July 1942 at Headquarters Eighth Army as the new BGS (operations). As Director of Military Intelligence in Cairo, he had noted the appalling and unexpected disaster to Auchinleck's operations at Gazala. Rommel was now only sixty miles from Alexandria, and it was known that despite his lack of sufficient supplies and petrol he intended to launch a final attack in the hope of reaching Cairo – an event for which both Hitler and Mussolini were making optimistic preparations and flamboyant pronouncements. If Rommel were to succeed, the possibility was opened up of an immense German pincer movement with one thrust southwards through a demoralised Turkey into Syria, Iraq and Palestine, there to join up with the eastern thrust of the Afrika Korps. This was dangerous enough, but in view of the impending launching of Torch, the Anglo-American landing at the western end of the Mediterranean, it was vital that Rommel's thrust should be held.

Nevertheless Freddie found the atmosphere at Tactical headquarters very discouraging. For some time past, due to failures of command and the losses thereby sustained, morale had suffered and, despite Auchinleck's prestige and the veneration in which he was held by many, decisive leadership seemed lacking. Many formation and regimental commanders had been out in the desert for a long time, and by now had experienced the failure of more than one 'Benghazi handicap'. For the next contest, theories abounded as to the tactics to be followed, many of them emanating from the top; all too frequently orders transmitted by the staff were treated as a basis for discussion. The Army composed of magnificent material, was 'brave but baffled', as Churchill later was to call them.

There was in addition a strange complication at the headquarters,

66

which greatly increased the bewilderment of the staff — the presence of Dorman-Smith, whose function was far from clear. Auchinleck had moved him up from Cairo as his personal advisor, but in practice with Whiteley in position as BGS (operations) there had been an intolerable duplication of staff instructions.

Freddie discovered that, in those confused days before his arrival, a variety of plans had been produced to meet Rommel's anticipated attack, including one which I had sketched out on Whiteley's instructions with the object of withdrawing Eighth Army to Khartoum. Thus in the worst case of a failure to defeat Rommel's attack, Eighth Army by withdrawal was to be 'kept in being'. Whiteley had instructed his planner to lock up the document and talk to no one about it. Concurrently one of the logistic staff, Lt-Colonel Miles Graham, had been carrying out a reconnaissance of routes of withdrawal based on the same concept, and a new site for the Army headquarters had been selected on the Nile, sixty miles south of Cairo.

Soon after his arrival, Freddie found himself faced with a succession of papers emanating from the fertile mind of Dorman-Smith which were sent to him by the C-in-C to examine. This wasted a great deal of his time; fortunately Auchinleck agreed, at Freddie's request, to return his mentor to Cairo, leaving the new BGS in sole charge of his vital function as head of the General Staff branches, with Hugh Mainwaring in Operations, 'Spud' Murphy in Intelligence, myself in Plans, and David Belchem in Staff Duties as his band of lieutenant-colonels.

The change-over was achieved without rancour. Since those days at Haifa, Dorman-Smith had continued to press on Auchinleck the great ability of Freddie de Guingand, and finally had recommended that he replace Whiteley. Thus the friendship of instructor and student had continued despite the awkward situation at Army headquarters. Dorman-Smith himself was ready to return to GHQ, and urged Auchinleck to get Eighth Army Headquarters on to a proper footing. Ironically he interpreted Freddie's cautious approach to his new and demanding responsibilities as evidence of a lack of self-confidence. In reality, this was due to Freddie's distaste for the unorthodox set-up at the Headquarters, the redundant position of Dorman-Smith and the undesirable influence he exerted over

Auchinleck. The four lieutenant-colonels answerable to Freddie were greatly relieved by Dorman-Smith's departure. Whiteley, with a recommendation from Auchinleck to the CIGS, General Sir Alan Brooke, returned to England, soon to reappear as a senior member of Eisenhower's staff.

Soon after Freddie's arrival a conference of Corps Commanders was held by the Army Commander with his new BGS (operations) beside him. It was decided that a pause was necessary before any offensive operation could be launched. One ingenious tactical plan had been under study by Dorman-Smith; this had involved the activities of numerous ad hoc battle groups supported from strongly defended observation posts – a concept of mobile operations which was quite impracticable in Eighth Army's current state of training.

Auchinleck confided to Freddie that he was considering returning soon to Cairo to reassume his appointment as C-in-C Middle East Command. His difficulty was to find a suitable successor to General Ritchie to command Eighth Army. Asked for his views, Freddie replied that a new man altogether was required and that only two generals had the necessary qualifications: Montgomery was one and Slim, one of Freddie's instructors at the Staff College Camberley in 1935, was the other.

A feature of Auchinleck's method of command had been to hold a daily conference with his principal staff officers in his map lorry every evening about 9pm. This was intended to keep the staff fully advised of the C-in-C's intentions. At this conference attended by the BGS (ops) and the four lieutenant-colonels, Dorman-Smith had invariably dominated the discussions, for which there had been neither an agenda nor an established pattern. Encouragement to the staff was lacking and the fog of war had seldom been lifted; morever the Army Commander became unduly involved in details. Freddie soon improved these sessions immensely by introducing a logical system. After Dorman-Smith's departure he radically changed the routine by having a staff conference of his own every morning at 7 o'clock, then a meeting with the RAF in the Air C-in-C's caravan, followed by a long private discussion in the evening with his Army Commander, at which he received instructions.

There was a great deal to be done by the staff: divisions which had lost tanks, guns and vehicles in the withdrawal to Alamein had to be re-equipped: new drafts of men had to be brought up from Cairo and absorbed: the logistical organisation controlled by the staff at Rear HQ had to respond to its new commitments: extensive stocks of ammunition had to be brought up and distributed ready for the defensive battle. Signal communications had to be redeployed and tested and, most important of all, training standards had to be improved.

The new BGS (ops) had acquired a well-founded understanding of Army/Air cooperation, derived from his exercises in Egypt in 1932 and in the studies made under Hore-Belisha in 1939; his ideas had further developed as a result of his experiences as a Joint Planner with his friend Group Captain Claude Pelly. But with the centre of Army Control situated amongst the camel tracks many miles from RAF headquarters, effective cooperation was extremely difficult. Nevertheless he concentrated on establishing good liaison with 'Maori' Coningham, AOC, and his senior Air Staff Officer, George Beamish.

By the beginning of August it was evident to me in my role as GSO I (Plans) that Freddie, starting in a low key, had quietly assumed firm control: he gradually established a dominant but easy relationship with all the officers at Army Headquarters including a number of personalities such as the heads of artillery, engineers, signals and administrative services, who had had long experience of desert operations and were senior in age. Notable amongst them were the chief administrative officer Brigadier Sir Brian Robertson aged forty-seven who, after serving as a regular officer in the Royal Engineers in the First World War had entered industry in South Africa and on mobilisation had come up with the South African Forces through the campaigns in East Africa: his deputy Lt-Colonel Miles Graham, aged forty-eight: and Brigadier C. M. F. White, the Chief Signals Officer aged forty-five. Brigadier F. Kisch who was older than any of them was a brilliantly inventive engineer officer who, after the First World War, had left the Army and become an enthusiastic Zionist in Palestine. Before very long these 'Desert worthies' would accept the authority of Freddie and cooperate with great enthusiasm. They would admire his quick brain, his sense of humour and his technique of quietly directing their efforts without in any way interfering in their activities.

On 5th August, Churchill and Brooke, the CIGS, arrived at Eighth Army's headquarters. Churchill was on his way to Moscow to meet Stalin, and hoped to be able to cite some large-scale offensive action to counter Stalin's criticisms of a lack of activity by the Western Allies. Auchinleck's wise refusal to promise any early offensive did nothing to meet this requirement. Initially Churchill had contemplated that Auchinleck should return to his proper role as C-in-C Middle East and that Lt-General W. H. E. Gott, tired and exhausted after immense efforts in battle should take over Eighth Army; but after further consideration of the problem and the tragic death of Gott, shot down by the Luftwaffe, the question arose of finding a new commander for Eighth Army and one who would work satisfactorily with Auchinleck in Cairo. The final choice was Montgomery. His relationship with Auchinleck, under whom he had served in England, was unsatisfactory, and this would have been awkward; but Auchinleck was relieved by Churchill and offered a newly-created command covering Iraq and Persia. This he declined to accept; but later he became C-in-C India.

Freddie, less than three weeks in the saddle, was aware of these possible changes. He had been fully aware of Auchinleck's refusal to respond to Churchill's demand for early offensive action; but seeking as always to avoid anything approaching a rupture had felt that his C-in-C had been unnecessarily abrupt, thus contributing to Churchill's annoyance.

Auchinleck was then summoned to meet Churchill, with Field Marshal Smuts, who was with him, and General Sir Alan Brooke the CIGS. Freddie noticed that he returned slightly worried, but during Auchinleck's usual stroll with his BGS (ops) after dinner the Army Commander discussed him future plans with marked enthusiasm. The next day the blow fell: a letter from Churchill was brought from Cairo, and Auchinleck after dinner announced to Freddie, 'I'm to go.'

Freddie had now been serving Auchinleck directly for over five months and had developed very warm feelings of friendship and loyalty towards him, which were reflected in a letter he left in Auchinleck's hand as he saw him off the next morning. The letter typical of Freddie's sympathetic, diplomatic style, read as follows:[1]

My dear Chief,

It was a great shock to hear your news this evening. The injustice of it all is difficult to believe. As you must realise I am utterly sorry that it should have happened, and I am convinced that they will regret the decision – a decision obviously arrived at to turn aside criticism from its rightful target. I'm afraid it is also a victory for the old privileged school.

As to the 'offer' [of the Persia-Iraq command] it is of course a decision that you alone can make. I don't wish to make comparisons, but my old boss Leslie H-B [Hore-Belisha] was offered the Board of Trade. But he refused. He felt he was right, but I always felt later he was sorry.

I do fully appreciate the other point of view. You may feel you are sitting on a stool between two chairs in which at one time or another you once sat. But who knows how the wheel will spin?

You know that it is only because of the help I knew I could get from you that I did not refuse this job [BGS Eighth Army] point blank. My lack of experience in this particular line was great.

Every possible good wish for the future, and my gratitude for all your kindness to me. You will be missed by many from this arid land.

Yours
Freddie de Guingand

This letter, tactful and generous, was obviously intended to staunch the wound, Nevertheless Freddie's final conclusion on the harsh verdict, conforming with the views of many of us who were present, was that the decision to bring in new blood was right.

The staff at Eighth Army Headquarters were relieved, some even delighted at this decisive change; during the interim, command of the Army had been placed temporarily in the hands of a corps commander, and after three days in limbo the situation had become highly critical; vital decisions were awaited on which depended vast preparations for the decisive battle that was imminent.

Montgomery, whom Freddie had last seen in France in 1939 when accompanying Hore-Belisha to visit the 3rd Division of the BEF, was summoned in great haste from England, where he had already been nominated to command First Army, which was preparing for Operation Torch at the Western end of the Mediterranean.

Freddie told us the news. I for one had never met Montgomery.

'What is he like?' I asked, and Freddie cautiously painted a picture of a commander who was very sharp, supremely confident and most decisive.

Montgomery arrived in Cairo on 12th August, and ordered Freddie by signal to meet him at the crossroad outside Alexandria at 7am the next morning.

CHAPTER SEVEN

Chief of Staff

After reading the signal, Freddie was to spend a restless night. Was it a summons to disaster or to glory? Since that day in 1939 when he had joined Hore-Belisha, his life had moved at a hectic pace through repeated challenges, many of which had seemed at the time unwelcome: the 'banishment' to Haifa, the abortive posting to the School of Combined Operations, then the job with the Joint Planning Staff in Cairo – admittedly his metier but interrupted by the strange Greek adventure – directing Intelligence in Cairo with no previous experience in its mysteries, then BGS (operations) in Auchinleck's darkest hour, to be followed now by serving a new Army Commander, whom he knew and admired, but whose personality and methods would be strikingly different from those of his predecessor – the friend whose agony in failure he had attempted to salve.

His mind went back to those carefree days in 1923 in the West Yorkshires' Mess when Montgomery had urged him to adopt a professional attitude to the business of war. He had not taken that advice very seriously at the Staff College. But Montgomery who had last seen him in 1939, briefcase in hand, smoothly conducting his political master into regions of the BEF where clearly he was not welcome, had continued to treat him as a valued friend. But it was well known that 'Monty' always insisted on choosing his own 'chaps'; in the intimate relationship essential between a Commander and his Chief of Staff, this proviso would surely be mandatory.

Montgomery without benefit of official approval had introduced his 'Chief of Staff system' wherever he went. But Freddie had never been a Chief of Staff, even of a division: the popular picture was of a trim, fit, dynamic figure experienced in battle, like that of Montgomery himself in 1918, when Chief of Staff of the 47th London

Division; there in his official position as GSO 1 (operations) he had been ordered by his Divisional Commander to assume the overall responsibility for all staff activity. Freddie did not match that picture: he was certainly not trim nor fit, but his previous masters had found in him some intellectual dynamism. Would the ruthless didactic, simplistic Irishman, self-confident and sometimes over-confident as in the Egyptian manoeuvres, accept as his *alter ego* the sophisticated, sensitive, Comte de Guingand?

However for Freddie it was no use brooding on his own position: he was now a seasoned professional and must act as such. What would Montgomery want when he met him next morning at 7 am? He noted down some points for urgent attention: the present defensive policy with its dangerous tendency of looking over the shoulder: the unsound technique of fighting in battle groups rather in divisions: the unsatisfactory set-up at Eighth Army headquarters with the confused duplication of functions: and the geographical separation of Army and Air headquarters. Freddie went to bed, excited at the choice of Army Commander, hopeful of great things to come, but dubious of his own survival in yet another appointment for which in his view he was ill-matched.

Montgomery's reaction to this historic meeting of the future partners was described in his *Memoirs* published in 1958.[1]

The BGS, of the Eighth Army was Brigadier (now Major-General Sir Francis) de Guingand. 'Freddie' de Guingand and I were old friends; we had first met in York when I was a major and he was a newly-joined second-lieutenant; we had met again in Egypt in 1932 and 1933, in Quetta in 1935, and in 1939 when he was a sort of military assistant to Hore-Belisha, who was Secretary of State for War. He had a quick and fertile brain and I had in the past regarded him as an outstanding young officer. There he was again, waiting for me as had been arranged at the cross-roads outside Alexandria, where the road from Cairo turned west-ward along the coast. He looked thin and worried; he was obviously carrying a heavy burden. I realised at once it was essential to re-establish the former close friendship before tackling the main problem; so I made him get into my car and I talked about our past days together, and we had a good laugh over several episodes I recalled. He quickly became less tense and after a while I said: 'Well, Freddie my lad, you chaps seem to have got things into a bit of a mess here. Tell me all about it.'

He then produced a document which he had written for me, giving the situation and all the relevant facts. I said, 'Now, Freddie, don't be silly. You know I never read any papers when I can get the person concerned to tell me himself. Put that bumf away and unburden your soul.'

He laughed and I saw at once that I would now get a first class review of the present situation and the causes of it – with nothing held back. We sat close together with a map on our knees and he told me the story; the operational situation, the latest intelligence from the enemy, the generals commanding in the various sectors, the existing orders of Auchinleck about future action, his own view about things. I let him talk on. Occasionally I asked a question but only to clarify some point. When he had done, there was a silence for a moment or two: then I asked about the morale of the officers and men. He said it wasn't good; the Eighth Army wanted a clear lead and a firm grip from the top; there was too much uncertainty and he thought the 'feel of the thing' was wrong. I did not press him on this point; I knew he was trying to be loyal to his past chief.

The time past quickly and in due course we left the coast road and turned south along a track into the open desert. We were quiet now and I was thinking chiefly about de Guingand, and I have no doubt he was thinking about me and his own future.

The magnitude of the task in front of me was beginning to be apparent. I knew I could not tackle it alone; I must have someone to help me, a man with a quick and clear brain, who would accept responsibility, and who would work out the details and leave me free to concentrate on the major issues – in fact, a Chief of Staff who could handle all the detailed and intricate staff side of the business and leave me free to command. I knew that if I once got immersed in the details of the 'dog's breakfast' that was being set in front of me, I would fail as others had failed before me.

Was Freddie de Guingand this man?

We were complete opposites; he lived on his nerves and was highly strung; in ordinary life he liked wine, gambling and good food. Did these differences matter? I quickly decided they did not; indeed, differences were assets.

I have always considered that two people who are exactly the same do not make the best team. He was about 14 years younger than I but we had been great friends in the past and as I looked at him, thin and worried as he was, the old affection returned. And he had a first class brain, which was capable of working at high speed. Furthermore he knew me and my ways, and that was important. If he was to be the man he must be given the necessary power; he must be Chief of Staff, not just Chief of the General Staff.

But the British Army did not work on the Chief of Staff principle; a commander had a number of principal staff officers under him and he was supposed to coordinate their activities himself. This was impossible in the situation now confronting me. How could I co-ordinate all the staff work of the desert campaign? That is what all the others had done and it had led them to lose sight of the essentials; they had become immersed in details and had failed.

Before we arrived at Eighth Army HQ I had decided that de Guingand was the man; I would make him my Chief of Staff with full powers and together we would do the job. I did not tell him then; I thought I would wait and announce it in front of the whole staff, so as to build him up in their eyes and and make clear the difference the new appointment represented.

I never regretted that decision. Freddie de Guingand and I went through the rest of the war together. Wherever I went, he came as my Chief of Staff; we journeyed side by side from Alamein to Berlin. As we went he grew in stature and I realised how lucky I was. He was a brilliant Chief of Staff and I doubt if such a one has ever before existed in the British Army or will ever do so again: although of course here I am prejudiced.

As we bumped over the desert track I came to the conclusion that I now had two tremendous assets. Behind me was Alexander, a firm friend and ally, who could be relied on to support me and do all that I asked of him – so long as it was sound, and I was successful. And by my side would be de Guingand, my trusted Chief of Staff. What was necessary next was to get good and reliable subordinate commanders below me.

Montgomery's arrival at Eighth Army will never be forgotten by those of us who were there. The myth that he, as the beneficiary of vast new resources, merely took over an Auchinleck/Dorman-Smith plan, carried it through successfully and thereafter wore a second-hand coat of glory has at last been laid to rest. What he took over was, in his own words, 'a dog's breakfast'; and we survivors of those days, who were present then, know it full well.

His premature assumption of command was welcomed by all who became aware of it, and particularly by Freyberg whom he visited in the vital area on the southern flank in the early afternoon of 13th August. Having told the New Zealanders that Auchinleck's planned withdrawal to 'defended OP areas' was cancelled, that their present positions would be *the* defence line to be held 'dead or alive', and that other units would be found from the Delta to man the vital Alam Halfa area, he went on to inform Freyberg that after defeating Rommel, the New Zealanders would take part in mobile offensive operations.

Montgomery then moved off to Headquarters Eighth Army where Freddie and the staff were waiting for him to speak to them. 'The effect of the address was electric – it was terrific,' Freddie was to write later: 'We went to bed with new hope in our hearts, and a great confidence in the future of our Army.'[2] As far as he was concerned the points for immediate action (which doubtless he recorded in his usual indecipherable notes) were:

> That he was no longer BGS (ops) but *Chief of Staff*
>
> All orders would be issued through him, and would be taken as coming from the Army Commander, and would be acted on at once 'without bellyaching'.
>
> That the headquarters was to move at once from the dung-strewn camel tracks to a decent place where the Army staff could be side by side with the headquarters of the Desert Air Force.
>
> That reinforcements of tanks were expected shortly at Suez.
>
> That Rommel's attack, expected at any moment, was welcomed, but preferably not within a week. If two weeks to prepare were available, we would be 'sitting pretty'.

Meanwhile they were to start to plan a great offensive, first creating a reserve corps, strong in armour, which would train *out of the line.*

The next day Freddie reconnoitred the new rearward site for Army headquarters at Burgh-el-Arab, where the staff would be relatively comfortable; greatly restricted in their use of fresh water, they could bathe in the sea. But far more important was the fact that they could join up with the Desert Air Force, which had lost some confidence in Eighth Army and had not been impressed with the headlong retreat to Alamein. Nevertheless in that retreat while their airstrips were being overrun in quick succession, they had put up a magnificent effort, which had minimised the effect of the German Air Force's attacks on Eighth Army's retreating columns.

Montgomery himself needed no education in the use of air power in support of Army operations, and he immediately took steps to repair the relations with the AOC, 'Maori' Coningham, who had done much to develop air support to the Army in the Desert. Freddie helped his commander enthusiastically, and by his intelligent understanding of air operations and his diplomatic skill he quickly brought Army/Air cooperation to a very high pitch of efficiency. Hugh Mainwaring, the GSO 1 operations, improved this further by introducing the so-called 'J' system by which situation reports in battle were transmitted on special radio links from forward report centres direct to Army headquarters. This permitted the RAF to support the Army much more quickly and intimately than before. A joint Army/Air operations room was then urgently established. Montgomery himself conferred regularly with the AOC, and Freddie with his SASO, to ensure they were fully appraised of the Army's operations and future intentions, and a regular staff meeting of both services took place every evening, at which the Army's requirements for the next day were considered, and Air resources, pre-planned and 'at call' were organised.

The Army staff, now fully motivated by the clear lead given by their new commander, met daily at 7 am under the Chief of Staff who immediately established a firm, sympathetic control. The meetings, though very informal, were highly expeditious. Freddie, sometimes a tousled figure emerging from his caravan, with his indecipherable scribbles written on a millboard, would walk to the operations truck to be greeted there by a dozen officers and, after a quick summary of the operational and intelligence situations, would run down his list tying up any loose ends. Thereafter those present would raise any further points, which would be dealt with decisively. The party would break up to pursue the actions for which they were responsible: if they looked at their watches they would find that only about twenty minutes had elapsed. Freddie himself having retired to his caravan might want to pursue other more complex matters with, for intance, the Chief Signals Officer or the Chief Engineer. He would maintain close personal contact with the brigadier in charge of administration at Rear Army Headquarters, giving him the Army Commander's future intentions, and obtaining reassurance that no insoluble logistic problems loomed ahead.

He would confer by secure telephone with the chiefs of staff of the corps and periodically would visit them; he would also ensure that GHQ in Cairo was kept fully informed of progress by the daily situation report sent by signal, amplified if necessary by personal telephone calls. I, as the sole planner, worked on a longer term basis under Freddie's direction.

The two weeks, at the end of which the Army was to be 'sitting pretty', were filled with intense preparatory activity by day and night. Freddie met the Army Commander regularly in his map lorry every evening, where he reported on the action taken by the staff, and discussed future requirements.

He still regarded himself as being on approval, and he recalled that Montgomery not long after his arrival had told him that some changes might take place, but that if he was one of them he would see that he got something good. Freddie, long after the war, wrote that the 'change' would have involved a previous staff officer of Montgomery's then in England; he assumed apparently that this was Brigadier Frank Simpson,[3] who in England had served Montgomery well; but the evidence is inconclusive. Montgomery did ask Alexander for certain chosen officers to be sent out to the Middle East Command. The list included Simpson, then Deputy Director of Military Operations in the War Office, and Brigadier Sydney Kirkman who duly joined Eighth Army. Simpson, keen to see service in an active theatre, was warned to go out to GHQ Middle East as Deputy Chief of the General Staff, but owing to the death of another brigadier in the War Office, the CIGS found he could not spare him. Montgomery would have welcomed having Simpson in Cairo as an effective 'rear link', a function Simpson was to perform much later in N.W. Europe, and he might have had it in mind to get him moved forward eventually from Cairo to become his Chief of Staff after he had become familiar with the North African Campaign. He wrote to Simpson to say he would try again later, but he never reopened the subject.

Nevertheless in Freddie's mind the existence of his phantom rival soured his feelings towards Simpson, who later in the war was to have such a special relationship with Montgomery. Montgomery's hint to Freddie was unfortunate: it introduced into their relationship the first of many enigmas. Nevertheless Freddie's outstanding performance as Chief of Staff immediately secured his position, which was further reinforced when the enemy intervened.

However, changes in Eighth Army at the very highest levels did take place with the arrival of two new corps commanders: Lt- General Oliver Leese who took over 30 Corps, and Lt-General Brian Horrocks, who took over 13 Corps. Their great capabilities were immediately recognised. One of the problems of high priority facing Horrocks was to provide a strong defensive system for the Alam Halfa ridge. The importance of this feature had been appreciated by Auchinleck as early as July, and it had been designated as one of the Dorman-Smith's 'Cowpats' – defended observation posts – but meanwhile little had been done to strengthen it except for the laying of some minefields and the erection of some wire. Montgomery decided immediately after his meeting on 13th August with Freyberg that the proper defence of this feature was vital and that 44th Division, which for three weeks had been receiving equipment and training for desert warfare in Egypt, must be brought up at once to hold the ridge. Freddie was told to arrange this move with GHQ that evening; he encountered opposition but after a personal talk on the telephone between Alexander and Montgomery the objection that the division was too green was withdrawn, and the move forward was agreed. David Belchem, Freddie's GSO 1 (Staff Duties), spent the rest of the night on the telephone tying up the details of routes, guides and administrative support. More minefields were then laid and wire erected, while labour units which had been allocated to prepared positions far back in the Delta were brought forward urgently to strengthen the defences.

On 17th August an appreciation by Rommel dated 15th August decrypted at Bletchley was read by Montgomery and Freddie. After estimating the relative strengths of the Afrika Korps and Eighth Army in artillery and tanks, and examining his logistic position, Rommel had concluded that he would be strong enough for a quick penetration of the front at the end of August. Since the necessary regrouping of his forces for the attack would have to be done at the last moment to secure surprise, a full moon was necessary: full moon would be on 26th August. Moreover, reconnaissance near the Qattara depression (i.e. on Eighth Army's southern flank) had been prohibited, indicating the probability, indeed the near certainty, that an outflanking movement would take place in that area.

Right: Exercises without troops at the Middle East Staff College at Haifa often took place near the orange groves of a Kibbutz.

Below: Major-General Davidson, Director of Military Intelligence in the War Office, visited Eighth Army in May 1942. Freddie as DMI in Cairo conducted him round the front. *Left to right*: Brig G.W.E.J. Erskine, BGS 13 Corps; General Davidson; Lt Col Hathwaite; Freddie; Lt Col R. Priest; Lt Col David Hunt; Lt Col F. de Butts.

Freddie as DMI Middle East was the 'official spokesman' in Cairo and was much admired by the war correspondents seen here at a Press dinner.

Auchinleck was quick to recognise Freddie's talents; having appointed him Director of Military Intelligence, he moved him some months later to the headquarters of Eighth Army as BGS (Operations).

Now that the timing and the thrust line of Rommel's attack were known, Freddie with Williams' assistance had the ingenious idea of trying to deceive Rommel as to the condition of the terrain over which his attacking units were likely to pass, and lead him into a trap. 'Going maps' were a normal feature of life in the Desert; they were coloured over-prints on ordinary contoured maps showing variations in 'going' in categories such as 'reconnaissance essential before movement: continuous low gear', 'fair going, 5–12 miles in the hour', 'firm and fast' etc. Freddie's plan was designed to lead Rommel up to the Alam Halfa Ridge through very soft sand by a route which in fact he eventually adopted. The faked map printed very urgently in Cairo was left in a blown-up scout car in the south, together with soldiers' kits etc. By the next morning the map had gone. There is some evidence that the plan may have succeeded: the German General von Thoma, after capture, reported at the interrogation centre that the British had planted a falsified map of the terrain on them, but Rommel's intelligence staff maintained that it had had no decisive influence on his movements, which were governed by other considerations.

Under Freddie's direction the Intelligence Staff had many other problems on their hands such as the further development and use of 'Y' – the tactical intercept service which served a vital purpose in supplementing and confirming the strategic Ultra messages – the collation of other sources such as Prisoner of War reports, and the organisation of photographic intelligence to meet the Army's requirements. Their success received a tribute in the post-war official history which stated:

> The new style of command, which did so much to raise the morale of Eighth Army . . . thus owed something directly to the possession of advance intelligence. Hardly less important, however, was the fact that the new commander took over as his intelligence staff a team that had been formed during July by the transfer of DMI Cairo to be Chief of Staff Eighth Army . . .[4]

The operations staff were busy with the daily issue of orders and situation reports and, with their RAF colleagues, were involved in the planning and conduct of Air Operations in support of forward units. I, as the GSO 1 (Plans), might well have found myself with little to do; however I was amazed when Freddie gave me in great secrecy the broad outline of Montgomery's plan for the next great offensive and told me to carry out urgently a detailed study and appreciation of what was to become the battle of Alamein.

Meanwhile there was great activity by the administrative staff in which Robertson and Graham cooperated with Freddie by informal personal contact, reinforced by the presence of their representative at 'morning prayers' at 7 am each day.

For us, the lieutenant-colonels, the whole atmosphere had changed: we had a commander who knew what he wanted and a chief of staff who was obviously in his master's mind. Moreover Freddie was at all times easily accessible, and it was a pleasure to seek his advice and to carry out his instructions.

During this period of urgent activity, very effective teamwork was achieved, led by the Chief of Staff who manifestly daily grew in stature but retained his informality, humour and modesty. 'Montgomery was a magnificent master to work for,' he wrote after the war. 'He never got excited, never lost his temper, gave you the task and then left you to carry it out without interference. Having made his decision he seemed to cast it from his mind. His staff always felt they had a hundred per cent support.'[5] Under Freddie's hand the staff machine began to operate more smoothly and efficiently than before.

From the night of the full moon, 26th August, we awaited Rommel's attack but none materialised. Rommel had asked for sick leave on 21st August, but on the 26th he reported that he would be able to exercise command during the planned operation but would need lengthy treatment later. A more serious impediment was his lack of fuel due to RAF attacks on Axis shipping. Nevertheless, shortly after midnight on 31st August Rommel launched his attack. Freddie, not yet fully cognisant of his master's habits, awakened him: this proved to be a mistake, and quite unnecessary as Montgomery commented, 'Excellent' and turned over in bed to resume his sleep.

The RAF had already achieved air superiority; now with their attacks pre-planned in great detail, they took a heavy toll by day and by night, bombing with flares. A great weight of artillery fire, planned and rehearsed, was also brought against the enemy. The bulk of Montgomery's armour was concentrated in a vital area previously determined on exercises and rehearsals; there, dug in for defence, they repulsed Rommel's armour and inflicted heavy casualties.

Freddie, as always in very close touch with his commander, on the evening of 1st September when Rommel's armour and supplies had been badly hit, had been summoned to Montgomery's caravan. There he pressed for a bold counter-attack by the New Zealand Division to cut off Rommel's retreat, but Montgomery, who was aware from Ultra that Rommel was going on to the defensive, would not risk it: their state of training he considered was not up to it. Freddie, like his staff, was disappointed but Montgomery was right. Later, the final operation carried out by the New Zealanders was expensive in casualties, contradicting Montgomery's insistent watchword: 'No more failures.'

On the night of 3rd/4th September Rommel, after further heavy losses, pulled out. His battle for Egypt had failed. Although there were some who felt then that more could have been done to destroy the Afrika Korps, the victory had an enormous psychological effect. The soldiers had seen and fallen under the spell of their new Army Commander, had heard him say what was going to happen, had trained and rehearsed for the battle where the enemy performed as forecast, and then had inflicted defeat on the 'invincible' Afrika Korps.

As for Freddie, he had proved himself. He knew now that he had the confidence of the Army Commander, had established good working relationships with the two corps and had the loyalty and admiration of all the staff. A new spirit of comradeship had been generated throughout the headquarters, and this was to prove an incalculable asset in facing the sterner challenges that lay ahead.

CHAPTER EIGHT

Partner in Triumph

After the victory of Alam Halfa, there was no time for relaxation, but Freddie attended on 6th September at Main Headquarters, Burgh el Arab, a thanksgiving service called by the Army Commander. On the next day, Montgomery wrote in his summary: 'Having called off the battle, all energies were then directed to continuing the plans for our own offensive and knock-out blow', and in his diary he recorded, 'Plans for formation of 10 Corps set in motion.' This *corps de chasse* was to consist of three armoured divisions.

The outline plan for the offensive had started to germinate in Montgomery's mind four weeks before, while he was packing his bags in London to fly out to Cairo; even while preparing for the Alam Halfa battle he had surprised Freddie and the Intelligence staff with his inquisitiveness about the enemy's minefields in the area of his future break-out. The staff work to satisfy the Army Commander had therefore been initiated already as second priority, despite preoccupations with the current defensive battle.

The command and staff routine which was to endure throughout the campaigns in Africa and Sicily was now firmly taking shape. The Commander was already preparing to establish himself at a Tactical Headquarters ready to move forward to battle so as to maintain close personal touch every day with his corps commanders. Two were generals of his choice: Horrocks and Leese. The third was Lumsden, the veteran of many armoured actions in the Desert who was to command 10 Corps, despite Montgomery's preference for Horrocks in that role. In the battle, Montgomery would use his ADCs initially as liaison officers, to move every day into the forward areas, there to make contact with the local commanders, assess the situation and make their personal reports verbally to the Army Commander every evening.

The Chief of Staff would also visit his Commander every evening, and at other times if the situation demanded. The ADCs, with whom he often relaxed after serious business had been done, welcomed his visits, finding him very good company. Freddie could adapt himself to any age group without condescension.

By this time, he had been in the saddle as Chief of Staff for twenty-four dramatic days, and had begun to learn how to handle his master, who had noticeably developed his professionalism and his astonishing self-confidence since those far-off days which they had enjoyed together in peace time in Yorkshire. Briefings were normally to be verbal, as for Hore-Belisha, although in rare situations Montgomery would be prepared to study a military paper. He was not to be bothered on matters of executive detail, which were wholly delegated to the Chief of Staff, who would issue instructions in the Army Commander's name with full assurance that he would be supported. On the rare occasions that Montgomery issued written directives to his corps commanders in conformation of verbal orders he would usually write them himself. He was, after all, a highly experienced staff officer. Freddie had already learnt that his commander, who normally retired early to bed was not to be disturbed unless there was a crisis demanding action on his part, and that he was happy to receive his brigadiers (Artillery, Armour, Engineers, Signals, Administrative, Medical etc) when they so wished; but in fact these occasions were to prove comparatively rare.

The head of the Intelligence Staff was to brief him verbally at an early hour every morning; thereafter the Army Commander would normally be absent from his headquarters for long periods visiting his forward commanders. Signals communication would be maintained with him by radio in emergency, and by secure telephone when he was at a subordinate headquarters.

Freddie, who was well aware of the enormous psychological strains imposed on a higher commander, realised the importance of avoiding unnecessary irritations in his dealings with his 'master'. He found that by concisely outlining the important factors of a situation and suggesting the options that were open, Montgomery would quietly listen to him without interruption. It was seldom that this was followed by any debate; normally the process of briefing led immediately to a clear decision. If this incorporated the advice or recommendation of the Chief of Staff, no reference to this was made and thereafter the decision emanated, for presentational purposes, entirely from the Commander himself. Much later in peacetime, when the comradeship of war no longer cemented so strongly the Chief of Staff's personal relationship with his commander, Freddie was to find this attitude ungenerous; but in war it is the function of the staff to provide recommendations to their commander without claiming credit, private or public, for carrying out their duty. The propriety of claiming credit in peacetime is more debatable.

Freddie when putting forward a recommendation which he hoped would change the Commander's mind had learned by now that the occasion must be chosen with care and that it should be private – an interchange *à deux* with no third party present. He had tried this after the riposte of Rommel at Alam Halfa but Montgomery had declined his advice. Montgomery, consciously or subconsciously, adopted a technique to present an image of a commander in complete charge of events, who made his personal decisions and never (or very rarely) changed them. This was in fact a great boon to the executive staff, and was in marked contrast to the confusion of the previous Auchinleck régime.

On Monday 7th September there was much to be done, and very little time in which to do it. Freddie knew that the battle of Alamein was to start with a night attack and for that a full moon was necessary. This he had been told indicated the end of September, a date which had been mentioned at Churchill's return visit on 19th August. How on earth could preparations be completed in three weeks? Here Freddie had to adjust his thinking from that of an executive staff officer of a brigade in 1932 to that of Chief of Staff of an army of more than eleven divisions in 1942. He realised that in Leese and Horrocks there were two excellent subordinates answerable to Montgomery, but the Army had to move into battle as one articulated machine with every part meshing correctly, and for this coordinating function he, the Chief of Staff of the Army, was responsible.

Montgomery had indicated broadly that as far as men and equipment were concerned he was not dissatisfied, but the training of the formations and particularly that of the newly-formed armoured corps of 1st and 10th Armoured Divisions needed much improvement. Fortunately for the Chief of Staff, the Commander personally assumed most of the responsibility for this aspect including – and this was unusual – the writing of his own training directives. In the next few weeks, Montgomery was to give highest priority to his personal supervision of this training, which was related specifically to the activities of the battle that lay ahead including the rehearsal of many of its anticipated features.

On the administrative side Robertson was known to be a highly effective and decisive brigadier, ably supported by Graham his deputy, who soon became an intimate friend of Freddie's. Graham, with a sense of humour which responded to Freddie's, and a taste for gambling, became a welcome safety-valve, releasing some of the immense pressures on the Chief of Staff. They were often to be seen in quiet periods with a backgammon board between them.

It was natural that Freddie, so recently a director of military intelligence, should give high priority to the implications of the intelligence picture. He found that Montgomery required little education in the magic of Ultra; the Army Commander fully understood its significance and was intent on exploiting it on every possible occasion. Freddie had great confidence in Major Bill Williams the GSO (II) Intelligence who later would succeed the GSO (I) Lt-Col 'Spud' Murphy, but rightly felt it was his duty to monitor the advice given by the Intelligence staff, who kept him very fully informed of the accumulating evidence about the enemy. This included his order of battle, his fighting strength and logistic situation, his equipment inventory, particularly of tanks and guns, his minefields development which was immense, and the location of likely targets for bombardment by artillery and the Desert Air Force. From time to time the Y Intercept service and Ultra would provide reliable indications of Rommel's intentions.

Freddie's warm relationship with Kisch, the Chief Engineer, enabled him to guide and encourage that unusual and brilliant man in the vital tasks of the engineers who had a major part to play in the battle in breaching the deep belts of enemy minefields.

In the rear areas of the Army's position, there were preparations for water supply, road and track construction and repair, the making of airstrips, the operation of the limited railway line to take some of the logistic strain off the roads, the construction of field hospitals and reinforcement camps and many other functions – all these had to be operating at maximum efficiency before and during the battle but even more important, had to be capable of development to match the anticipated needs of an immediate advance of many hundred miles thereafter. Forward surveys of terrain and water sources, many of them culled from reports of the two 'Benghazi handicaps' had to be studied and a vast amount of stores and material distributed ready for immediate deployment. In the forward area of the battlefield, it was the task of the Engineers to prepare tracks for the forward move of assaulting formations to the edge of the enemy's minefields and there, with infantry in close support, to cut the enemy's wire, lift and disarm the mines and form wide tracks, marked by tapes, through which infantry and tanks could continue to advance to a distance of several thousand yards. Kisch, receiving from Freddie not only a comprehensive interpretation of the Army Commander's intentions, but also friendly support and encouragement, carried out a major programme of equipment trials and subsequent training to establish and to disseminate the most effective methods for achieving this hazardous mine-lifting operation.

Montgomery had already indicated that the next battle was to be a protracted and violent affair extending over ten days, and that considerable casualties, several thousands in number, would have to be accepted. Measures to mitigate the effects of this had to be prepared as a high priority; Freddie had learnt that the Army Commander took a keen personal interest in the effective evacuation and treatment of the wounded, and their replacement by reinforcements sympathetically inducted into their units. This was primarily the responsibility of Robertson who, tall and distinguished like his father the field-marshal, who had risen from trooper to become CIGS under Asquith, had a daunting manner and was not a man to welcome interference in his responsibilities. Yet Freddie again established an amicable and effective relationship, which enabled him to monitor Robertson's activities with a light touch, as was necessary in Freddie's capacity as Chief of Staff.

Montgomery, who had enquired on arrival, 'Where are the RAF?', had immediately moved his headquarters to join up with that of the Desert Air Force, and re-introduce the Joint Operations Room. He had then gone out of his way to develop a' friendly relationship with his fraternal *prima donna*, Air Marshal 'Maori' Coningham. But this was not an easy task: their personalities were too competitive. Initially he had regular discussions with him, reinforced by social contacts in the Mess; then more and more he delegated to Freddie the task of consultation and cooperation with the Royal Air Force in support of the land operations. Montgomery soon reposed great confidence in Freddie, who, well-versed in these matters, played his cards brilliantly both with the AOC and his Senior Air Staff Officer. Priority was given, during the weeks leading up to the battle, to maintaining air superiority, and this was magnificently achieved, together with effective attacks on Rommel's airfields and his supply lines by sea and land. As the day of battle approached, increasing priority was given to ground attack against enemy formation; this was to lead eventually to a massive pre-planned night assault by bombers as an immediate preliminary to the Army's night attack. Coningham, with long experience of supporting Eighth Army in the fluctuating battles of Auchinleck's regime, led his gallant Air Force with great success at this period.

Nor were the potentialities of the Royal Navy overlooked. A Naval Liaison officer had been permanently attached to Army Headquarters as the representative of the C-in-C Mediterranean. With the near superiority which had been achieved in the neighbouring coastal waters, it was manifestly prudent to make preparations for some naval activity to take place during the battle, be it a serious landing or a feint. But the lack of adequate assault craft seriously circumscribed the scope of any operation.

Lastly, but by no means the least important, was the requirement for a Deception Plan, which it was hoped might deceive Rommel as to the timing and principal axis of Montgomery's assault, which to me at least appeared to be alarmingly obvious. The working-out of the plan was delegated by Freddie to me his GSO 1 (Plans); I had never been involved before in such matters and was not very confident that any plan would succeed, but with Montgomery's declared support much weight was given to its implementation. This support was essential, since the successful implementation of the plan, which started in mid-September, involved every formation of the Army in much tedious and seemingly pointless activity; only through full support of subordinate commanders was it carried out week by week with unfailing discipline. Thanks to Freddie's enthusiastic involvement, and the denial by the Desert Air Force of enemy tactical reconnaissance over the battle area, it proved entirely successful.

'We were very deception-minded in those days,'[1] Freddie recorded much later; but he was referring frivolously to a less serious event which had occurred when Churchill, returning from Moscow had stayed with Montgomery at Burgh el Arab on 19th August. This had been the occasion when Montgomery had vacated his caravan – a rare event which he was to repeat in NW Europe for the Prime Minister and King George VI – and positioned it close to the beach so that he could take the aged Prime Minister to bathe in the sea. Hand in hand and naked I saw them picking their way across the sandy beach before breakfast. An evening swim before dinner sometimes followed; for such a dinner party, Montgomery, claiming ignorance about alcohol, asked Freddie to supervise the drinks. Having no brandy in the Mess, an ADC had been hurriedly sent to Alexandria and had returned with a local brand, thought to be somewhat lethal, which was then poured into an empty bottle graced with a well-known French name. Churchill had enjoyed it all immensely, and after retiring well after midnight, by which time Montgomery was in his bed fast asleep, the Prime Minister had risen early on the morrow, bright as a lark. Freddie, the life and soul of any party, had been happy to deputise as host far into the night, but at 7 am was alert and ready for his usual staff conference.

As the busy days rushed by, Montgomery continued with his procedure of maintaining close personal contact with his corps and divisional commanders, together with visits to nearly every unit and talks to the soldiers themselves. There was no fretting over planning details which were confidently left to his Chief of Staff, who, in his executive role, functioned virtually as a deputy Army Commander. Thus Montgomery, returning to his map lorry after lengthy tours in which he concentrated on the aspects of morale and training, had ample time in the evenings for cool, calm reflection on the battle that lay ahead. On 13th September he was seen by one of his liaison officers walking backwards and forwards in the sands of Burgh el Arab, like Napoleon with his head down, his hands behind his back. And we all said, 'Master is giving birth.' He came back into his caravan and in about four hours . . . he wrote his whole operation instruction for Alamein.

That evening Freddie issued orders for the thirteen commanders of corps and divisions of Eighth Army together with the Army staff to assemble on 16th September at Main HQ, and there the plan for Alamein was announced with Montgomery's usual clarity and self-confidence. There were a few questions but confidence on all sides seemed very high and no queries were raised on the tasks set for each commander.

Nevertheless on 16th September an objection came from the same source that had tormented Auchinleck – the Prime Minister. Freddie was present when General Alexander the new C-in-C Middle East Command arrived from Cairo with a telegram from London in which Churchill pressed for the offensive to start at an earlier date, which meant at the full moon in late September. Freddie, so perceptive of personal relationships, now observed a new aspect of his master's character: his determination to call the tune even with Churchill when the success of his operations was at stake.

The reply to Churchill drafted by Montgomery stated that if the attack was to be launched in September the troops would not be sufficiently trained, and new equipment would be wasted, and in all probability failure would result; but if the attack took place in October then victory was assured. This blackmailing tactic succeeded and after much protest the Prime Minister agreed. The last piece had now fallen into place. Thirty days were left to complete the training and preparations for the battle on which the whole future of the war, not to mention the Prime Minister, depended.

By now Freddie's team, trained on the job, was responding with great coherence to the clarity of Montgomery's demands. Seldom had a commander before a battle been so well served with intelligence about the enemy facing him. Activity rose to a new crescendo and all the agencies available, photographic reconnaissance, Y intercepts, interrogation of prisoners, and the invaluable Ultra played their part. The official history of the intelligence activities of those days, based both on British and German sources, has now

been published (1981) and it is possible to appreciate the scene that
was being unfolded to the eyes of Montgomery, and to Freddie,
Murphy and Williams, the only figures in Eighth Army that had
access to Ultra. When Ultra information was substantially
supported by intelligence from other sources, the picture would be
reproduced, but with the source disguised, in Eighth Army's
Intelligence summaries; but there were always fears in Whitehall
that this irreplaceable source might be compromised. Hence in some
instances such as the absence on leave of Rommel on 8th October
and his temporary replacement by Stumme, information was sent
out on a very restricted distribution.

The photographic reconnaissance carried out by the RAF
produced excellent results, and a comprehensive picture of the
enemy's defences was continuously built up together with further
alarming developments which came to light during the weeks
leading up to the battle. Churchill, who read his Ultra signals in
London, drew Alexander's attention as early as 23rd September to
the possibility that Eighth Army would find a greatly increased belt
of fortifications in depth instead of the crust through which the
assault was to be completed in one night. The Prime Minister's
forecast was not far off the mark, and this was to have a significant
influence on the final plan.

The Y service which was now very highly developed, and could
operate at maximum efficiency in the prevailing static situation,
produced a splendid harvest, contributing to the definition of the
enemy order of battle, the location of units, the position of gun
batteries determined by direction finding, and in many cases the
short-term intentions of subordinate commanders.

Attacks by the RAF and the Navy on Rommel's supply line across
the Mediterranean had been most effective, and the appalling
difficulties facing him in respect of his petrol supply and
reinforcements were periodically disclosed to the Army Commander
and his Chief of Staff by Ultra signals throughout this period.

In the minds of the Army Commander and his Chief of Staff, two
major factors were now becoming dominant: first the standard of
training of the armoured units of 10 Corps as viewed by Montgomery; second the strengthening of the deep defensive belt of anti-
tank mines and obstacles in the enemy's position. On 5th October

the Intelligence staff drew up their latest and most accurate analysis of the defensive lay-out. Half a million mines were to be laid by the enemy to form not only a series of conventional belts but also dividing walls to form 'boxes' intended as traps for assaulting troops. As a result of this information Montgomery reconsidered his tactics for the first phase of the operations.

Already amongst the staff, rumours had been current that some of the commanders of armoured units had begun to doubt their ability to continue breaking through the enemy's deep defensive position after the assault on the first night. In the temporary absence of Montgomery who, typically, had taken a day off to give a lecture, Freddie had attended a conference at 10 Corps in his capacity as Montgomery's deputy. He was horrified to hear Lumsden, the commander of the *corps de chasse*, regarded by many as the expert in armoured action, calmly announce that he did not agree with one point in Montgomery's plan, namely that tanks should be used to force their way out of minefields. Freddie, amazed at such a statement so late in the game, and fearing a return to the old Eighth Army habit of accepting orders 'as a basis for discussion', warned Lumsden that the Army Commander would permit no variations from his orders. He sensed immediately that in Lumsden's reaction lay the seeds of disaster. Was Montgomery, who had set off so jauntily to give a lecture, living in a fool's paradise? He decided that he must report to Montgomery Lumsden's statement, immediately on his return to headquarters. As a result, Montgomery after much discussion changed his policy for the employment of armour in the first phase of the battle – instead of advancing as a *corps de chasse*, hopefully against only light opposition, through lanes cleared by 30 Corps, they were to work with the infantry of that corps in protracted 'crumbling' operations which eventually would break through the deep enemy defensive belt. The major change, startling as it was, did not affect the staff arrangements, and was conveyed by Montgomery in personal interviews with the corps commanders concerned.

Measures to maintain security had been carefully assessed by Freddie and approved by the Army Commander, and as D day approached all leave was stopped. But the Army Commander noticed that his Chief of Staff was in a bad way. Not surprisingly the strain through fourteen weeks of supervising the vast amount of detailed preparations had taken their toll, and Freddie, who some said lived on his nerves, was not sleeping well. He was sent off for a short break which he took as the guest of the C-in-C Mediterranean in Alexandria. The staff preparations at Army level were now complete so on his return to Army headquarters he decided to take three of his staff officers to have a good lunch with him at the Union Club in Alexandria, while the Operations Officer 'minded the shop'. The atmosphere was in strange contrast to the battle scene only eighty miles away. After the near panic of 20th June when 25,000 troops had surrendered at Tobruk to the Germans, normal life in the Egyptian Delta had been resumed; now at Alexandria an orchestra played in the dining room where well-dressed ladies were being entertained by young naval officers. After the rigours of the desert the menu and the wine of Freddie's lunch party were excellent.

After a restful night and breakfast in bed, Freddie returned to the battlefield on 22rd October. Montgomery now left Main HQ at Burgh el Arab and moved forward to his Tactical Headquarters. His Chief of Staff, contrary to his usual practice of basing himself at Main Headquarters with daily visits to Tac HQ, decided he must be closer to his commander at the outset of the battle and organised a small headquarters in a superannuated Italian pillbox near the coast road close to the headquarters of 30 and 10 Corps and Montgomery's Tac HQ. The work of the GSO 1 (Plans) was over, so I was ordered to go with him; Mainwaring the GSO I (operations) was in charge of Main HQ.

On the day before the battle, Montgomery held a Press Conference. Freddie, who had been the official spokesman when DMI in Cairo and was a seasoned performer in that role, watched over him; in future years on many occasions he was to warn his chief of pitfalls that might lie in that particular path. Montgomery explained his plan, and how he intended to fight the battle, and demonstrated his great confidence in the outcome. Freddie was surprised that some of the war correspondents, who had not yet gained that faith in Montgomery which soon was to follow him all the way to Lüneburg Heath, showed some scepticism. So often in the past Eighth Army's vaunted successes had turned to dust.

On the afternoon of D day, 23rd October, Freddie and I drove up to the Italian pillbox where a small number of vehicles had been dug in and slit trenches prepared. Buried telephone cables ensured secure communications with the Corps and with Main HQ. Freddie had some food with Leese and his BGS at 30 Corps HQ, and checked with Main HQ that no surprises had occurred; then we both went out about 9.30 pm to watch the beginning of the battle, due to start at 9.40 pm. We then returned to the pillbox and went to bed. Freddie, who never slept easily, dozed fitfully.

Early on the 24th we received telephoned reports of the progress of the battle. It was clear that the attack had achieved complete surprise. Rommel was on sick leave in Germany, and did not re-assume command until 25th October. Secrecy had evidently been maintained, and concealment of all the vast preparatory measures had been effectively carried out.

So far Montgomery's battle had gone well. 30 Corps had fought its way to the dominant Miteiriya Ridge on its left and, although held up short of its objective on the central sector, was right through the enemy minefields on the right in the Australian Division's sector. 10 Corps had advanced as planned and was now positioned in considerable strength alongside the foremost infantry, although it had not yet gone beyond the Miteiriya Ridge, as had been hoped.

Freddie in his forward headquarters could do little more than assess the progress of the battle in relation to Montgomery's clear intention which was to get the armoured divisions out into the open as top priority. But progress towards this goal seemed very slow, and Montgomery spoke to Lumsden, commanding 10 Corps, urging more offensive action in no uncertain voice. But by nightfall he was reasonably satisfied that the activities of the armoured divisions, though 24 hours behind schedule, were conforming to his plan.

On the night of 24/25th October, Freddie still at his forward post, was in very close touch with the battle situation while his Army Commander as usual was sleeping soundly in his caravan. He learnt that a night attack at 10 pm by Freyberg's New Zealand Division had been only partially successful in moving forward over the Miteiriya Ridge with his armour leading, but had then been held up by lack of support from 10th Armoured Division. At 1.40 am the commander of that division which had suffered some casualties, referred the question of a further attack to his corps commander, Lumsden, who gave no clear decision. An hour later, I woke up to find Freddie fully dressed and looking worried. 'What's going on?' I asked. Freddie replied guardedly: 'Things aren't so hot, I'm getting the corps commanders to come and see the Army Commander.' It was then that Freddie had decided that the battle had reached a crisis which only the Army Commander could solve, and immediately by telephone convened a conference at Montgomery's Tactical HQ for 3.30 am; he then went to wake his master, and described to him the critical situation. Montgomery said, 'They're coming along at 3.30? I agree with you – quite right, I'll be there.'

To awake the Army Commander was acceptable only in the direst circumstances. In Montgomery's pamphlet 'High Command in War' he was to write:

> The wise commander will see very few papers or letters; he will refuse to sit up late at night conducting the business of his army; he will be well advised to withdraw to his tent or caravan after dinner at night and have time for quiet thought and reflection.
> It is vital that he should keep mentally fresh.

It is interesting that Freddie, whose personality was the antithesis of Montgomery's, often found his relaxation in playing chemin de fer with the young officers at Tactical Headquarters late into the night.

On this occasion he had rightly identified a moment of crisis: after the war he described what he called the 'first stepping stone to victory' as follows:[2]

> I led the generals along the little path to the lorry. Inside, Montgomery was seated on a stool carefully examining a map fixed to the wall. He greeted us all most cheerfully, motioning us to sit down, and then asked each corps commander to tell his story. He listened very quietly, only occasionally interrupting with a question. There was a certain 'atmosphere' present, and careful handling was required. Lumsden was obviously not very happy about the role his armour had been given.

The reference to Lumsden was a diplomatic understatement by Freddie. There had been a sharp clash of wills; Montgomery had

had to make clear to the corps commander and his divisional commander that the armour must get forward and get through. 'The firm decision to make no change in the plan at that moment was a brave one, for it meant accepting considerable risks and casualties,' Freddie recalled later.

Although Montgomery has subsequently been criticised for demanding too much from his armoured units, and although he was immediately forced to modify his tactical concept for offensive action in the next phase, Freddie's intervention in the early hours of 25th October was well timed and well-judged. Afterwards he rightly maintained that Montgomery's firmness at this juncture was decisive; without it, the principal thrust on which all depended at that time might have failed. Leese supported that view.

The unpleasant crisis, recognised by the perceptive Chief of Staff and handled so decisively by the Army Commander, strengthened the bond between them.

However, the immediate result on the ground was very different from the Army Commander's intentions. Far from getting out into the open beyond the Miteiriya Ridge, the armoured corps by mid-morning was stuck and unable to act as a shield for 30 Corps' crumbling operations. Montgomery, greatly disappointed with the action of the armour, withdrew it gradually into reserve leaving Leese with his infantry to make the running. He now showed his genius by rapidly modifying his plan and giving priority to a northern thrust by 9th Australian Division in the area of the Coast Road; this resulted in Rommel making a series of useless and expensive counter-attacks against the centre, which seriously weakened his forces in that area. In Freddie's post-war account he named this operation as the 'second stepping stone', and here the description was apt.

On the evening of 26th October Montgomery regrouped in order to bring the New Zealand Division into reserve preparatory to a final assault. This was Freddie's 'third stepping stone'. If this description, derived perhaps from Freddie's fishing experience, were to give the appearance of a calm progress towards a far bank, it would be highly misleading: intensive fighting in scenes of great confusion was continuing by day and night. Only thus could the powerful capability of Rommel's Panzer Army be gradually destroyed in Montgomery's dogfight, which he had forecast would last up to ten days.

At Freddie's daily conferences, note was taken of the mounting casualties in Eighth Army, which the New Zealanders, Australians and South Africans could afford even less than the British, and the losses in tanks – a dominant factor in Eighth Army's ability to continue offensive action. At the outset the Army had had an immense quantitive superiority in tanks, but losses had been heavy. However, many of the tanks were recovered and urgently dispatched to the rear for repair; the efficient conduct of this operation was never far from Freddie's mind.

Montgomery's battle plan, although now greatly modified, had always envisaged a final major thrust after the enemy had been sufficiently weakened by the 'crumbling operations'. Soon the axis of this thrust would have to be determined: Freddie's brain was more imaginative than Montgomery's in assessing Rommel's situation 'over the hill', and he been watching closely the moves of the Panzer divisions, particularly 21st Panzer Division. It was at some stage expected to move northwards, there to join the rest of Rommel's armour for a possible mass counter-attack. The intelligence staff were able to assure Montgomery on 26th October that it had still not moved. It appeared that the deception plan, and Rommel's preconception that the Eighth Army's major thrust would be in the south, combined with the activities of British armour in that area, had retained it there. However, on 27th October, intelligence from Direction Finding, Y and Ultra all indicated that 21st Panzer Division was on the move, and at 13.15 hours its headquarters was located on the northern front. This made it possible for Montgomery to move his armoured division from Horrocks' 13 Corps to the northern sector, ready for the final assault and the break-out into open country beyond the minefields.

On the night of 28th October, the Australians delivered a powerful attack northwards through the narrow salient they had previously created known at Army Headquarters as 'the thumb'. Freddie and his staff officers, marking the repeated German counter-attacks against it, had been very concerned that 'the thumb' might be cut off at its base, and had been amazed at the confidence with which Montgomery, returning from a visit to the Australian Division, had asserted that they had the situation well under control. However, the Australian attack did not reach its final objective, the sea, but was held on the line of the railway. Nevertheless it was sufficient to produce from Rommel a forecast of impending disaster; already on that morning he had informed his commanders that they were engaged in a life and death struggle.

On Thursday 29th October, preparations continued for the final attack, code-named 'Supercharge', which Montgomery intended should be staged on the axis of the Coast road. It was for that purpose that the Australian 9th Division's offensive had been sustained in that area. However the intelligence picture now showed very clearly that the German divisions were concentrated in that area and that the Italian divisions to the south, which had previously been stiffened by German units, were standing on their own without what Williams called their German 'corsets'. To the intelligence staff and to Freddie it seemed preferable that the final attack should be delivered not at the concentration of German divisions near the coast road but further south in the neighbourhood of the boundary with the Italians. Freddie himself was doubtful of the capacity of Eighth Army to defeat Rommel's concentrated divisions in a frontal attack, but he could hardly parade these fears before Montgomery, who would undoubtedly tell him that he, the Army Commander, was better able to judge such a question than his Chief of Staff. Yet, strongly influenced by the opinion of Williams, Freddie was convinced that a shift of the axis further south might make all the difference between success and failure. Montgomery, having imposed his will successfully on his corps commanders and, despite major changes in his plan having so far swung the battle his way, was in no mood to change his ideas. How was this to be done?

It was at this juncture that an unexpected complication intervened: the arrival from Cairo of Alexander, McCreery, his DCGS, and Casey who was Churchill's Minister of State for the Middle East. Churchill in London had been alarmed by reports of the withdrawal of Montgomery's armoured divisions into reserve, interpreting this not as the necessary preparation for a further offensive but as a sign of stalemate. In view of the imminence of Torch, the Allied landings in NW Africa, due on 8th November, the moment was critical and he had signalled Alexander urging immediate action.

Montgomery allayed Alexander's fears but Casey, after a discussion with Freddie and Williams, proposed sending a signal to Churchill indicating that success was still in doubt. Freddie prevented this with some very blunt speaking.

The subject of the change of axis was then raised; McCreery, who approved of the proposed change, volunteered to discuss it with Montgomery, only to be warned off with some vigour by Freddie. The Chief of Staff had now learnt that such acts of persuasion stood no chance of success when conducted by outsiders, particularly if attempted by McCreery whom Montgomery invariably disparaged; they must be handled *à deux* at the right moment by one of Montgomery's own team. The delegation departed and Freddie soon pulled it off.

After these distractions had been dealt with, Montgomery on the morning of 30th October wrote his directive for operation 'Supercharge' to take place on the night of 31st October/1st November. However, there was great congestion in the battle area and many units were uncertain of their precise locations on the map as there were few recognisable features, and visibility was impaired by dust storms with haze produced by the movement of tanks combined with the smoke of burning vehicles. Freddie ordered me to inspect the battlefield in company with Lt-Colonel Ray Queree, Freyberg's GSO 1, and despatch to the rear those units not required for Supercharge, thus releasing positions for other units to come forward. Armed with the personal authority of the Army Commander we were not, throughout the long day, confronted with any disagreement.

Montgomery at Freyberg's request then authorised a postponement of 24 hours. The attack went in at 1 am on 2nd November and after desperate fighting achieved success. Rommel began to withdraw the remnants of his Afrika Korps leaving the Italians, immobilised and without transport, to surrender. On 4th November Freddie was present at dinner not only with the victorious Montgomery but also with von Thoma, the captured commander of the Afrika Korps. As he was to write later:

El Alamein was the proving ground of British military renaissance in the Second World War. Without it one frankly cannot imagine the feats

which were subsequently achieved. Behind us stretched a pathetic cata-
logue of bungled efforts and ultimate failures: the defence of Belgium,
Dunkirk, Norway, Greece, Crete, Dieppe and the loss of North Africa
to the very gates of Cairo. Democracy had shown itself a poor opponent
in the field of battle, when one must be willing to lay down one's life.[3]

After the battle Churchill ordered that church bells should ring
throughout Britain, and the name Montgomery rose in a crescendo
of popularity. His Chief of Staff, anonymous but perpetually active
behind the scenes, had made an outstanding contribution to the
victory. He had faultlessly carried out the duties of a chief executive
but, more important, with talents in contrast to his 'master's' he had
established a partnership in which the dogmatic Irishman now
listened with keen attention to what his Chief of Staff had to say.
This was a feat which few others could have achieved.

It seemed that Freddie, with his innate frivolity now leashed, his
brilliant brain working at top pressure and his skills in persuasion
fully deployed, might prove to be the perfect complement to his
chief.

CHAPTER NINE

The Willing Horse

After the battle had been won, Freddie on 3rd November 1942 received an immediate award of the DSO, in recognition of his outstanding services in the battle of Alamein as Chief of Staff Eighth Army. The ribbon was sewn on his battledress by his batman alongside the OBE which had been awarded to him a year before in Cairo. This recognition by Montgomery gave him fresh impetus for the ceaseless work that lay ahead; although always cheerful and in good humour he was beginning to feel the strain. Nevertheless the pursuit of a defeated enemy who had repeatedly dragged the reputation of British arms in the mud for close on two years was a subject for great rejoicing. Unfortunately, despite the overbrimming confidence of the Army Commander, it was not carried out with the tactical mastery that Freddie had expected.

On 5th November 1942, three days before the Allies landed at the western end of the Mediterranean (Operation Torch), Eighth Army's pursuit continued with armoured car regiments and armoured divisions, while Montgomery in his Tactical Head-quarters moved close behind them; but they failed to cut off the remnants of Rommel's forces. Freddie, the planner, had not been happy about his Master's arrangements for exploiting the situation when, as was clear from Rommel's increasingly desperate reports relayed by Ultra to Eighth Army, disaster was about to overtake the Afrika Korps. He had instructed me as his planner to prepare a scheme by which units not involved in the closing stages of the 'dogfight' might be kept in readiness to carry out a rapid and daring pursuit of the retreating Germans. A force of 96 tanks with infantry, guns, ground staff for a fighter wing of the Desert Air Force and a naval liaison officer, together with petrol and supplies, had been organised: it was intended to reach Tobruk and be self-contained on arrival for seven days. Montgomery, however, was never attracted by the plan, and declined to use it. Freddie, years after in 1978 commenting to Nigel Hamilton on the failure of the pursuit. recalled:[1]

> I thought he ought to have rounded up the enemy . . . During the battle of Alamein, taking bits and pieces from various corps, I built up a reserve – tanks, armour, guns, troops, etcetera, and had them all formed up and ready; I used to see the commander, General Gairdner, every day . . . But every day Monty would say he wanted some more troops and he'd pinch them from my 'Grapeshot' reserve and so when the great moment came – the breakthrough – it wasn't available. He just used Freyberg's forces to push on, instead of using fresh troops and armour.

However there must be considerable doubt whether Grapeshot as constituted would have succeeded.

A set-back, minor in the scale of events at that time, was the capture by a German rearguard of Hugh Mainwaring, head of the Operations Branch with Dick Carver, the Army Commander's stepson and another officer. I was fortunate to be appointed head of the Operations Branch.

In the pursuit, great expectations had been pinned on the operations of the Desert Air Force, but although Freddie was closely involved with Air Commodore George Beamish, the SASO, in the planning of this aspect, the air strikes against enemy vehicles proved to be not as effective as had been hoped.

Fortunately at this juncture a new Senior Air Staff Officer, Air Commodore Harry Broadhurst arrived to replace Beamish. Broadhurst, from Air Marshal Trafford Leigh-Mallory's Fighter Command in the UK, was well-qualified to further the evolution of air power in the land battle. As a wing commander in May 1940 he had had hard practical experience of the Luftwaffe's tactics in support of the *Blitzkrieg* in Belgium. Later, as Deputy SASO Fighter Command, he had flown in the Dieppe Raid and, after writing a report recommending changes in operational methods, had lectured on the subject in Montgomery's presence at Army Cooperation Command.

His arrival on the desert scene was momentous but bizarre. Leigh-Mallory was loth to lose him; but on arrival in Cairo with a high reputation as a courageous and successful fighter pilot,

Broadhurst found that Coningham did not want to change his SASO and that Tedder had agreed with him. Following a lunch 'to cool him off', a signal was despatched to the Air Ministry, and the posting in replacement of Beamish was then quickly confirmed.

After this unpropitious start, Broadhurst worked in tandem with Beamish for a week or two but, not surprisingly, his relations with him and with his chief were distinctly cool. Montgomery, however, went out of his way to welcome him.

On meeting Claude Pelly in Cairo, Broadhurst received from him not only a valuable briefing, but also a warm recommendation about Pelly's old friend Freddie. Thus a close relationship was initiated between the new SASO and the Chief of Staff of Eighth Army which was to prove immensely valuable until the war's end. Montgomery in 1943 described this vital relationship as follows:

> . . . the Army and Air Staff must sit together at the same headquarters. There must be between them complete mutual confidence and trust. Each has to understand the problems and difficulties of the other. My headquarters and the headquarters of the Air Support Force must be together. When I go forward with a small headquarters, there must be good telephonic communication back to our combined headquarters.
>
> The confidence, trust, and integration of the two staffs is quite remarkable. The SASO and the Chief of Staff have to be great friends. If there is any friction there, you will be done. You have to be great friends, not merely to work together. And so it must go downwards. The machine is so delicate that it can be thrown out of gear very quickly. That mutual confidence and trust, starting with the Air Vice-Marshal and myself, must go right down. . . .[2]

Freddie, for his part, found that the newcomer to the Desert Air Force was a kindred soul and, professionally, a great improvement on his predecessor. He welcomed him warmly and made him at home in the Joint Headquarters. The friendship between them would develop still further when Broadhurst would assume command of the Desert Air Force in February 1943, at the age of thirty-seven. Broadhurst formed an equally happy relationship with Montgomery but, appreciating Freddie's skill in handling his master, worked always on the principle that in controversial matters 'never move without Freddie'.

As SASO he soon found himself in disagreement with the existing policy for the use of fighters; they were still operating as if to gain air superiority, whereas he reckoned that that had already been achieved, and top priority should be given to attacking the enemy's retreating columns.

On 13th November 1942 Tobruk was occupied by Eighth Army; Rommel, threatened by the immense strength of Montgomery's forward armoured units, had decided not to attempt to stand there. This opened up the possibility, well-known to everyone in the Army, of sending a force across the Cyrenaica 'bulge' to cut the road south of Benghazi and thus entrap enemy forces withdrawing on the coastal route. Tedder, an infantryman in World War 1, unwisely sent Montgomery a signal from Cairo stressing the importance of this manoeuvre. Freddie remembered to his dying day this 'meddling airman's presumptuous message' and 'its deplorable effect on Montgomery' which, he wrote, could easily have been avoided had Tedder 'flown up to see him, congratulated him on his victory, questioned him about the RAF's performance from the Army's point of view, asked him about his needs and, in privacy, conversed about Montgomery's future proposals. Yet Tedder never learned his lesson'.[3]

This criticism of Tedder by Freddie, first made public in 1947 and further emphasised in 1979, was a severe condemnation of a man whom he had known well and had much admired in 1941. However the qualities of sensitivity and tact, so manifest in Freddie, were not to be found in every war-time Commander-in-Chief, however intelligent.

But by now at the end of 1942 the strain of events was beginning to tell on the Chief of Staff. After the capture of Benghazi on 20th November, Montgomery, noticing his frail Chief of Staff, decided to take him with him on a jaunt to visit Benghazi, inspect the port and confer with Leese, the leading corps commander. The party consisted of their two caravans, the map lorry, and signals communications, and was accompanied by Montgomery's ADC and liaison officers. Describing this trip nostalgically in 1964 Freddie recalled:[4]

We set out on a lovely November morning for Benghazi, spending one night on route in a small and sheltered valley. It was wonderfully relaxing to get away, even for a few hours, from the hectic atmosphere of operations and plans; to leave an environment where one could not call one's soul one's own; being at everyone's beck and call during the whole twenty-four hours. That evening stands vividly in my memory, for I could luxuriously reflect upon the past few weeks, and I believe that it was only then that I realized to the full what the Eighth Army had achieved. It was pleasant to gossip quietly with my Chief while our batmen got busy with our evening meal. Before we retired to bed we obtained a 'Situation Report' over the wireless, and, later, Montgomery's liaison officers arrived to tell their story. Things appeared to be going well south of Benghazi.

Freddie then described how, next day, they drove into Benghazi, chatted with Church dignitaries at the Cathedral scarcely damaged by the war, and sat down with Montgomery to a picnic lunch, topped off in his case with Italian wine. He recalled the lack of pomp and ceremony, and indeed of security arrangements. 'Montgomery behaved more like a tourist than a victorious Army Commander.' They reached Leese's headquarters at dusk. His account continued:

Little time was lost in getting down to business and our future plans were discussed in great detail. How could we turn the Agheila position? How long would it take to concentrate sufficient force and adequate administrative resources? There was still the question of establishing the Desert Air Force far enough forward to ensure adequate air support to cover the next advance.

We ate a good dinner in Leese's Mess, after which George Walsh (BGS 30 Corps) and I got down to detailed planning as the result of the decisions arrived at between our respective chiefs. About 11 pm I strolled over to my caravan to turn in, and hardly had I got undressed than I experienced an attack of acute pain – a repetition of several I had had over the last year or so. After some time it eased but I felt on the point of collapse. My trusted Chief Clerk, who was with me all through the war and used to sleep under a lean-to attached to the side of my caravan, heard some peculiar noises and arrived to find me in a pretty poor condition. He rushed off to find the Corps HQ's doctor who arrived in due course and gave me an injection which soon gave me some blessed sleep.

After breakfast I was once again examined by the doctor who decided that I must be evacuated to hospital in Cairo. . . . It was, as I had always thought, a gallstone. I was naturally very distressed at being invalided back to Cairo, for I began to conjure up thoughts which spelt the end of my time with the Army I had grown to love so well; to say nothing of the end of my association with its remarkable Commander. I handed over to my friend Bobby Erskine [Brigadier G. W. E. J. Erskine, BGS 13 Corps], which was reassuring for I knew he would prove a first class Chief of Staff.

After a couple of weeks' treatment a Medical Board dealt with my case, and I was told that they would recommend three months' sick leave and suggest a rest in South Africa. So this was the end, and I began to picture spending the rest of the war as a 'Base Wallah'. But I had not at that time appreciated fully the amazing determination or the character of my Chief. He flew to Cairo about the 8th December and came along to see me. I told him of the decision of the Medical Board and, in that typical way of his of refusing to accept anything which interfered with his plans, he asked me when I thought I would be fit to rejoin him? I replied that at the moment I did not feel too good but I guessed two or three weeks rest would do the trick. 'All right, Freddie, I'll talk to your doctors,' he said. The talk produced miraculous results, for my three-months sick leave was changed to three weeks on the condition that I was 'worked gently' to start with. So, in a matter of hours, the outlook entirely changed and I felt I had received a high-powered injection of some new stimulant.

Freddie was of course a willing victim of this exploitation, and he could not foresee that on several future occasions Montgomery would again 'talk to the doctors'.

On the next day Montgomery followed up his visit with a letter from the British Embassy which, short and simple as it was, made Freddie feel that he was wanted once again in Eighth Army.

British Embassy,
Cairo

9-12-42

My dear Freddie,

I enclose a copy of the treatise on how to fight battles. The printing people have done it well.

Get well quickly and come back to me.

Yrs ever,
B. L. Montgomery.[5]

With the prospect of several weeks leave, Freddie's mind had now turned to matrimony. During his time in Cairo he had met a close friend of long standing, Mrs Arlie Stewart, whose husband in the West Yorkshire Regiment had been killed at Keren in Abyssinia in 1941. She had then moved to Cairo and had been serving in one of the Intelligence organisations. Freddie had known her for many years; but now approaching his forty-third birthday he was still unsure whether to take the plunge. Cabling to his old friend Hawkins for advice whether at his advanced age he should do so, he received the robust reply: 'You will be too old if you don't.' They were married in Cairo on 17th December 1942. Montgomery encouraged the marriage, and thereafter was kind and helpful to Freddie's wife.

Some days before the event, Freddie had written to Montgomery who was quick to reply on 18th December. He was glad to hear that Freddie was out of hospital and might be back in one month. He should certainly get married and have a quiet honeymoon in Jerusalem. Knowing his man he went on, 'But you must be quiet and not rush about to parties etc.' There followed a light-hearted description of how he had ouflanked the Agheila position, and he then ended his letter with a significant warning to his Chief of Staff, prone to burn the candle at both ends, 'Don't overdo it on leave.'

For their honeymoon Freddie and his wife flew to Jerusalem to stay at the King David hotel, and later were invited by the Emir Abdullah of Trans-Jordan to his winter camp in the Jordan valley where Freddie got two days' shooting and his wife some riding, heavily escorted by armed warriors.

Meanwhile Montgomery, compelled for logistic reasons to pause in his advance, was as usual looking some months ahead. His eyes were fixed on Tripoli, the next objective for Eighth Army and, as he hoped, the last, since he expected First Army in a few months' time to advance from the west and join him there. In a letter written to Brooke on 28th December 1942 he emphasised the logistic limitations governing his advance. He also expressed concern that the invaluable experience of battle which had been gained by his commanders and staff officers should be disseminated amongst those in the United Kingdom who were not engaged in land operations but were training for the Second Front. In a manuscript note to this letter, he nominated half a dozen officers of high quality whom he recommended should be sent home for this purpose: amongst them was Freddie.

Montgomery, although invariably seeking to dominate the scene, was also remarkably observant, and to many of those surrounding him appeared to have an uncanny knack of knowing every thing that was going on in every corner of his far-flung army. By now he knew a great deal about his Chief of Staff, based on his previous friendship and the five months of his professional association; he recognised in Freddie a lack of physical robustness, further diminished in his view by his peace-time habits – 'Wine, women and gambling', the last being equated with late nights. So in a letter, dated 28th December 1942, to Brooke he recommended for Freddie in due course a less physically demanding appointment in England. He added, 'I do not know what I should do without him as he is quite 1st class', but 'he has been out here a very long time and really ought to go home'.[6] He strongly recommended him for the appointment of Director of Military Intelligence in the rank of major-general in the War Office. Brooke's reaction evidently was negative; although some of the other officers on Montgomery's list duly returned to England, Freddie remained. Such a change even if accepted by Brooke could not have been immediately contrived; so three days later on 1st January 1943 Montgomery sent a letter by hand of officer to Freddie on his honeymoon in Palestine:

Eighth Army
1-1-43

My dear Freddie,

I am delighted to hear all is going well. Here we are all getting tee-ed up for the big stuff. My leading troops are only about 200 miles from Tripoli, and 200 miles is nothing to us.

I shall be delighted to see you back again. If you join up here by 14th January it might be worth your while. But get well first as life will be somewhat hectic about that time. I expect you will read between the lines.

We are now in contact with the Bosche on the line of the main Buerat position about forty miles west of the Wadi Gebir.

Yrs. ever,
B. L. Montgomery.[7]

This letter finally removed from Freddie's troubled mind any
lingering doubts that he might not be wanted back by his Chief.
Amused by the transparent attempt to preserve the secrecy of D-Day
for the great advance to Tripoli, he was delighted with the warmth
of the letter, and recognised the importance which Montgomery had
attached to it by arranging special delivery by officer over a distance
close on a thousand miles.

He returned with his bride to Cairo, and was back at Eighth
Army Headquarters on 14th January. Montgomery immediately
took him to his caravan and explained with his usual clarity the
plans for the advance to Tripoli. Freddie writing in 1964 of this
event said: 'I had to admit somewhat grudgingly perhaps that
everything had gone along very well without me – a sobering and
useful experience.'[8] But this was not the whole story: Freddie's
staff officers working under his stand-in had noticed a significant
change. Although the deputy was very pleasant, Freddie's profound
comprehension of changing battle situations and his swift reactions
to them were lacking. Moreover Bobby Erskine, the BGS of 13
Corps, was not adept at handling Montgomery, and this was
Freddie's forte.

Freddie had been absent from duty for about seven weeks, but
the timing of his gallstone trouble had been fortunate as no very
important actions had taken place in his absence. In future he would
not be so lucky; his frail health was to let him and his Commander
down at too many critical junctures in future operations.

During the later stages of the advance to Tripoli, when
Montgomery with his Tactical Headquarters was cracking the whip
far ahead, Freddie who had never liked the split headquarters but
had accepted it in good spirit found it difficult for Main HQ to keep
in touch. This problem was to recur in a severer form during the
closing stages of the operations in NW Europe.

On 23rd January Eighth Army entered Tripoli. By this time the
Army's logistic problem had become acute. The delay in opening
the port of Benghazi had forced Montgomery to 'ground' 10 Corps
and use their transport for carrying forward supplies for 30 Corps
all the way from Tobruk.

Montgomery, aware that Churchill would visit Eighth Army on
3rd February, decided to use the pause for holding a review of his

victorious troops with a march through the city and an exercise. The theme was, 'How I win my battles'. When taking the official surrender of the city without ceremony on the 23rd, he omitted to invite a representative of the Desert Air Force which had contributed so greatly to the success of the joint operations, and Freddie again was quick to notice this tactless omission. Montgomery had certainly been very busy at the time and the Air Headquarters was very far away, but it was an occasion when a tactful move would have paid handsomely. Soon thereafter the necessity to coordinate the activities of Eisenhower's forces from the west with those of Eighth Army led to a change of organisation under which Coningham joined Eisenhower, and Broadhurst was promoted from SASO to become Air Officer Commanding the Desert Air Force.

This event, taken with the scrutiny of past operations demanded by Montgomery's exercise, provided Broadhurst and Freddie with the opportunity to review the effectiveness of air strikes against enemy armoured and soft-skinned vehicles. Freddie reminded him with good humour of the ineffectiveness of the air strikes immediately after Alamein, and Broadhurst, not slow to retaliate, referred in equal good humour to the paralysing effect on Eighth Army's advance of the German 88 mm anti-tank gun. He then suggested to Montgomery that a trial be carried out using a typical column of captured enemy vehicles. This was agreed, and Freddie responded enthusiastically. The results of the air strikes were poor, and from that moment a serious technical study of the problem coupled with further training of fighter pilots in low-flying (the antithesis of their normal role) was intensively put in hand by Broadhurst.

Fortunately he also received reinforcements in the shape of two American Groups of Warhawks, a group of American light bombers equipped with their latest aircraft, the B.25, and half a Polish squadron equipped with the latest Spitfires, which completely outclassed the German fighters. The Germans could not tell the difference betwen the two types of Spitfire and, after a few successful interceptions by the Poles, they assumed that the Desert Air Force had been re-equipped: this had a crushing effect on the Luftwaffe's morale.

Freddie for his part reviewed with the operational staff the activities of the Army's 'tentacles' and of the J service to ensure that with the more mobile operations now being undertaken at greatly increased distances from headquarters the necessary information for identifying and controlling bomb-lines etc might be more speedily acquired.

These activities were to contribute to the success of the third most critical battle of the North African Campaign – Mareth, which was already looming.

Freddie's cooperation with the Desert Air Force, which was a significant battle-winning factor in subsequent operations of the war, was further helped by the fact that Broadhurst had selected as his SASO Claude Pelly, the very able and intelligent Air Staff Officer, with whom Freddie had worked in close concert when both had been planners in Cairo in 1941. It was a powerful combination; from their previous experience they knew all the 'back doors' into GHQ as well as their custodians, and could thus obtain preferential treatment for the forwarding of resources, including personnel specially selected by their commanders. Soon the change in atmosphere brought about by Broadhurst highlighted the unpopularity in Eighth Army of his predecessor, Coningham; Pelly's dislike of Coningham was equally intense.

At Tripoli both Main and Tac Headquarters were located together in an area south of the city. Montgomery concentrated on planning his exercise, to which senior officers, American and British, were invited from Tunisia, and others from Cairo and the United Kingdom. Freddie with Robertson and Graham was meanwhile much concerned with the logistic build-up, on which the timing of future operations now depended, and with the combined activities of the Royal Navy and Army to open the harbour, which as usual had been rendered inoperable by the enemy.

The preparation of the exercise, which involved almost all staff branches and certain selected commanders, provided an excellent opportunity for personal liaison after a long period of contact solely by radio or telephone. Freddie's influence, based on his instinctive capacity to analyse and comprehend the problems of others, combined with a light touch which obviated any suggestion of interference, was a great asset in this situation, complementing

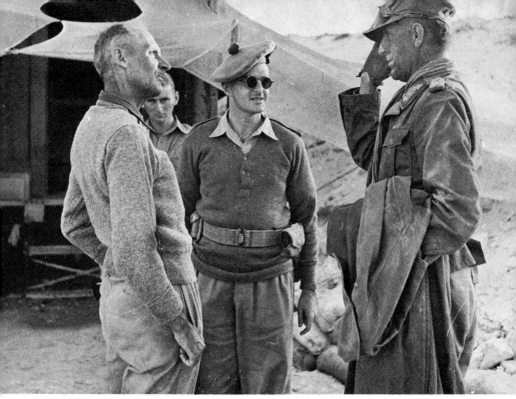

On 4th November 1942 General von Thoma, commander of the Deutsche Afrika Korps, surrendered at Alamein. Monty invited him to dinner and Freddie was present. Shown acting as interpreter is Lt Col 'Joe' Ewart and in rear is Capt Poston, one of Monty's liaison officers.

Left: Freddie accompanied Monty on this trip to Benghazi after the town had been captured by 30 Corps under Gen Oliver Leese (seen here). Freddie commented on 'the lack of pomp and ceremony, with Monty behaving more like a tourist than a victorious Army Commander'. *Right*: The Army Commander with his Chief of Staff has a quick lunch of hard-boiled eggs.

After Monty's exercise in Tripoli ('How I win my battles') there was an Eighth Army dinner to celebrate. Left to right at top table: Maj-Gen 'Pip' Roberts, Freddie, Horrocks, Monty, Coningham, 'Bobby' Erskine, 'Slap' White.

The Army Commander and his indispensable Chief of Staff after a victorious advance of 1500 miles from Alamein.

Montgomery's leadership as the victorious commander intent on passing on to others the benefits of his hard-won experience. This was a genuine trait which had manifested itself very early in Montgomery's career and would continue to the end of his life. Nevertheless it was hardly to be expected that all those summoned to Tripoli would be happy to sit at his feet. Some of them, indeed, considered that the event was a glaring example of self-glorification.

In a letter home, with the arrogance of youth I summed up this period as follows:

> We have had a party here for various generals from near and far – 'Senior jobs' as our AOC calls them, for whom various lectures and demonstrations were arranged by the victorious and efficient Eighth Army. It is amusing to compare the present attitude bred by success and a great deal of publicity to the old days when it seemed that many people were not aware that a war was being fought out here, and it was regarded as a very primitive colonial skirmish. Our reputation now is such that we simply cannot afford to make any mistakes.

Morale was very high and good 'Public Relations' was indeed an important objective of Montgomery's; on that aspect Freddie always kept a watchful eye. He was greatly helped by a young major, Geoffrey Keating, already a veteran of many battles and bearing the wounds of some. Officially he was in charge of the Army Film Unit, but he was so successful with senior commanders and the Press that he virtually ran the Public Relations of Eighth Army. He was readily accepted as one of the team both by Freddie and Montgomery. Light-hearted and amusing, he assumed the additional duty of a court jester, and in this role was indulged by Freddie.

The Chief of Staff, now much improved in health after his convalescence in December and January, continued to grow in stature. With a team of young but seasoned staff officers, who had served him almost unchanged through six months of operations, he was able to take many important initiatives in support of his commander's broad intentions. Meticulously he continued to coordinate all Eighth Army's activities which, with the arrival of First Army in Tunisia, were now becoming more complicated. His services during this period were recognised by the award of a CBE.

Eisenhower, at the western end of the Mediterranean, did not attend Montgomery's exercise, but sent his Chief of Staff General Bedell Smith, whom Freddie found very congenial. He was a highly intelligent and sophisticated officer with diplomatic skills akin to Freddie's; their close friendship, which grew from that time onwards, was to be an asset in many stormy scenes in future Anglo-American relations. Freddie was to meet Eisenhower himself on 31st March at Tac HQ after Montgomery's victory at Mareth; after the visitor's departure he passed on to some of the staff Montgomery's mischievous summing up: 'Nice chap, no soldier.'

During the exercise from 15th to 17th February, Montgomery had other matters on his mind which he discussed with his Chief of Staff. The first was Husky, the invasion of Sicily, a strategic objective seemingly leading nowhere, which the staff had viewed earlier with dismay, assuming wrongly that a cross-channel invasion would be possible in the summer of 1943. But by now Montgomery was reconciled to Husky, and in his discussions with Alexander, the overall land force commander under Eisenhower, he only emphasised that full use should be made of the Eighth Army's resources and of the mystique of its title. Never averse to criticising those outside his team, he commented on the indifferent performance of both British and American Forces in Tunisia, which had culminated in the American disaster at Kasserine just at the time that his visitors were dispersing from the Tripoli exercise.

Thus it was no great surprise to Montgomery to receive on 22nd February a cry for help from Alexander. Montgomery immediately responded, and despite the lack of the full logistic resources that had been planned, he rushed divisions forward to confront Rommel at Medenine. As Freddie wrote in 1946: 'The Army Commander's reaction was immediate and generous . . . He always responds wholeheartedly to an appeal . . .'.[9] The forward moves that took place included the advance of the small French contingent under Le Clerc which anticipated the deployment for the Mareth battle.

The 'copy-book' defensive victory at Medenine, assisted by Ultra, followed on 10th March. Thus Montgomery's outline plan for the Mareth battle with its coastal thrust by 30 Corps and 'left hook' by the NZ Division, conceived in mid February, was not disturbed.

General Le Clerc after his remarkable march of a thousand miles from Chad had arrived at Tripoli on 1st February with his small, mixed contingent of Free French colonial troops and had immediately impressed Montgomery, Freddie and the operations staff with his spirited determination and obvious efficiency.

Freddie, since his days as DMI, had maintained personal touch with the Long Range Desert Group which had carried out many operations on the southern flank of Eighth Army and, with Williams he had already made a close study of the possibility of outflanking the formidable obstacle of the Wadi Zigzaou; this feature, with the dominant hills providing enemy observation from above, and elaborate man-made defences in the wadi, blocked the entry to Tunisia by the coastal route. He had interrogated Arabs and French soldiers, who declared that the Desert route to the south was unbelievably difficult, but after studying air photographs, the Long Range Desert Group had been given in January a special assignment to reconnoitre the intended 'left hook'. Thanks to their highly developed techniques of movement, the LRDG had reported that the route though difficult was possible, provided improvements could be made to a particularly critical defile known as Wilder's Gap, named after the LRDG officer who had discovered it. Thither Le Clerc's detachment had been sent to ensure that it did not fall into enemy hands.

It was particularly difficult for Freddie as Chief of Staff that, while all these preparations for the Mareth battle were being supervised by him, Husky again intruded in the shape of a visit by Admiral Bertram Ramsay, who had been selected as the commander of the Eastern Task Force for Sicily, and Lt-General Miles Dempsey, commanding 13 Corps, which had been earmarked for the operation. Freddie who had not met either of them before was greatly impressed with both. Ramsay, who had been the naval commander at Dover responsible for the Dunkirk evacuation, was to become a well-known figure to all the Eighth Army 'gang', and was also admired by Montgomery whose 3rd Division of the BEF had been evacuated by him from Dunkirk. The date for Husky had already been decided as July, and Dempsey was deeply involved with Ramsay in Cairo, studying provisional plans worked out by a staff known as 'Force 141' in Algiers.

Montgomery with his Chief of Staff examined the map of Sicily for the first time, and they agreed that the provisional plan, made without the influence of a responsible commander, involved too great a dispersion of the assaulting forces, and that it was high time that the future commander of the British force for Husky should have a representative with the planners in Cairo.

But their immediate task was to concentrate on the pressing problems of the current operations. As the D day for the battle of Mareth approached, Broadhurst and Pelly, his SASO, watched the weather reports anxiously. These were ominous, with a forecast of drizzle and fog which would greatly hamper the Desert Air Force's ground attack techniques by obscuring enemy targets. These techniques now included the 'Cab-rank' system, in which RAF officers in armoured cars were established as controllers with the leading ground troops. They had radio communications to close support aircraft already airborne and to the headquarters of the forward formations on the ground. Thus an air strike requested by the forward troops could often be made in a matter of minutes. This highly effective technique was one of the improvements brought about by the RAF's new commander. But now he had to inform Montgomery before the battle that he would not be able to give the air support required due to the weather. He asked for a postponement: but was told somewhat curtly by Montgomery that he would stick to his programme. Having discovered how difficult it was to persuade Montgomery to change his mind, he resolved that in future he would approach Montgomery through Freddie who, he recognised, was exceptionally skilful at handling his master.

By 20th March, Freyberg's Corps as it was now entitled, had moved well forward towards the enemy's defensive position on the southern flank – a gap between two hills codenamed 'Plum' in Eighth Army. The enemy's formidable defences at the Plum defile had been detected by a Photographic Reconnaissance sortie of the Desert Air Force on 7th March.

An air of uncertainty hung over this battle which was most unusual in Eighth Army. Freddie was unable to tell us which of Montgomery's thrusts, the Wadi Zigzaou frontal assault or the left hook via Plum was the main attack, and he did not share his Commander's confidence about the frontal assault. Before the battle, Montgomery judged that the enemy could not hold his position against the combined effect of two thrusts, but in the event he underestimated the strength of the Wadi Zigzaou defences.

On the night of 20th March, 30 Corp's frontal attack went in at 22.30 hours. The great strength of the defences, the difficulties of mine-lifting particularly in torrential rain, some mismanagement by the divisional commander, and the staunch resistance of the Italian Young Fascist Division stiffened by German troops resulted in only a partial lodgement by 50th Division across the rainfilled Wadi; and this was subsequently beaten back by a counter-attack by 15th Panzer Division, whose movement to the battle, although discovered, could not be broken up by air strikes owing to the weather.

Very early in the morning of 23rd March, I was awakened at Main HQ by the telephone beside me. George Walsh, the BGS 30 Corps, told me that the assault had failed, and the remnants of 50th Division had been withdrawn across the wadi. I went to Freddie's caravan and wakened him with the disastrous news. Further sleep was impossible. This was the first failure since the days of Auchinleck, and it was a great shock. Having driven the enemy 1,500 miles from Alamein, were we now to get bogged down so close to Tunis where the final curtain must fall?

At 2 am Montgomery was wakened, and shortly afterwards Leese arrived in person at Tac HQ to confirm the failure of his attack. After a brief discussion, he was told to return in the morning for a conference at 9am.

Montgomery immediately told his personal staff, 'Send for Freddie.' On arrival at Montgomery's map lorry, Freddie found that the Army Commander's usual composure had been badly shaken. For more than an hour the disaster was discussed between them; Freddie was then told to return to Main Headquarters to examine what could be done to strengthen Freyberg's 'left hook' and Montgomery retired to bed.

The incident in the map lorry made a profound impression on Freddie. He never forgot the stunning impact which the disaster had had on Montgomery. It was a situation, often encountered in war, where a Chief of Staff is called on to provide that moral and intellectual support to his Commander which only an intimate can give. If Montgomery sought encouragement and reassurance from his Chief of Staff, Freddie would have provided it in full measure, as in duty bound.

At the corps commanders' conference the next morning which was attended by Broadhurst, Montgomery with his self-confidence restored ordered Leese to close down his front, and Horrocks to take charge of the 'left hook', reinforcing the NZ Corps with his 1st Armoured Division. Freddie back at Main Headquarters held a conference to implement the new plan; staff work concerned with the moves such as tank transporters, anti-aircraft protection, traffic control etc was quickly organised.

Freyberg's corps on 24th March, 200 miles away, was now confronting a formidable defensive position at Plum to which locality two German reinforcing divisions, one of them 21st Panzer, had been moved. 15th Panzer was to follow them on 25th March from the Mareth Line. All these reactions by the enemy were made known to Montgomery by Intelligence, supplemented by air reconnaissance. Freyberg was not optimistic about penetrating the Plum defences and signalled that a set-piece attack with massive artillery support would take up to seven days. The move up of medium gun ammunition which Freyberg demanded would take several days, by which time further enemy reinforcements could be moved across. It seemed to Freddie and the staff that Eighth Army, so near its final success, might now be 'bogged down', with appalling results.

To surmount this problem of delay which could be fatal Freddie, anxiously twisting his forelock almost to destruction – a sure sign of desperate worry – groped towards the idea of a 'blitz' air attack, using fighter bombers in substitution of the artillery shells which could never arrive in time. He and Broadhurst discussed the problem, and despite the risk of heavy pilot casualties from the enemy's dual-purpose 88 mm guns which were known to be guarding Plum, he found Broadhurst most sympathetic and constructive. There had been talk of such a technique before; but using air power instead of artillery was not accepted in the RAF as correct philosophy. However the Desert Air Force now had complete air superiority, and the training and skill of pilots in the ground attack role had been greatly improved. In the crisis which faced Eighth Army, Broadhurst agreed to the plan, for which he would provide forty light bomber squadrons for an opening bombardment on the narrow frontage of the attack, followed by sixteen fighter bomber squadrons attacking ground targets, particularly enemy headquarters, at a density of two squadrons for a period of two and a half hours. The specialist squadron of 'tank busters' would also take part, and five squadrons of Spitfires would operate as top cover.

Broadhurst's problem was how to persuade Montgomery to accept this novel plan with its risks largely unknown. He and Freddie agreed on the tactics: Broadhurst would say what the Desert Air Force could do and Freddie would 'sell' the idea to Montgomery so that he adopted it as his own. This achieved the desired result, and the next two days were spent in innumerable preparations. The Intelligence staff produced from air photographs special maps for the pilots, showing the exact locations of enemy guns, transport, defences and suspected headquarters. Broadhurst sent his squadron leaders on preliminary flights over the battle area to accustom themselves to the geography. An experienced RAF officer was sent up to go forward in an armoured car to control the 'cab-rank', and special arrangements were made in connection with landmarks and coloured smoke signals to show the position of our own troops. Broadhurst himself visited his squadrons to brief them in their critical role; he was received with immense enthusiasm.

Freddie, whose fertile mind was supplemented by a meticulous attention to 'loose ends' was exercised over the peculiar command arrangements for the battle. After Montgomery's conference, which of course had not been attended by Freyberg, Horrocks before his departure had put some proposals for the attack by phone to Montgomery who had curtly told him through the staff officer, 'Don't bellyache, get on with it.' It seemed to Freddie that Horrocks was to be in charge; but would Freyberg, who occasionally defended his status as the senior general of another nation, react awkwardly? To help to smooth out this situation Freddie sent the following letter[10] accompanied by the Army Commander's blessing in the form of two bottles of brandy. The gesture, though well-meant, was not welcomed by Freyberg.

Main HQ,
Eighth Army
MEF.
March 25th 1943.

My dear Generals,

(I feel as if I am writing to the old combination – Hindenburg and Ludendorff).

This letter gives you the Army Commander's views as to future operations.

'Supercharge'[11] is virtually your course No. 1 . . . with stronger and more intimate air support than we have ever tried before.

The Army Commander wants you to go 100 per cent for 'Supercharge' and produce a simple cut and dried plan, and we will give you the maximum air support possible.

The Army Commander stresses the need to keep your joint resources concentrated and not dispersed; that is why he did not like the Kebili project as it placed a mountain range between the two divisions.

He feels that if we can break into this front facing you, you can take considerable risks, and by pushing on deep, the enemy will be forced to pull back from the hills.

We are sending over Darwin, Burton and Alex Wallace to help you tie up the air support for 'Supercharge'. The RAF have ordered an armoured car to report at NZ HQ, and it is proposed that Darwin should be located in it, and be stationed 'cheek by jowl' with Comd. 8 Armd Bde. or whoever else is in a position to get the latest information as to how the air support is working. It is important that he should be able to see the battle area from a good OP and he will then be able to give the pilots the 'low-down' as to how they are doing. It is also important that he keeps in the closest touch with one of our Commanders as he must have an up-to-date picture. Sitting back here it would look as if 8 Armd. Bde is the right location.

The following are the main points which have arisen during a conference held with the RAF this morning:

(a) The RAF are prepared to allocate all their Spitfire Sqns. and 16 Kittybomber Sqns.[12] to support your break-in and break-through.

(b) The length of time they can operate over the area continuously depends upon the Spitfire Sqns. These can operate continuously for two hours. Therefore you can expect Kittybomber attacks throughout this two hours' period at the density of 2 Sqns.

(c) The important thing will be to decide on the correct timing. We feel it might be best to start this intensive air effort about zero minus 30 mins. This should thoroughly disorganise the defence at the psychological moment and allow the fighter bombers to continue supporting the attack during the most difficult period. You may, however, feel you would like a longer preparation beforehand, but it is probable that your artillery will be able to deal with this.

(d) It will be most important to give the Air Force, as soon as possible, the maximum information as to your plan of attack, and the areas and centres of enemy resistance, guns, etc, that you wish to be attacked.

(e) It is hoped that other air resources will be employed on bombing enemy aerodromes during this period and so interfere with enemy air re-action.

(g) The tank busters we feel should be used in the preparatory stage owing to the complication of employing them during the concentrated blitz.

(h) The weather should allow a similar night effort as was put over the enemy facing you last night. From reports received things seem to have gone extremely well, and we feel that two nights like this will not improve the enemy's fighting value. Only the worst type of weather should interfere with the support laid on.

The Air Force are going flat out on this low strafing. It may be very expensive owing to flak and enemy opposition, but they have agreed to do it because the Army Commander has told them it is the big thing at this stage of the campaign. They will not be able to stage such an intensive air effort two days running.

Yours ever
F. W. de Guingand

Lt Gen Sir B. G. Freyberg, VC
Lt Gen G. B. Horrocks.

On D day, which had been postponed by 24 hours to 26th March to facilitate the vast and detailed preparations, there was an appalling dust storm which necessitated the moving of RAF squadrons just before take-off to different air strips. Nevertheless the operation although slightly reduced in strength proceeded as planned and was highly successful in opening the way for the combined forces of Freyberg and Horrocks to pass through the defile; by 29th March El Hamma and Gabes were captured.

Montgomery in his *Memoirs* published in 1958 paid tribute to the magnificent work of the Desert Air Force in these words:[13]

The outstanding feature of the battle was the blitz attack on the left flank, in daylight on the afternoon of 26th March. It was delivered at 4 pm with the sun behind it and in the enemy's eyes. A dust storm was blowing at the time, the wind also being behind us and blowing the dust on to the enemy. The enemy was making ready for our usual night attack; instead he was assaulted in the afternoon with great ferocity.

The attack was simply conceived; it was dependent on surprise, on complete integration of land and air forces, and on a willingness to take risks and to face casualties.

The air forces played a notable part in the attack, using twenty-two squadrons of Spitfires, Kitty Bombers and Hurricane tank-busters, operating in the area beyond the artillery barrage; in that area every vehicle, and anything that appeared or moved, was shot to pieces. Brilliant and brave work by the pilots completely stunned the enemy; our attack burst through the resistance and the battle was won. On this attack we took 2500 prisoners, all Germans; our own casualties were only 600, and we lost only 8 pilots.

There was of course no reference to the part played by his Chief of Staff.

Freddie's contribution to the Mareth battle had been superb. We now know with certainty, and suspected at the time, the enemy's strategic position was untenable due largely to his inferiority in the air and the stranglehold on his supplies; but his ability to make both the British and Americans pay dearly for any mistakes during their advance remained formidable to the bitter end. The tactical outcome of Montgomery's initial attack with 30 Corps had been disastrous, and all those who were closely in touch with the Army Commander knew it. In the minds of some, the awful possibility had begun to form that Eighth Army after its magnificent triumphs might even now become bogged down, with unpredictable results on the campaign in North Africa and the future conduct of the war. Freddie's contribution, apart from his routine supervisory role as Chief of Staff, had been first to prove the practicability of the 'left hook' and to become virtually its sponsor, secondly to support his commander sympathetically at a rare moment of dismay, and thirdly to initiate with Broadhurst's great cooperation a battle technique which had obviated a second potential disaster.

There could be no doubt that by now the willing horse was not only an admired and trusted figure in the eyes of the corps commanders and all the staffs but, as Montgomery's partner, had shown himself to be indispensable.

CHAPTER TEN

Invasion Expert

Husky, the assault on Sicily, only three months away, now began to dominate our thinking. Freddie was not at the top of his form as his stomach pains were giving trouble again, but Husky was a challenge which appealed to him; his work as a joint planner and his experience of the evacuation of Greece had given him insight into many of the problems that would arise in an amphibious assault. This operation was going to be doubly important: first as the opening move in the process of knocking Italy out of the war and secondly as a rehearsal for the Second Front.

Relations with the Royal Navy and the Royal Air Force would be of paramount importance. He had already met Ramsay who was to command the British 'Eastern Task Force', and his Chief of Staff, and he liked the look of them. Ramsay knew well how to delegate; as Chief of Staff in 1938 to the C-in-C Home Fleet he had unexpectedly applied to retire, saying to his master, 'You don't need a Chief of Staff, you do all the work yourself.' As proof of the point, his master had died a year later.

Relations with the Royal Air Force were difficult, partly because of Tedder's belief that by guarding their independence and exploiting their flexibility they could best serve the interests of the land forces. Thus the intimate direct support of Army formations received low priority, and the goodwill between Army and RAF, earned in the desert, began to turn to distrust.

Maori Coningham for the RAF would have the principal Allied Tactical Air Force role to play under Tedder and Eisenhower; this was unwelcome, but Freddie had managed to sustain a diplomatic relationship even with that *prima donna*. Initially the Americans and Canadians would be on their own, but once landed, their operations would be coordinated with those of Eighth Army by Alexander, under Eisenhower's overall direction. After the Tunisian experience

Freddie had his doubts, but he could only wait and see how effective that arrangement would be.

The assault operation was to be on a scale never previously attempted; there were innumerable problems and time was short. The worst complication was the staff's deep involvement still in the current battle in Tunisia. 'Paper' plans for Husky were being made in London, Algiers and Cairo; but Montgomery and Freddie were both much exercised as to how the war in Africa might be quickly terminated so that practical plans, devised by the responsible commanders with their staffs, could now be evolved.

As early as 17th March, Montgomery had written to Brooke giving his view that the plan devised in London for Husky would have to be recast, and that experienced fighting divisions must be used for the operation. The need to recast was accepted by both Alexander and Eisenhower a week later; but by 3rd April Montgomery was still complaining of 'woolly thinking' about the plans being made by Force 141 the planning staff in Algiers, and Freddie was worried by the slow ponderous procedures to decide the issues involved. On 10th April Montgomery again asked Alexander the key question: which Army was to play the major role in the final liquidation of the Axis forces in Tunisia? Two days later it was agreed that the main effort should be made by First Army, and that Eighth Army should be permitted to send divisions back to Egypt to train for Husky.

In the middle of April Montgomery, increasingly apprehensive that a 'dog's breakfast' would emerge from the Husky planning, sent Freddie back to Cairo to act as his deputy. He was promoted to major-general, and as I was to act for him as Chief of Staff in Tunisia I was promoted to brigadier. Montgomery intended that Eighth Army's commanders, staffs and troops should have an easy time before Husky as the pace had been very hot since August 1942. The pace had certainly had an effect on Freddie's health, and at this period he was seen gulping down three medicines at once. Alexander, fearful that Montgomery himself might prematurely pull out of the Tunisian battle to take charge of the British part of Husky, told him that he would regard that as a disaster.

Freddie, after the good news of his promotion to major-general, returned from Sousse to Sfax and stayed for the night with Leese and Walsh his Chief of Staff at 30 Corps. Typically he had celebrated his good fortune by drinking champagne and playing poker far into the night. He was looking forward to returning to his wife and the fleshpots of Cairo, which he reached on 15th April. There, the contrast of good food at the Mohammed Ali Club, the attractions of the sophisticated Gezira Club with its green lawns and swimming pool, the purchase of new clothes for his wife and himself, and dinner parties with dancing at Shepheard's Hotel – all these pleasant activities obliterated temporarily the stress of his 1500 mile trek from Cairo to Tunis when at any hour he must anticipate calls from his innumerable clients.

The reaction of the *bon viveur* to his illnesses was unusual; he could not be called a hypochondriac as they were very real, but he seemed to take an obsessive interest in their manifestations, had an irrational faith in his many pills and developed close friendships with his assorted medical advisors, so much so that he was often in doubt whose advice to accept.

He certainly needed some days of rest and recuperation before facing the appalling muddles which characterised the planning of Force 141 in Algiers; the confusion was reflected also in the reactions of Churchill and the Chiefs of Staff in London and of the Combined Chiefs of Staff in Washington. Neither Eisenhower nor Alexander, who admittedly were primarily occupied in terminating the successful campaign in North Africa, took a grip on the Husky planning in the period February to April 1943. The degree of indecision even reached the ears of Attlee, the Deputy Prime Minister in London, who was not normally involved in such affairs: in a minute to Churchill he had asked whether anyone of commanding willpower was directly in control of the joint planners: should not their deliberations be directed to essentials by some ruthless and forceful personality? The personality, in the shape of Montgomery, was at hand.

On 17th April 1943 Freddie in Cairo was hard at work planning with Ramsay and with Air Vice-Marshal Keith Park, AOC Malta, who was to be Eighth Army's airman rather than Broadhurst. He was to find that Ramsay, then aged sixty, and his Chief of Staff were splendid collaborators, but there were only ten weeks left to plan and prepare the expedition. They were all located in a building, code-named George, which was in the centre of the residential part of

Cairo. The planning group was called Force 545 for cover purposes, and security was strict and elaborate. Freddie immediately called on Ramsay and gave him a letter of authority from Montgomery. Ramsay was most friendly and helpful, and Freddie explained that after studying the Force 141 Plan and conferring with Dempsey he intended to write a new appreciation. This document commented once again on the excessive dispersion of the original plan and the need for a more concentrated assault. Very soon Freddie was joined by some additional staff officers withdrawn from Eighth Army. The BGS (operations) remained in Tunisia as acting Chief of Staff Eighth Army, still engaged in the last stages of the African Campaign.

Freddie's appreciation duly reached Montgomery in Tunisia, and on 23rd April, the Army Commander flew to Cairo for consultations with his commanders and his Chief of Staff. Freddie with his planning staff put on a presentation of the plan as conceived at that stage, with Ramsay and Dempsey present. Montgomery, who had already recommended one change to the Force 141 plan, sat silently sucking in the presentation, interrupting only very occasionally with a question. He then had further private discussions with Ramsay and Dempsey, and by dinner time had made up his mind. After dinner at the British Embassy, a signal was drafted recommending to Alexander a further variant of the plan. Ramsay, who did not dissent, was committed somewhat unwillingly to agreement in a paragraph of the signal: later he was called to order by his superior for having done so.

This 'Montygram' (as they were known to Freddie and the Army staff) was in very strong terms. Montgomery declared that he was prepared to carry the war into Sicily with Eighth Army but must do so in his own way. The fight would be hard and bitter, and the assumption of previous planners that opposition would be slight was a grave error. Hence his army must operate concentrated in corps and divisions in supporting distances of each other. The proposed western landings must be given up and the whole initial effort be made at the eastern end of the island. The capture of airfields and ports would then follow. 'Time is pressing and if we delay while above is argued in London and Washington, the operation will never be launched in July . . .' These points were rubbed in: the style was repetitive and hectoring.

The message on arrival in Algiers came as a bombshell to Eisenhower, Alexander, Cunningham the Naval C-in-C, and to Tedder, whose disapproval Montgomery had provoked by demanding that Broadhurst should command the air operations in support of Eighth Army instead of Park, the more senior air marshal in Malta. In the event Broadhurst sited his headquarters alongside Park's and the staffs worked closely together. Park was in fact in the better position to defend the base in Malta and cover the amphibious landing.

Hearing that there was opposition to his proposals in Algiers, Montgomery then suggested that with Ramsay he should fly to Algiers to explain their revised plan, but unfortunately at this critical moment he fell sick. He signalled to Freddie ordering him to take his place at the Algiers conference. A special plane was ordered and Freddie flew to El Adem to refuel. While taking off in chancy weather the plane crashed. Miraculously no one was killed, but Freddie was badly shaken and concussed and was flown to Cairo in an ambulance plane.

As a third attempt to get the invasion plan settled, Leese was then sent to Algiers at very short notice to present Montgomery's arguments. No one met him on arrival at the airfield and he was forced to hitch a lift. At the meeting neither Tedder or Cunningham was prepared to accept Leese's advocacy of Montgomery's arguments, and strong disagreement was expressed on all sides.

Freddie after the plane crash had remained unconscious for some hours and had been delivered to his flat in Cairo where his wife, already alarmed at her husband's condition, had been startled by the arrival of a posse of staff officers intent on recovering Freddie's briefcase containing the invasion plans. Fortunately the briefcase, which appeared to rate a priority higher than that of the damaged general was soon discovered intact. After X-rays and treatment, the Chief of Staff was ordered by the doctors to take two weeks' leave and, in a shaky condition, left with his wife for a fishing holiday in Palestine and Syria. His depression was much relieved by a letter from Montgomery written from his own sick bed in Tunisia on the fatal day of the plane crash:[1]

Freddie with Captain Geoffrey Keating, commander of the Army Film Unit, who virtually ran the Public Relations of Eighth Army, and was indulged by Freddie as a 'court jester'.

Eisenhower meets Monty for the first time after the victory at Mareth. Also present: Harry Broadhurst, Freddie and Horrocks.

Generals Freyberg and Horrocks, who combined to win the Mareth battle.

After suffering concussion in an aeroplane crash, Freddie was sent on sick leave; with his wife Arlie he went fishing in Syria.

28-4-43

My dear Freddie,

I am terribly sorry about your accident. I am sending Belchem to Cairo. You are to stay in your house and be completely quiet.

Belchem will do the whole thing and come and see you if he wants advice on any point.

It is absolutely essential that you take it easy and get well.

I am in bed myself with a temperature and sore throat, so the whole show is breaking up.

Cheer up.

My kind regards to your lady wife.

Yrs ever,

B.L. Montgomery.

This letter reflects the very warm relationship which now existed between the Army Commander and his indispensable Chief of Staff. Montogomery must have felt severely frustrated lying on his sick bed while the critical argument over the invasion plan was still unresolved, and D day was only ten weeks away. Yet, sensing Freddie's inevitable depression, he composed this jaunty sympathetic letter designed to allay Freddie's anxieties and to cheer him up.

Meanwhile in Tunisia the Axis forces continued to fight desperately against annihilation. On 29th April, Eighth Army's contribution to the final battle, an attack against the very strong defensive position of Enfidaville was carried out, but resulted in failure. A conference was held the next day attended by Alexander, McCreery his Chief of Staff and Broadhurst, and Montgomery's new plan was agreed: two divisions and an independent brigade were sent on a wide outflanking movement to attack through First Army's sector, with Horrocks to run the battle. This operation was to produce on 12th May the final triumph of the North Africa campaign, and all German resistance ceased.

But Montgomery, who by now had been relieved of responsibility for operations in Tunisia and had recovered from sickness, was not to be thwarted. To obtain agreement to his revised plan for Husky he now proposed a visit to Algiers on 2nd May taking me with him as acting Chief of Staff Eighth Army. At Eisenhower's headquarters he skilfully seized an opportunity in the lavatory to put his arguments to Bedell Smith and quickly convinced him. He then formally presented his case to Eisenhower, who agreed on 3rd May. Characteristically, but not without some military logic in support, he then suggested to Brooke that he should be given command of the entire Anglo-American land forces, totally ignoring the political realities of an international endeavour.

Meanwhile Freddie recovering from concussion was enjoying with his wife a well-earned rest in Palestine and Syria. From Jerusalem they drove to Baalbek where he had three days' excellent fishing on the Orontes river, recalling a similar holiday when he had been the bachelor adjutant of the West Yorkshire Regiment in Egypt in 1932. Good rainbow trout were caught in the swiftly flowing river fed from the melting snows of the Anti-Lebanon. It was a wonderful place for convalescence.

Within a few days of his planned date of return to Cairo Freddie received another letter from Montgomery:[2]

> British Embassy,
> Cairo.
>
> 12-5-43
>
> My dear Freddie,
>
> I am in Cairo checking up on Husky. Before coming here I visited Algiers and got various things agreed as the result of the acceptance of my plan.
>
> I then visisted Alexander and got everything I wanted agreed to. There is now no need to worry on any matter. I have had conferences here and have explained the whole business to everyone; the foundations and framework of the whole project are now firm.
>
> I am quite happy with the Air matters.
>
> In fact everything is going along so well that I myself am going off to England on Sunday next, 16th May: Army HQ pulls out of the battle that day and goes back to the Tripoli area. Oliver [Leese] will be in charge here while I am away; Belchem is running everything quite excellently. Richardson will be at Algiers as my representative at Force 141.
>
> Now about yourself.
>
> It is absolutely vital that you should get quite fit before you come back.
>
> You are not to worry about the business, or even to think about it. It is quite unnecessary for anyone to go up and see you, and keep you in touch.

There is nothing to worry about; everything is now splendid. You must stay where you are; amuse yourself; have a thorough good rest; and be back here on 1st June and not before. I will be back myself by 5th June at Tripoli (Main Army).

I shall come to Cairo about 8th June, and go off with Ramsay to the rehearsals about 11th or 12th June.

Show these orders to your wife and tell her that I rely on her to see them carried out. You are far too valuable to be wasted, and I would be 'in the soup' if you came back too soon and cracked up again later.

So stay where you are and be back here by 1st June.

Good luck to you,

Yours ever
B. L. Montgomery.

Once again this was a letter that would warm the heart of any convalescent Chief of Staff. The protracted confusion in settling the outline plan of the invasion had apparently been ended at last, and the vast mass of detailed planning was now being pushed ahead by the young staff officers whom Freddie had led and developed over the last nine months. Montgomery, the land force commander designate of the 'Eastern Task Force', was about to go off to England for his well-earned rest, and was due to return to Tripoli on 5th June, only five weeks before D-day. This demonstrated his great confidence in his staff, although now temporarily bereft of their leader.

The letter contained for Freddie his Master's sympathetic instructions and, as always, argument was out of the question. So off he went again with his wife for another two weeks fishing in the hills above Beirut.

Despite Montgomery's reassuring letter, the detailed planning both at George and in Algiers was not without its problems. Belchem, aged only thirty-two, had to lead the staff of all three services many of them much senior to him. Though ably supported by Graham the administrative head, he had to cope with some 'bellyaching' by certain senior staff officers; this had to be firmly dealt with. Planning with the RAF was expectionally awkward due to the command system on which Coningham had insisted. In the absence of Freddie, Broadhurst found that the previous close army/air liaison deteriorated, and he was far less certain of the Army's future plans.

On returning to Cairo on 31st May, Freddie received another letter from the Army Commander, who had returned from England, informing him that due to the visit to Eighth Army of King George VI he would be unable to attend a final coordinating conference called by Eisenhower and that Freddie was to present Eighth Army's plans and 'would do it very well'. This he did after his usual meticulous preparation. The performance of General Patton who was the Commander of Seventh Army, the US Western Task Force, surprised him by its brevity; never much given to planning, the American's contribution lasted only a few minutes.

Montgomery, back from England a few days later, was in no way inhibited in telling Freddie in Cairo of the popular acclaim he had received on his leave at home. Master's self-confidence, always prominent, appeared now to have developed still further, and Harry Broadhurst, whose squadrons were to operate from Sicily after the landings, was relieved that Freddie was back in the saddle; he regarded him as the only person who could exercise some control over Montgomery, whose vanity had been much inflated by the hero-worship that he had received.

In preparation for the assault landing there followed the well-known sequence of Montgomery's verbal orders to commanders, followed by studies of possible eventualities and a round of rehearsals. By the end of June, Eighth Army Headquarters had moved to Malta, and Freddie sailed in a cruiser with Ramsay to join the staff already well-installed there in the Lascaris tunnels. Montgomery was to join them from Tripoli early in July.

The complexities of Husky which had faced the staff of Eighth Army, and particularly the Chief of Staff, had been considerable. For embarkation many ports had had to be used: Haifa, the Suez Canal ports and Tripoli: for these, GHQ Middle East in Cairo had been responsible for loading. In addition Sfax, Sousse and Kairouan (for Airborne troops) had been used, controlled by Supreme HQ and Alexander at Algiers. Finally the Canadian Division and certain units from the UK had been loaded there and controlled by the War Office in London. The various commanders concerned had also been widely dispersed. Eisenhower was in Algiers; Alexander, the overall land forces commander, was in Tunis; the Naval C-in-C Cunningham was in Malta, while Tedder the Air C-in-C was also in Tunis.

During the planning phase in Cairo, Freddie had found that the arrangement for obtaining intelligence of beaches and defences had been most unsatisfactory. But later excellent results were achieved by low altitude oblique photography by the RAF. Further beach intelligence was successfully acquired using a new scientific method of calculating the slope of beaches from the intervals between the crests of waves, supplemented by the courageous and hazardous operations of the Combined Operations Pilotage Parties who visited the beaches by submarine. All these techniques were again to prove their worth in planning the invasion of NW Europe.

On 10th July, despite the lack of tactical surprise, the invasion was carried out with great success except for disaster with the airborne forces, which tragically were dropped often in the wrong localities due to mismanagement and difficult weather conditions. Freddie himself had a busy and adventurous time. Montgomery as usual decided to go ashore early and left Malta on 11th July to find that a muddle had occurred over his headquarters' vehicles, with the result that he was homeless in Sicily for twenty-four hours. The Chief of Staff, after receiving a very sharp signal, put the matter right in very quick time.

The next day Freddie with Graham visited the beaches in a destroyer and made contact first with the Canadian Division which, new to Eighth Army, had fought magnificently. He then returned to the headquarters ship and sent out signals to try to locate his commander, but this was unsuccessful. Continuing the search he moved on by ship to 13 Corps and from there went by car to 30 Corps HQ where he at last found the Army Commander with his Tac HQ near a landing ground. They spent a noisy night under bombing by the Luftwaffe.

In the first phase of the operation Eighth Army had met with only light opposition and progress had been satisfactory. In the second phase from 12th July to 21st July progress on the eastern side of the island was much slower due to the effect of mines and demolitions combined with the natural defensive strength of the terrain. It then became clear from the enemy's signal traffic that he was on the point of abandoning Western Sicily, and that he intended to reinforce Eastern Sicily; thereafter Patton with his Seventh US Army made rapid progress up the west coast towards Messina. In order to coordinate the operations of the British and United States Armies, Montgomery decided to visit Patton at his headquarters at Palermo, flying with Freddie and Broadhurst in his recently acquired Flying Fortress aircraft crewed by the US Air Force. They made a difficult landing at Palermo which required a heavy use of brakes, but on the return journey Broadhurst informed them that the brakes now were ineffective and they must divert to a larger airfield. Even so they had to use the grass field surrounding the runway to make yet another hazardous landing. Freddie seemed to be a Jonah with aircraft.

Meanwhile negotiations for an armistice with the Italian Forces were being undertaken by Eisenhower's headquarters. For security reasons Freddie and his Army Commander were the only people who were kept informed of the progress of these events. This was achieved by secret meetings between Freddie and Alexander's Chief of Staff. These developments placed a further responsibility on the Chief of Staff.

But even to Freddie, the highly experienced and clear-headed planner, future objectives were shrouded in confusion; this was partly due to uncertainties as to Italian reactions when the German forces were finally driven from Sicily. Nor could it be decided which Allied formations would be available to move into Italy until the end of the Sicilian campaign. Nor were there any firm figures for the availability of landing craft and shipping to undertake the landing operations in Italy. Originally it was intended that the invasion of the mainland should be carried out by Eighth Army only with two corps, one across the Messina straits and the other on the northern coast of the 'toe' of Italy. Towards the end of July a third possible operation was added: an assault landing at Salerno. Eventually on 17th August these options were reduced to two: Eighth Army at Messina, (Operation 'Baytown') and the US Fifth Army with a British corps at Salerno, (Operation 'Avalanche').

Freddie, who, in addition to his executive functions in the current battle, had to lead in the resolution of these problems, was puzzled and worried about the Messina operation. By this time it was becoming apparent that Eighth Army, diminished by the transfer of a corps to the Americans for Avalanche, was to have a secondary role. The US Fifth Army, whose objectives were the capture of Naples and the advance to Rome, was manifestly dominant and was to have top priority. Thus it was that Freddie and his staff cast envious glances towards Salerno, and were most unhappy about Messina and operations in the toe of Italy.

As early as 10th August, Freddie had stated that it was not clear what was to be achieved by the crossing at Messina. Moreover the conclusions of an Eighth Army planning conference went further by declaring that if Avalanche was a success, then that front should be reinforced for there was little point in Eighth Army laboriously fighting up the east coast of southern Italy. Eventually Freddie concluded from a further planning conference that 'Baytown' ought to be cancelled and used merely as a threat, since lack of naval and air resources made an assault simultaneously with Avalanche impossible; during the interval between the two assaults, the enemy would have ample time to withdraw their divisions to the Naples area, using rearguards effectively to delay Eighth Army.

On 16th August Patton reached Messina and found that large numbers of Axis troops had succeeded in escaping across the Straits. The Sicily campaign was now at an end and Italy was under threat, but Montgomery harboured no illusions about the effect on operations if the Italians were to capitulate. He shared his Chief of Staff's uncertainty about the object of Eighth Army's next campaign. Never loth to confront his superiors, he sent a powerful 'Montygram' to Alexander demanding enlightenment: 'I have been given no clear object for the operation . . . all I can do with present resources is a major raid across the Straits – request definite instructions.'[3]

Freddie was not worried by this high-handed approach as he understood the strange relationship between the two men, under which the nominal subordinate acted frequently as the superior. Alexander's reply was far from satisfactory in Montgomery's eyes: 'Your task is to establish a bridgehead across the Straits, and engage enemy forces in the southern tip of Italy in order to draw Axis divisions away from Avalanche' – 'daft' as Montgomery wrote later in his diary.

Freddie, although frustrated by the lack of sensible direction from above, was able at this time to enjoy some distractions which kept his spirits up. The Army Commander for the first and last time in the campaign had occupied a beautiful villa in Taormina for his

Tactical Headquarters, and Freddie spent a number of happy nights there, enjoying as always the good life, admiring particularly the beautiful dinner table, the excellent porcelain and the artistic appointments of the Fascist owner. He frequently travelled there from Main HQ in Broadhurst's captured speed-boat, bathing and picnicking en route. After dinner when business was finished, he would foregather with the ADCs and liaison officers, and often play chemin de fer, using a miniature pack of cards and a shoe given him years before by Mrs Hawkins at Le Touquet. They 'made a killing' of an eminent Permanent Under Secretary, who forfeited all his French francs, his lira and his pound notes; nevertheless the PUS, bearing no grudge, repaid the unforgettable hospitality he had received by successfully fighting financial battles in Whitehall on Eighth Army's behalf.

Thus, faced with an uninspiring future, Montgomery and Freddie were reconciled to 'get on with the business'. The now familiar tasks of beach reconnaissances, the organisation of landing craft and logistic shipping, the planning of artillery and air bombardment and the training of assault units were duly carried out. The assault across the Messina Straits took place on the night of 2nd/3rd September with a heavy artillery barrage. Opposition turned out to be negligible; and Freddie, who had once again held in his coordinating fingers the threads of every activity,[4] asked himself where was the operation getting them and was it really necessary?

Montgomery publicly put the best face he could on the difficult winter campaign that lay ahead. In his personal message to the Army he referred to Eighth Army's great honour in being the first troops to land on the mainland of Europe. 'They would knock Italy out of the war.' The Italian Armistice was indeed announced on 8th September. But both to the Army Commander and to Freddie a landing to capture Naples was the real prize, and Montgomery had written enthusiastically to Brooke about this possibility as long ago as July. Moreover, the event of the Second Front planned for the summer of 1944 had already engaged their minds, and Montgomery had suggested to Brooke that he and Alexander would make a 'good team'. It would have been strange if Freddie, who, habitually looked ahead as far if not further than his master, had not also speculated on his future position.

By now Freddie had been Eighth Army's chief executive through sixteen months of critical but victorious operations of ever-increasing complexity. Throughout that time, Mongomery had placed immense reliance upon him using him to amplify, transmit and supervise all his verbal instructions. Evidently he had satisfied his exacting master. On 14th October his name had again appeared in a list of awards: he was made a Commander of the Order of the Bath. But the strain of his service, coupled with the dismal weather of an Italian winter and the lack of strategic promise in Eighth Army's operations had not left Freddie unmarked. Invariably he worked very late but, even so, suffered from insomnia. His personal clerk, Sergeant Harwood, whose law studies had been interrupted by the war, was often summoned by Freddie from his nearby slit trench at midnight.

'What shall we talk about tonight?' Freddie would enquire, and Sergeant Harwood would willingly oblige with some topic from his civilian experience – anything other than war. Soon Freddie was ready for sleep.

Often he would be seen in thick battledress with a heavy muffler round his throat, and bags under his eyes, arriving at Tac HQ for an evening's visit and dinner, the meal to which one brigadier from Main Headquarters was customarily summoned each day. But Freddie's visits, perhaps because of the difficult communications, became less frequent; and often it fell to a young staff officer, after receiving Montgomery's orders and the plan of his moves for the next day, to transmit to the Chief of Staff the Army Commander's verbal instructions on a wide range of tactical and confidential matters of great urgency and importance. It was disquieting that Montgomery should adopt this new technique, and surprising that Freddie would accept such instructions through an intermediary; but it was characteristic of Freddie that once he had established a relationship of confidence with an individual, age and status assumed little importance.

After attempting unsuccessfully to come to Fifth Army's assistance during their crisis at Salerno, Eighth Army continued laboriously to fight their way northwards through rivers, minefields, mud and demolitions to the river Sangro and the enemy's 'Gustav' Line, which they reached at the end of November 1943.

En route, the anniversary of the Battle of Alamein was not forgotten.
Freddie had marked the occasion by addressing an appropriate letter
to the Army Commander from his staff:[5]

>   HQ Eighth Army
>   23rd October 1943
> My dear General,
>   On this first anniversary of the Battle of El Alamein, I would like, on
> behalf of your staff at Army HQ, to send you our warmest good wishes
> on this great occasion; and to express our gratitude for leading us
> through the past year with such wisdom, inspiration and success.
>   We look forward to the future with solid confidence in your
> leadership.
>   (Sgd) F. W. de Guingand
>   Major-General Chief of Staff

During this period, Freddie had to cope with a number of visitors,
since it was Montgomery's habit, and a very sound one, to avoid
distraction from outsiders other than those of the greatest
importance. A group of Russian officers turned up, nominally to
study Eighth Army's techniques but in Freddie's opinion 'to see
whether we were fighting'. They were soon convinced of this, and
were said to have commented: 'We have seen enough bravery for
one day; we now would like a little sleep.'

Portal, the Chief of the Air Staff also arrived, and on his way to
Montgomery, disclosed to Freddie some information about the
threat of the German V weapons. He was followed by Churchill,
Brooke and Eisenhower. Later Freddie tried to elicit from Brooke
some indication of the choice of commander for the Second Front.
'No fly that we dropped produced any reaction. But then he is a
keen fisherman and knew the game.'

But the most welcome visitor of all was a strange, unshaven
'Italian peasant' with a dirty plum-coloured coat, an old straw hat,
a stick and a vino bottle in his hand, who arrived in a truck from
13 Corps. He walked up the steps of Montgomery's caravan and
announced himself by saying: 'Good evening, sir.' Montgomery
looked up and not recognising him said in a gruff voice, 'Who are
you?'

He replied: 'Hugh Mainwaring, sir.'

'Good God! Come in and sit down. Where have you come from?'
'Fontenallato, about fifty miles south of Milan.'

Montgomery then called Freddie on the telephone: 'Come here.
I have got Hugh Mainwaring with me.' When Freddie arrived,
Montgomery said: 'We must have a party in my Mess tonight.
Invite everyone who knew Hugh in the Desert . . . .'

The dinner party was a wonderful reunion with about twenty old
friends, and Montgomery was in tremendous form . . . After dinner
he got up and said: 'I am going to bed now. You will have more fun
here without me. I will lend you some pyjamas for the night;
someone else will fix you up with some bedding. Attend my
conference in the morning and tell them all you know.'[6]

Then suddenly out of a clear sky Freddie heard the good news that
Arlie his wife, en route to England from Cairo by sea, was expected
in Augusta, Sicily, for a day or two. After a long interval of
separation, they spent three happy days at Taormina as the guests
of General Crerar, the commander of the Canadian Corps; thence
Freddie returned to the mud of the Sangro battlefield, and his wife
continued her slow journey to England.

Compared to the great mobile operations under bright North
African skies, where skill in manoeuvre on a Napoleonic scale had
been possible, the slow frustrating winter operations, conducted
often in appalling weather and sometimes resulting in heavy
casualties were a torment to Montgomery and Freddie. So it was
immensely heartening to the Army Commander to receive a signal
on Christmas Eve 1943 ordering him to return to England to take
command of 21st Army Group in preparation for the cross-channel
invasion of Europe, the long-awaited 'Second Front'. Eisenhower's
appointment as Supreme Commander had been announced two
days previously. The choice of Montgomery was crucial: Churchill
and Eisenhower would have preferred the amenable Alexander, but
Brooke and Grigg, the Secretary of State, insisted on the victor of
Alamein.

Mongomery was a great believer in working through seasoned
teams and decided at once that for the nucleus of his staff he would
need Freddie, Graham his Chief Administrative officer, Williams as
head of Intelligence, Richards as tank advisor and Hughes his head
chaplain. I was with Mark Clark, but would join later.

Montgomery told Freddie the great news on Christmas day at Tactical Headquarters, and afterwards they had dinner together with a few of the faithful around the table. Freddie, despite the stress of the last sixteen months, 'worked to the bone' in Montgomery's phrase, was delighted, and Master on whom the strain had been greater, was jubilant.

Years later Montgomery was to recall that moment and write:

> I could not possibly have handled the gigantic task that lay ahead without the trusted Chief of Staff who had been at my side since Alamein.
> He knew me and my ways, and that was all-important.[7]

Yet Montgomery's assessment, simplistic as usual and not without vanity, concealed a critical choice. He was well aware that Freddie's health, always questionable, had not been improved by the incident two years before at Benghazi, after which the doctors had recommended without avail a long convalescence in South Africa. Later there had been the aeroplane crash, followed by the strain of operations in the debilitating heat of the Sicilian summer, and a taxing winter campaign in Italy; and this was the man whom he had proposed in 1942 for lighter duties in the War Office.

But how could he face the prospect of 'running in' a new Chief of Staff? Not only was Freddie now superbly competent in the business of assault landings, he had also established fruitful relationships with Ramsay and Broadhurst. Moreover he led a devoted band of able staff officers and was himself desperately keen to continue. There was another aspect: the relationship between him and his Chief went far deeper than mere professionalism: strong emotions of loyalty and affection were involved.

After the war, Montgomery, discussing his successes was often heard to declare: 'Get yourself a first class Chief of Staff: work him and keep him until he goes mad – then get another one.' In Freddie's case Montgomery's boast was to prove in 1944 uncomfortably near the truth.

CHAPTER ELEVEN

Serving the Alliance

The task of launching the Second Front was indeed gigantic. There were fifty-eight enemy divisions located in France: how could the forces of the Allies, British, American and Canadian, perilously landed from the sea be established in sufficient strength to withstand immediate counter-attacks and form a secure bridge-head? This was now the problem confronting the Eighth Army team: Sicily again but writ large – very large indeed.

However before the party was to leave for England in the Army Commander's private aeroplane, there was one act Freddie was called on to organise: Montgomery's farewell to his Army – 'the brave but baffled' Army that he had taken over from Auchinleck, that he had trained and led to victory and on which his personality had been indelibly stamped. Freddie staged this event in the Opera House at a small town called Vasto; a great audience was assembled as if for one of the familiar briefings before a major battle. Broadhurst of the Desert Air Force, who had with Freddie's help transformed the relationship between the army and the supporting air force, was invited with the corps and divisional commanders. He had been told by Slessor, Tedder's successor, that he would be retained in the Mediterranean Theatre as it would be bad for morale if all commanders were seen to leave. However, some weeks later, he was posted to England, to be welcomed by many old friends of Eighth Army.

When Montgomery came to write of this farewell in his Memoirs[1] in 1958, he confessed: 'I should have difficulty myself in describing the occasion.' He went on to quote Freddie's account of it in *Operation Victory*:

I drove with him to the hall, feeling as I always do on such occasions, sad and sentimental. My Chief was very quiet and I could see that this

141

was going to be the most difficult operation he had yet attempted. We arrived inside and he said, 'Freddie, show me where to go.' I led him to the stairs leading up to the stage. He mounted at once, and to a hushed audience commenced his last address to the officers of the Army which he loved so well.

He started very quietly, apologising in case his voice might let him down for, as he said, 'this is not going to be easy, but I shall do my best. If I happen to have difficulty in speaking on occasions, I hope you will understand.' I felt a lump coming in my throat, and one could feel everyone in his audience was perfectly tuned in to his mood. He then very simply and rather slowly explained about his coming departure, and what responsibilities lay ahead. He touched on the past – on the successes we had gained together, and of the things he considered important, and which guided him during his command. He summed up the situation, and expressed his thanks to everyone for the support he had received, and for the way they had fought.

He then asked them to follow the new Army Commander, Leese, as they had followed him. There were no great feats of oratory and no false note. It was exactly right and I found it intensely moving. He finished quietly by reading his last of many personal messages to the Army – his message of farewell.

We cheered him and then he walked slowly out to his car. I followed feeling very uncomfortable, for I had tears on my cheeks and we were riding in an open car. We drove back to Main Headquarters, which was only a few yards away, where some of the senior commanders had been asked to come and have a chat. It was a wonderful gathering of old friends. As my Chief talked to this trusted few I could not help thinking of Napoleon and his Marshals, for here surely was to be found the same relationship, born and tempered by mutual esteem and success in battle. Later Freyberg, Dempsey, Allfrey and the others departed, and I had a feeling that something rather terrible was happening – I was leaving this great family. But then again I remembered that I was leaving in company with the one who had given us that inspiration, and that guidance, and so although sad I felt content with fate.

It was on 31st December 1943 that the Army Commander with his Chief of Staff and key staff officers flew to Marrakesh where Montgomery spent the night with Churchill who was convalescing there. He found the Prime Minister in bed, reading a copy of the plan for the invasion of NW Europe (Overlord), and was asked to comment on it. After dinner he pleaded for an early night, and then wrote out some terse and prescient criticisms, which he presented to Churchill after breakfast before leaving for London.

Meanwhile Freddie, who with the other chosen 'chaps' had had a good dinner and a comfortable night in a hotel, flew in advance to Prestwick in Scotland. He was surrounded by devoted friends, and took the opportunity to relax during that long flight with a drink and a game of chemin de fer. He looked forward to joining his wife, last seen at Augusta, and he knew that in a few weeks' time he was to be a father.

But despite the atmosphere of relaxation, foresight was one of his great strengths, and during that journey he pondered over the new challenge that was to face him as soon as he arrived in London. By contrast with his diffidence at the interview with Auchinleck in 1941, when he had been ordered to become Chief of Intelligence in Cairo, he must on this occasion after two years of intense experience have felt a measure of confidence that he could meet the challenge. He certainly 'knew his Master's ways', and was satisfied that his task would, as always, be eased by the granting of quick and clear decisions and by the absence of any fussy interference in the immense load of work delegated to him.

But the size of the task was daunting. It looked as if Montgomery was to be overall land commander for the entire Allied assault; hence it would be on Montgomery's Chief of Staff that would fall the responsibility for ultimate coordination of the plans of the Allied forces by land, sea and air. In Cairo in 1941, as a joint planner with the Royal Navy and the Royal Air Force he had been concerned only with writing agreed recommendations for submission to the Commanders-in-Chief, Middle East Command. In London he would have massive executive responsibilities akin to those of Husky, but on a vast and unprecedented scale. Moreover as Chief of Staff to the overall comander for the assault phase, he would be involved in coordinating the activities of the Canadian and American allies, particularly the United States 12th Army Group under General Omar Bradley, whom he had met in Sicily. That was one interface between the Allies; the second was between Montgomery and Eisenhower, the Supreme Commander of Overlord. Freddie had been just as frustrated as his chief by the lack of operational decisions from Eisenhower's headquarters in the later

stages of Husky and at the beginning of the Italian campaign;
but the prime responsibility for that deficiency had rested with
Alexander, about whom Freddie had few illusions. However in
Overlord there would be no Alexander. The 'Master of the
Battlefield' would be directly under the man whom at their first
meeting he had categorised as 'Nice chap – no soldier'. Some oiling
of the wheels, a task familiar to Freddie, would no doubt be
required: the objective of serving the Alliance figured in Freddie's
sophisticated mind more prominently than in Montgomery's.

As to the other British services the familiar and trusted figure of
Bertram Ramsay provided some reassurance. Not only was his
capability admired by all of Montgomery's gang but, after some
light-hearted sparring over the planning of Husky, he and
Montgomery now collaborated splendidly. The RAF set-up was still
unknown but Freddie could legitimately hope that inter-service
cooperation, on which the success of the amphibious assault would
vitally depend, would be devoid of those absurb frictions which in
early days had arisen from the *amour propre* of three services in
rivalry, fed by the personal ambition of various *prima donnas*. Much
had been learnt from Husky and Baytown about effective methods
of ensuring intimate cooperation between the Army's assaulting
formations and the naval craft and shipping that would get them to
their beaches. Much had also been learnt of Army/Air cooperation
by which the RAF would first achieve air superiority over the
invasion area, without which any landing would be impossible, and
then carry out their tasks of strategic interdiction and close tactical
support which would vastly increase the potential of the land forces.
Full understanding of these matters now existed not only at the top
but well down to regimental level in the veteran Eighth Army
divisions, some of which at Montgomery's insistence would take
part in Overlord.

Freddie arrived in London on New Year's Day 1944. After four
years' absence he was much struck by the warm comradeship shown
by the man in the street to anyone with the Eighth Army star on his
African ribbon, and by the cheerful sense of purpose that seemed to
motivate most of the population. On 2nd January he reported to
'Cossac', the Allied staff which for a long time past had been
planning the assault into NW Europe. There he met Lt-General F.

Monty and his staff in Malta before the assault on Sicily. Front row *L to R*: Ken Ray (Chief Engineer), Freddie, Monty, Graham. (The author is in the second row between Freddie and Monty.)

Freddie with his 'partner' Miles Graham, responsible for personnel and logistics.

In this portrait drawn by S. Morse Brown in Italy, Freddie, under heavy pressure at this time, is seen wearing the CB, awarded after the victory in Sicily, and the CBE and DSO.

Top: Freddie emerging from the Map Lorry.

Bottom: Monty's farewell to Eighth Army on 30th December 1943 at the Opera House in Vasto. It was an unforgettable occasion and Freddie was moved to tears.

Monty with Freddie and Miles Graham prepare to leave the Sangro battlefield for England and 'The Second Front'. Sergeant Harwood (Chief Clerk) with his back to the camera.

After arriving in England Freddie was summoned to an investiture at Buckingham Palace. On either side of Freddie are his wife (with muff) and his sister (Mrs Frere). Miles Graham, with his wife and daughter, completes the group.

E. Morgan, the Chief of Staff of Cossac, and Bedell Smith, who had been sent ahead to London by Eisenhower. They agreed that a presentation of the plan, comprising an assault of only three divisions and two airborne brigades should be made by the Cossac staff to Montgomery on the morrow. Freddie and Bedell Smith as well as Montgomery had already appreciated that the Cossac assault was on too small a scale and that the capture of Cherbourg, the essential port, was not assured at a sufficiently early date.

The presentation on 3rd January took place in St Paul's School, which was the headquarters of 21st Army Group, with living quarters and messes in Latymer Court, a block of flats opposite. Montgomery criticised the plan severely, demanding a five-divisional landing, and suggested the use of additional beaches in Brittany. After further examination, landings in Brittany were abandoned and the plan stabilised in the form that was finally adopted. Nevertheless provision of the extra landing craft for the larger assault became highly controversial; they were eventually obtained by postponing and trimming Anvil, the proposed landing in the south of France, which had always been strenuously opposed by Montgomery and Freddie, and by postponing the date of Overlord from May to the beginning of June, in order to take advantage of a further month's production of landing craft. Freddie played a major part in these negotiations.

On 10th January he took over officially as Chief of Staff of 21st Army Group. At Montgomery's request he remained a major-general, notwithstanding that the previous Chief of Staff had been a lieutenant-general, as was the head of COSSAC. Both were much older than Freddie. Montgomery's hardly valid objection to any upgrading was due to possible developments at lower levels where various brigadiers still in their early thirties might have felt that they would have a claim to the rank of major-general. The decision was to have unfortunate repercussions on Freddie after the end of the war.

Montgomery's intention, during the twenty-two weeks of preparation leading to the June D-day, was to delegate the entire staff work to Freddie and his subordinates, and to leave himself free to instruct and motivate his commanders, British, American and Canadian, and inspire their troops for the decisive operation which was to end the war in Europe. He himself had been a most efficient staff officer in his early career, and he fully appreciated what was involved; it says a great deal for Freddie that his master un-reservedly placed this heavy load on his shoulders, confident that with only the minimum of supervision he would discharge it meticulously and successfully. Montgomery with his habitual ability to dissociate himself from the consideration of any situation where his decisions were not required, immediately after his first formal study of the Overlord plan took a day off to give a lecture to the Staff College. Long after the war he recalled

> The work involved was terrific and the strain on the staffs was very great. I used to think that my experienced staff under de Guingand played a major part in ensuring that the problems which arose were handled in a practical and realistic manner. I doubt if a better and more experienced planning team existed anywhere in those days . . .[2]

On 11th January Mongomery addressed his staff at HQ 21st Army Group. He announced the new set-up: Eisenhower, the Supreme Commander, with Ramsay, himself and Leigh-Mallory as the naval, land, and air commanders. He then explained his 'System' speaking from notes as follows:

> (I) keep clear of all details; indeed I must
> Great responsibilities
> Have a Chief of Staff, with full powers; he gives all decisions on all staff matters once I have made my plan. Everyone is under him
> I see no papers – no files.
> I send for senior staff officers; they must tell me their problems in ten minutes.
> I do everything verbally . . .[3]

Two days later he summoned the corps and divisional commanders that made up the four armies for Overlord; they were First United States and Second British for the assault with the Third United States and First Canadian for the follow-up. They were to stop experimenting and prepare for battle. He would lay down the general form; everyone must accept it and act on it; all bellyaching must cease. They were to give him their confidence. American doctrine was their own affair . . .[4] and once again he explained his use of verbal orders and his Chief of Staff system.

Freddie's position had now been declared to all concerned. He was to be the principal coordinator and decision-maker on all the matters that Montgomery referred to as 'details'; these were in fact an enormous list of essential requirements without which the assault could never take place. They included the equipment of units, with decisions on their special scales for the immediate assault; modifications such as waterproofing for the amphibious landing: allocation of special devices for demolition of obstacles: allocation of specialised vehicles such as D D tanks: priorities for the allocation by the Navy of landing craft: allotment of concentration areas: provision for logistic support including the use of the artificial harbour Mulberry and of Pluto, the oil pipe-line: communications networks from concentration areas through to the positions of formations ashore: assessment and distribution of intelligence and maps: Public Relations: Security arrangements: the organisation for the control of Build-up (BUCO), the timings of forward moves to the embarkation points: arrangements for postponement; preplanned programmes for air support: the operations of the Airborne forces, and many other matters too numerous to mention.

While Freddie was facing up to the problems presented on this list, many of which had of course been analysed by the Cossac staff, arguments about Anvil, the planned landing in the South of France over which Freddie acted as Montgomery's advocate before Eisenhower, and about the date of D-day and the command set-up were in train at the highest levels, including the combined Chiefs of Staff in Washington. Eventually on 21st January Eisenhower approved Montgomery's plan; the creator of it immediately broke away from St Paul's School to carry out a series of visits to formations to motivate them for the battle ahead. This left Freddie in sole charge, acting virtually as Deputy Commander.

Every morning he held a conference for his own staff but including also liaison representatives from the Navy and the Air Force, and often representatives of Government organisations such as the Ministry of Shipping. He would give out decisions already reached and instructions regarding conferences and visits, while those attending could raise points for decision and coordination.

This saved an immense amount of paper work. In parallel with this coordination of Army business there would be at a high level joint meetings with the staffs serving Ramsay and Leigh Mallory to resolve current planning problems where more then one service was involved. By February these staffs produced an initial *joint* plan, which was accepted by the Commanders-in-Chief.

As a happy interruption amidst all this hectic activity, an unusual event took place: the baptism of Freddie's daughter Marylou, who had been born on 18th February. Afterwards a tea party was given in the Commander-in-Chief's offices, which were cleared for the occasion. When inspecting the scene before the guests arrived, Montgomery, now a godfather, pointed to the 'Pending tray' which unaccountably still remained on his desk, and said to Freddie, 'I've left it there so that you can park the baby when it gets tired' – the Commander-in-Chief was looking ahead as usual.

Freddie, inevitably, was closely concerned with the Cover Plan for 'Overlord', code-named 'Fortitude'. The objects of the plan, which proved to be highly successful, were first to persuade the enemy that the assault was to take place to the east in the area of the Pas de Calais at a date later than the 'Overlord' D-day, and secondly that Allied troops once landed in Normandy were only a diversion for a subsequent main landing in the Calais area. As DMI in Cairo, Freddie had studied Shearer's successful deception activities, and had himself arranged the false 'going' map before the Alam Halfa battle and, later, had enthusiastically supported the successful deception plan for the Alamein battle. Hence he gave much more than lip service to Fortitude. On one occasion he was found in his office at 5 am, whitefaced in a greatcoat, demanding that a staff officer take down immediately a new idea to improve Fortitude – an idea that he had thought up in the middle of the night.

The plan required activities by all three services which were carefully controlled and monitored by a joint committee of deception experts of which Freddie was a member. The locations of assaulting formations were adjusted where possible to lend credence to a Pas de Calais landing, and the usual tricks of a bogus headquarters with diversions of wireless traffic were carried out. Dummy landing craft were erected, hard standings were prepared and faked embarkation exercises were carried out. These activities were supplemented nearer the 'Overlord' D-day by raiding operations by the Royal Navy. Freddie himself had to recommend the targets in the Calais area and elsewhere for preliminary attack by heavy bombers; for a time he endeavoured to keep them clear of his beloved Le Touquet and of the villas of his friends, although obviously these were likely to be bombed in the circumstances of 'Fortitude'. Eventually he had to give way to the cruel necessities of war; and the Hawkins' villa with many others was destroyed.

Considerable attention was given to the organisation and training of Montgomery's tactical headquarters, and Major Paul Odgers an officer from Eighth Army's Tac HQ in Italy was summoned from Italy for this task. Freddie viewed the build-up of Tac HQ with some misgivings. Although for the commander of an army and, particularly for Montgomery in that role, the exercise of day to day personal command demanded a small mobile headquarters far forward in the battle zone, it did not necessarily follow that the Commander-in-Chief of a group comprising four British and American armies should adopt the same procedure. A C-in-C's directive to his commanders should be stated in much broader terms and be effective over longer periods; he should certainly not get involved in the detail of their battles, and a Main Headquarters in a rear area would be better placed for the analysis and presentation of massive intelligence reports and for the consideration of the logistic limitations which were likely to be a major factor. Freddie could hardly have overlooked the possibility that Montgomery, who was already demonstrating an increasing disregard for the opinions of others, with the one exception of Brooke, might happily distance himself from his Main Headquarters and attempt to run the campaign single-handed. However it was obviously impossible to convert Montgomery to this view; as second best, Freddie persuaded his chief to accept a senior colonel from the operations staff to command Tac HQ, but unfortunately the background and personality of that officer were to prove unsatisfactory and resulted all too soon in his removal. For this difficult task of top-level liaison between Montgomery and his Main Headquarters, only a senior officer whom Montgomery had known and trusted from past experience would have sufficed. Had such an officer – one of that family of old associates – been installed, the functions of Main

Headquarters and of the Chief of Staff in later phases of the campaign might well have been discharged more satisfactorily.

The attitudes of the supporting Air Forces, nominally under the command of Leigh-Mallory, created recurrent difficulties. Taken together, the United States and British Air Forces, Bomber, Tactical, Air Defence, Transport and Maritime were enormous, 4500 Fighters and Fighter/Bombers with 6000 Bombers, and there were some commanders among them who still maintained that Germany could soon be defeated by strategic bombing alone and that invasion by armies was unnecessary. Leigh-Mallory was over-whelmed by the combination of Eisenhower, Tedder his Deputy Commander and Coningham, C-in-C of the Tactical Air Forces. Montgomery was averse to dealing with Tedder or Coningham, and tried to deal with Broadhurst or Leigh-Mallory: Freddie was the balancing factor amongst all these prima donnas. In certain cases, action in support of the armies failed to attract the high priority that the soldiers considered necessary, and this attitude was to influence for a time both the planning and execution of some of these tasks. Much of the argumentation about and negotiation of these issues fell to Freddie supported by his operations and planning staffs and, despite many crises, particularly over the airborne operations, acceptable solutions were eventually achieved.

In the resolution of all these questions in which problems of nationalities and personalities as well as strategies were involved, Freddie showed a sure touch; perhaps it was that 'foreign sophistication', wrily observed in 1909 by his schoolmates, which made his cooperation with American allies so successful – not that to them he was anything but a 'Britisher' with what they supposed was a 'Huguenot' name. He was greatly admired and liked by the Americans and Canadians, and he found them pleasant and easy to deal with. His talent in this regard was a priceless asset to his master who, as Land Force Commander for the entire assault operation and its immediate exploitation, was promulgating his operational plans with the utmost decisiveness and was determined that his subordinates of any nationality, British, American or Canadian, should execute them in the closest conformity with his concepts. At this stage, Montgomery himself with his forceful personality and aura of victory about him, drew enthusiastic and loyal response

from his American and Canadian subordinates; but at the slightest
sign of friction the diplomatic Freddie would intervene and, relying
on the warm acceptance extended to him by Eisenhower and his
close friend Bedell Smith, he would forestall any difficulty.

A small hand-picked team of US Army staff officers headed by
Colonel C. H. 'Tic' Bonesteel had been introduced into 21st Army
Group headquarters at an early stage of planning. In addition, as
a further step to foster smooth relations, Montgomery had asked
Eisenhower to provide him with an American ADC which, he said,
was 'only fair' as the Supreme Commander had a British Military
Assistant at his headquarters. Two young American officers were
carefully selected and sent for interviews by Montgomery, who
immediately asked that he might keep both. Ray BonDurant was
retained by Montgomery, and Edwin Culver, known to all as 'Bill'
went to serve Freddie, and soon grew to admire his warm
personality, informality and sense of humour.

Forty-two years later he commented: '. . . in keeping the Allied
effort truly "Allied", Freddie's contribution was greater than that
of any other allied officer, other than perhaps Ike himself.'

At the beginning of April, Montgomery, in retrospective mood,
confided to his diary that the period of planning since January had
involved hard work, but that by now 21st Army Group had become
an Allied HQ; it was well organised with the experienced officers he
required, and de Guingand and Graham worked in very well with
the Americans. In February he had found that Freddie with his flair
for advocacy had been a forceful but tactful representative at
Eisenhower's conference on the vexed problem of Anvil, and
increasingly he used him to attend conferences at Supreme
Headquarters Allied Expeditionary Force acting as his deputy.

On 7th and 8th April at St Paul's School, Montgomery held an
indoor exercise with all his senior commanders, at which various
developments of the operation, including many possible
emergencies, were considered. Freddie of course was on hand,
retaining in his memory a vast amount of detail about the planned
activities of each of the four Allied armies.

It was hardly surprising that the the strain imposed on him, magnified
by his indifferent health, sometimes became all too evident to those
closest to him. His Military Assistant at that time, Lt-Colonel Harry

Llewellyn, who had been one of the liaison officers established at
Eighth Army's Main HQ to try to ensure that the staff there were
kept as well informed as Montgomery at his TAC HQ, recalled a
picture at St Paul's of a sickly man after a very long day's work
taking a short snooze at midnight in his office, with the blue light
turned on outside – DO NOT DISTURB. Eighteen years later
Montgomery would write 'Freddie . . . revels in responsibility: he
accepts it readily.'[5]

So it was with a sense of relief on all sides that on 28th April
Headquarters 21st Army Group moved to Southwick Park near
Portsmouth and camped with their caravans and office trucks in the
park, reproducing the familiar style of Montgomery's Main
Headquarters at war. Freddie rightly was given a bedroom in an
adjacent house. Tac HQ was close by, and the Naval headquarters
was adjacent. The headquarters of Leigh Mallory the Air C-in-C
was at Stanmore where I was Montgomery's representative, while
the headquarters of the Allied Tactical Air Forces, with a small
supporting staff from the Army, was at Uxbridge.

As before the battle of Alamein, there was now something of a lull
before the D-day, still fixed for 5th June, was reached. Montgomery
as C-in-C and Freddie as the Chief of Staff of the highest
headquarters with immediate operational control of the assault had
fulfilled their responsibilities, but time was now needed for the
subordinate commanders and headquarters of all three Services to
discharge their duties. If Freddie on 1st June 1944 looked back to
those hectic days of planning in March he would have recalled the
timetable which he had then issued. This had given in outline the
dates governing the intricate procedures required to deliver the vast
force of twelve divisions to a hostile shore and to sustain them
thereafter. All these preparations had how been successfully set in
motion.

Montgomery by his visits had inspired and motivated all the
military forces taking part, including the Americans, and at this
stage was happily accepted as their indomitable commander.
Freddie by his quiet diplomatic work had welded the Allied staffs
into a cooperative team with mutual confidence established
throughout.

Shortly before D-day there were visits by King George VI and by

Churchill to 21st Army Group HQ, and bets were laid in Montgomery's betting book as to the date when the war would end. The optimists went for the end of 1944. Then hour by hour the Allied Commanders-in-Chief of all three Services closely watched the weather forecasts and, after deciding on 4th June to postpone by one day because of high seas with strong winds and cloud, Eisenhower courageously announced at 4.15 am on 5th June, 'We will sail to-morrow.'

The great initial success of the Normandy landings surprised both the Chief of Staff and his Commander-in-Chief. The enemy once again had been cleverly misled: Rommel had gone on leave on 4th June, and landings had not been expected in the rough weather, which Ramsay had described as sinister. The Allied air forces had done their vital work and the airborne forces had performed magnificently. By 10th June the bridgeheads had been joined up into one continuous lodgment area sixty miles long.

Montgomery, in the initial phase commanding all four armies, was determined to conduct operations by his well-tried methods: instructions, verbal as always, would be delivered personally to his subordinate commands, followed up by periodical memoranda confirming his intentions. His Tac HQ, self-contained in every respect, had been established very early across the Channel. Bradley at this period was happy to acquiesce in Montgomery's dominant position, having been closely associated with him and Freddie throughout the planning period leading to the assault. By now he admired Freddie as a skilled and tactful interpreter of Montgomery's commands and as a diplomatic intermediary whenever there was any possibility of inter-Allied friction.

A change now came over Freddie's role. It was clear that Main Headquarters 21st Army Group could not be moved to Normandy for many weeks: in the build-up schedules there were many fighting units of much higher priority. This was irksome, but there was plenty to be done. He was the Controller-in-Chief of everything still in England and responsible for supervising, expediting and, if called upon, adjusting the build-up of the reinforcing formations and of every form of administrative support.

He was also to be Montgomery's link with Leigh Mallory, the C-in-C of the Allied Air Forces, through whom the immense air power, American and British, could be brought to bear. He had a similar role to play with Ramsay, whose headquarters remained in the Portsmouth area. Furthermore the International Press would be eager always to arrive immediately on the scene, but for some days to come they too would be content with Freddie as 21st Army Group's official spokesman.

However the most significant aspect of his role in this period was that he was to be Montgomery's constant link with Eisenhower, whose headquarters would not get across the Channel until a date even later than HQ 21st Army Group, and thereafter would for a long time remain in Brittany far removed from the battle front. As Freddie's headquarters was the first to receive the latest situation reports on operations together with the comments and intentions of Montgomery, the C-in-C of the Allied Land Forces, it was natural that Eisenhower and his Deputy Commender Tedder should pay frequent visits to that headquarters to discuss progress. At this early stage, liaison and cooperation were excellent on all sides, and Montgomery's frequent personal signals to Freddie reporting progress of the battle, revealed his intentions and often demanded of Freddie supporting activities which he was confident would be instantly arranged, if practicable.

His reliance on Freddie is well illustrated by two messages typical of the many he sent to his Chief of Staff at Southwick Park. The first is a letter dated 10th June:[6]

Top Secret	Headquarters
Personal	21 Army Group

My dear Freddie,

I cannot possibly come out to Ramsay's ship tomorrow, nor is there any need for me to do so; for one, beyond the pleasure of seeing Ramsay, it would be a waste of time. You have my letter sent by Johnnie, and my intentions and plans will now be clear to you.

It is quite impossible to send any Commandos back yet. I am directing the left of First Army on CAUMONT as a first priority, then ST LO next. Everything in going very well and I am well satisfied. The Canadians are a bit jumpy just at present, but they will settle down as they gain experience.

I have issued enclosed Personal Message. Give it to the Press your end, and have it given out by the BBC. Send copies to Second Army Main for distribution to Second Army formations still in England, and send a copy to First Canadian Army.

Do not let any VIPs visit me, or anyone not actually concerned with the operations on land e.g. War Office PM'B' etc. [*Montgomery's code for Churchill: Mr Bullfinch*] I have two Army Commanders who have never commanded Armies in battle before, and a large number of inexperienced Divisions and Generals, and my time is very fully occupied; I have not time to spare for visitors. I would like to see Miles Graham [*Maj-Gen in charge of Administration*] and also Slap White [*Chief Signals officer*].

The roads have been far from safe, due to snipers left behind by the enemy. So far 8 women snipers have been killed.

Night bombing is going to be a nuisance; we had a very near miss at Tac HQ last night, and Sgt Ship had a narrow escape in the Mess Tent.

Yrs ever
B. L. Montgomery.

The second is a 'most immediate' signal of 11th June:[7]

First Army doing well and has reached Airel and Balleroy. My general object is to pull the Germans on to Second Army so that First Army can extend and expand. Two things now important. First to increase and improve our build-up. Second to do all possible by air and other action to delay enemy build-up against us. Would like a demonstration against Granville area tomorrow night from the sea if you can arrange it.

B.L.M.

And on 12th June he wrote again to Freddie:[8]

I am enjoying life greatly and it is great fun fighting battles again after five months in England. . . . My views about accommodation, messes, etc: I have decided that the only Major-Generals to be members of my mess will be yourself and Miles; the others are all to be elsewhere. I will not have a crowd in my mess; my personal staff, Chief of Staff – no more. You must set up another mess down the road. I cannot have B Mess at Tac overcrowded. In fact Tac HQ has got to remain small and self contained.

In fact, by VE day, Tac HQ would grow enormously, due largely to the increase in communications requirements.

A week later, despite his preoccupation with the battle, Montgomery wrote to the Military Secretary at the War Office as follow:[9]

> I wish to put forward the names of the undermentioned officers to receive the awards stated, as an immediate recognition of the great and outstanding services that they have rendered.
>
> These officers have worked with me since January last in the preparation of operation OVERLORD, its launching and the battle on land.
>
> It is not possible for me to pay adequate tribute to the services they have rendered.
>
> I request most earnestly that their names may be submitted to the King for the immediate bestowal of the honours stated:
>
>
>
> Major General F. de Guingand
> CB, CBE, DSO
> Chief of Staff 21 Army Group   . . . KBE
>
>

Eisenhower, who by now had had ample opportunity to appreciate Freddie's exceptional service to the alliance, wrote to him on 1st July:[10]

> Dear Freddie:
>
> I saw in the paper that you had been awarded the KBE, I cannot tell you how delighted I am that your great contributions to the war effort have been so splendidly recognised.
>
> Many congratulations.
>
>
>
> Sincerely,
> Dwight D. Eisenhower
>
>

Freddie in his reply referred to the patient and unstinting support invariably received from SHAEF: much patience indeed would be needed in the months ahead.

Freddie would receive the accolade of knighthood from the King's own hands at Eindhoven four months later. He had served his master well, and had served the Alliance even better.

The critical first phase of the assault had been successfully concluded, and thirty-two years later, when much had been written by historians about 'Overlord,' a tribute was printed, for which Freddie as the grand coordinator of the assault should receive a major share of the credit.

The complexity of Overlord constituted one of the greatest dangers. A thousand things could have gone wrong: a rendezvous missed, a signal misinterpreted, a turn in the weather for the worst. Meshing together so many intricate pieces into a relatively smooth operation of such magnitude – even to the extent of maintaining the security which contributed to attaining tactical surprise – played a large part in the Allied success.[11]

However, when later the battle appeared to be slowing down and a stalemate, always feared by the planners, appeared to threaten, whispers were heard, 'Has Montgomery failed?' The repeated attacks on the Caen area were criticised as failures to achieve a breakthrough preliminary to an advance to the Seine. This however had never been a feature of Montgomery's plan. And what of the airfields south-east of Caen which, the critics erroneously said had been *promised* to the Air Force at an early date? Were not Montgomery's phase lines now shown to be hopelessly optimistic, and was there not a risk that the battle of Normandy, so favourable in those early days, might soon with the arrival of German reinforcements founder in defeat?

A particular subject of criticism was the battle, code-named 'Goodwood', on 18th July. To support the corps taking part, a massive air bombardment by heavy bombers had been requested for what the Air Force wrongly assumed was to be a decisive breakthrough east of Caen. Freddie, who may well have found that he had had to overplay the importance of this novel support, vital and difficult to acquire, was adamant throughout those fractious days that his master's battle plan of maintaining pressure at Caen but reserving his main thrust for the break-out far to the west, as declared on 15th May at St Paul's, was developing inexorably, slowly but successfully. However there were others in high places who either did not fully comprehend the plan, or expected instant miracles in the long drawn out battle, which Hitler and Rommel had correctly recognised as 'decisive for the Fatherland'. It became Freddie's unwelcome task to counter these misapprehensions, and to shield his master as far as possible from their impact when Montgomery needed to retain all his poise and to exercise all his powers of concentration free of outside distractions. This aloofness of Montgomery as some regarded it, created a situation in which Freddie's diplomatic skills were taxed to the full.

However he was in no position to ward off visits by Churchill and by Eisenhower accompanied by his deputy, Tedder. It is incontestable that Tedder, at this time, deprived of the 'promised' airfields and lacking confidence in Montgomery's conduct of operations was attempting to influence Eisenhower towards removing Montgomery from his position as overall land force commander. Yet Freddie who was in frequent contact with Tedder, and was a sophisticated operator in the field of human relations, appears to have been unaware at that time of Tedder's intentions. Writing in 1946, he recalled:

> Tedder was being pressed by the Air Commanders to see that the airfield sites South-East of Caen were captured. This no doubt made him somewhat apprehensive at times. But in the talks he had with me, there was never any suggestion that he considered Montgomery was making a mess of things.[12]

Perhaps Tedder shrewdly kept his opinions and intentions to himself. It was only much later in 1964 that Freddie quoted the account of Tedder's intrigues, recorded in the official history,[13] and revealed that Eisenhower himself was swayed by the criticisms levelled at Montgomery's conduct of operations.[14]

Fortunately Montgomery, well aware of what was afoot, was able with the backing of Brooke and Churchill to defeat the intrigue and, three weeks later, to bring off at Falaise the biggest Allied victory of the war. Perhaps for Freddie who had so staunchly supported his master's operational policy, this exposure to mischief-making in high places, reminiscent of his days with Hore-Belisha, carried a warning: despite Montgomery's incontestable expertise as a master of the battlefield, he was not invulnerable to critics lurking at the highest levels of the ramshackle hierarchy which existed at the pinnacle of the Allied Expeditionary Force.

It was years after the event that Freddie, near the end of his life, learned from Bedell Smith that his own name had been tossed into the ring as a possible successor to Montgomery. He rightly commented, 'I couldn't have done it: there is all the difference in

the world between being a chief of staff and a commander.'[15]
Freddie's most ardent British admirers would agree; our American
allies viewed this matter differently.

However this threat to Montgomery's position as Commander-
in-Chief of the US and British land forces, serious as it had been,
was quickly submerged in the euphoria of victory which
immediately followed. Forty-three enemy divisions had either been
eliminated or severely mauled. Of the commanders of armies, corps,
and divisions twenty had been killed or captured. Prisoners
amounted to 210,000, while enemy killed or wounded were
estimated at about 240,000. 3,500 and 1,500 tanks, with a vast
amount of other equipment, were captured or destroyed. This
catastrophic disaster to the Wehrmacht prompted expectations in
21st Army Group of a rapid end to the war before the onset of
winter, and Freddie himself fell in with this optimism.

CHAPTER TWELVE

Victory and Eclipse

Montgomery's magnificent success at Falaise, though incomplete in that some of the Wehrmacht escaped over the Seine, was sufficient to convince Hitler's military leaders that they had lost the war. Hitler himself declared, 'August 15th was the worst day of my life'.[1]

The operations in north-west Europe then entered a new phase which would be marked by tragic errors of strategy. Freddie was much involved in these contentious issues, and after the war blamed himself specifically for the delay in gaining early use of the port of Antwerp; but had it been possible for his erstwhile influence on Montgomery to have been applied at this period more effectively, some chapters of the tragic story might have been written differently. Two factors, as the war proceeded would make this impossible: the remoteness of the dictatorial Commander-in-Chief cocooned in his isolated tactical headquarters, and the mounting mental exhaustion and physical breakdown of his Chief of Staff.

After the Allied break-out from Normandy and the race to the Seine, contact between Montgomery's two headquarters, Tac and Main, began to deteriorate. In the old days in the Desert, Montgomery, seated before his personal maps in the map lorry had always responded readily to Freddie's physical presence beside him and had listened closely to his recommendations, invariably well-prepared and skilfully presented. Afterwards at dinner with his ADCs and his personal staff, the Army Commander might sometimes pull the leg of his Chief of Staff; 'Freddie at times you do throw out some "extraordinary"[2] ideas'; but Freddie would happily stand his ground.

The critical link between them had first been broken when the Army Commander sailed to Normandy and his Chief of Staff inevitably remained with Main Headquarters at Southwick Park.

160

e Chief of Staff explains the
verlord' plan

D-day of Overlord at HQ 21
my Group at Southwick
ouse: David Belchem,
l Williams (*behind*),
eddie and Miles Graham.

eddie briefs Air Chief
arshal Leigh-Mallory,
in-C Allied Air Forces.

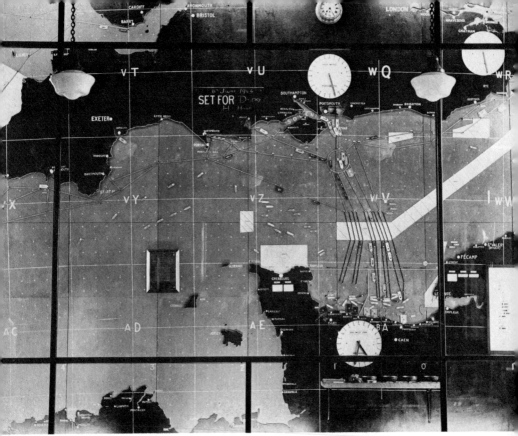

Invasion Chart at Naval headquarters Southwick Park.

The Chief of Staff 21 Army Group; until 1st September 1944 he was the staff coordinator of four Allied Armies.

Freddie receives from General Eisenhower the United States Legion of Merit.

Awards by Eisenhower to Monty, Dempsey (*on left*) Crerar (*in centre*) and Freddie (*on right*).

Left: Freddie at Tac Headquarters, Eindhoven, receives the accolade of Knighthood of the British Empire from King George VI. This award had been gazetted in June 1944.

Below: Freddie with his devoted personal staff officers: Major Bill Bovill his Military Assistant, and his American ADC Captain Bill Culver (Capt Edwin Culver III).

Signals were despatched between them and, at an early stage, telephone calls were exchanged almost daily, supplemented by Freddie's visits in his own aeroplane supplied by the Americans. All this ensured a liaison which though second-best was adequate and controversy did not supervene because the operations followed a long-thought-out and agreed pattern. Freddie at that time had done noble work in minimising outside interference in the steady development to victory of Montgomery's battle plan.

In August, when the whole of France was open to exploitation, new options began to develop. My planners had recommended through Freddie that 21st Army Group's major thrust should be directed through Maubeuge and the Aachen gap thence northwards round the Ruhr. For that thrust we envisaged a total force of twenty-six divisions.

On 18th August Montgomery had recommended in a signal to Brooke that the whole of 12th and 21st Army Groups, after crossing the Seine, should keep together as a solid mass of forty divisions. 21st Army Group should clear the Channel coast, the Pas de Calais and West Flanders and secure Antwerp. The American Army Group should be directed on Brussels, Aachen and Cologne, with their right flank on the Ardennes.

This signal marked the beginning of the 'Northern Thrust' controversy, in which Montgomery demanded without avail that overriding priority should be given to securing the Ruhr by an enveloping movement from the north. Eisenhower repeatedly wavered, and eventually compromised on a 'Broad Front Strategy' which ultimately led to three main thrusts directed on the Ruhr, Frankfurt and the Saar, with inadequate resources to support all three.

Montgomery further argued, as a corollary to his proposition, that the major northern thrust of British and American armies should be carried out under a single commander, and that that man should be himself or, if that were unacceptable, Bradley.

Freddie in his Main HQ near Bayeux became heavily involved in advocating Montgomery's proposition to Eisenhower who was still 400 miles away, located with his headquarters near Cherbourg. The Chief of Staff was in a difficult position: just at the time when his contact with Montgomery was beginning to deteriorate, his liaison with SHAEF had become particularly close, largely through his friendship with Bedell Smith whom he frequently visited. Nevertheless he remained Montgomery's loyal advocate, while recognising all too clearly the force of the political factors which he felt Eisenhower could hardly ignore.

It was in that capacity that Freddie in August was sent by Montgomery to SHAEF headquarters, where he had meetings with Eisenhower on the evenings of 20th and 21st August. He found that the SHAEF planners had already decided, without consulting Montgomery, on a broad strategy, and this had been backed by Eisenhower, who was disinclined to change his views.

On Freddie's return, Montgomery learnt that at those meetings, in addition to decisions about the new command system under which, as foreshadowed in England, Eisenhower was to become the overall Land Force Commander, the US 12th Army Group was now to be employed, not towards Aachen and the Ruhr but towards Metz and the Saar. This clearly revealed that Montgomery's concept of forty divisions in a concentrated thrust towards Aachen had not won the day; and so Freddie was sent back on 22nd August to see Eisenhower again, armed this time with Montgomery's 'Notes on future operations', in which he restated his arguments and argued for retention of his personal command over all operations directed north of the Ruhr. Eisenhower, pressurised by Bradley who was no longer a supporter of Montgomery's concept, and influenced also by the desirability of linking up with the Anvil forces which had landed successfully in the South of France, opted for a compromise solution. At a meeting on 23rd August Montgomery was given authority to coordinate operations on his flank with Bradley, and the use of the Allied Airborne Army by him was foreshadowed, but the policy of 'broad front' was maintained.

Freddie after the war declared that he had been arguing a lost cause; and he recalled that the strategy of the 'northern thrust' was the only issue on which he and Montgomery had disagreed. However, on the original basis that Montgomery's thrust would be given overriding priority, which implied that Patton's successful advance in the south would be halted, Freddie in his own mind had reached the same conclusion as his chief. But once the halting of Patton had been ruled out, Freddie himself had concluded that the available logistic resources without the use of Antwerp would be insufficient.

This controversy, magnified at a later date by references in the memoirs of the protagonists, was to become one of the principal causes of the final rupture of Montgomery's relations with Eisenhower, and after the war it was also to become a bone of contention between Freddie and his chief.

In the event, there was a confusion of purpose at the very moment when the Wehrmacht was desperately piecing together new *ad hoc* divisions from the remnants of the old; this delay in decision was followed by a series of compromises under which Montgomery was allotted some reinforcing US formations to strengthen his right flank, without power of command and fewer than he had demanded for the task. Although no one could predict then or assert now that Montgomery's concept would have succeeded, it can be argued that in view of the prize at stake – victory in Europe in 1944 – the attempt should have been made in late August while the Wehrmacht was still reeling from the defeat in Normandy. That it was not made was due primarily to the formidable political obstacles barring the way to such a decision; they were brushed aside by Montgomery but were fully appreciated by Freddie.

Montgomery, supported by Brooke and Grigg, the British Secretary of State of War, viewed his choice of strategy as of vital importance, and repeatedly challenged Eisenhower, demanding 'why public opinion (in the United States) should make us want to take military decisions which are unsound',[3] In this attitude he was supported by Simpson, who on his frequent visits from the War Office reflected the views of Brooke.

Freddie could have countered with a long list of reasons why political factors could not be ignored: the much publicised successes of US Forces to the south of 21st Army Group, including the appearance of Patton as a national hero: the rapidly diminishing strength of the British forces due to diminished manpower and every other resource: adverse public opinion in the States if a large proportion of the victorious US forces were now to be placed under British command while the rest were to be doomed logistically to inactivity, and finally Eisenhower's personal reputation if he now were to be seen as Supreme Commander surrendering the responsibility of controlling the land battle throughout the Allied front. The tragic outcome of this impasse was the adoption of the broad front strategy leading after some further errors to the continuation of the war into 1945 and the capture of Berlin by the Russians.

Throughout August, strategic policies remained confused, while the Wehrmacht after massive defeat was hastily reorganised to defend the Fatherland.

In the atmosphere of indecision combined with euphoria, the importance of securing Antwerp and its approaches was underrated. An airborne operation at Tournai had been planned in August and, on 2nd September, I drew Freddie's attention to a change in the operational situation which indicated that the new object of the Tournai operation should be to give infantry strength to the Second Army right forward so that they could continue their thrust to Antwerp. My planning staff went on to recommend that the Polish Airborne Brigade should be removed from the proposed Tournai operation (which in the event never took place) and be used for an airborne *coup de main* at Antwerp.[4] The Royal Navy were also pressing for the early use of Antwerp.

Freddie, after the war, blamed himself for not emphasising to Montgomery the vital importance of the early capture of the port and its approaches, and Montgomery himself in his *Memoirs* admitted that he had underestimated the difficulties of opening up the approaches, and had reckoned that the Canadian Army could achieve this during the advance to the Ruhr.[5]

At the beginning of September Montgomery, intent on exploiting the situation in the hope of defeating Germany before the onset of winter, made the first move which culminated a fortnight later in the battle of Arnhem. After a conference with Allied Army and Army Group commanders on 3rd September he signalled to Freddie on that afternoon that Second Army was to advance on Wesel and Arnhem, and that he required an airborne operation of one British division and the Poles on the evening of 6th September or morning of 7th September to secure bridges over the Rhine between *Wesel and Arnhem*.[6] Four hours later he signalled again indicating a need for a 'considerable Airborne drop to make certain of getting over the Meuse and the Rhine'. He summoned Lt-General Browning, the Airborne Corps Commander, and Freddie to report on 4th September.

The story thereafter is well-known.[7] The substitution of Arnhem itself for Wesel because of strong enemy flak at Wesel: Montgomery's three postponements of the operation: Browning's entreaty that his Airborne Division be used so as to play some part in active operations before 'the end of the war': Eisenhower's directive to exploit success by breaching the Siegfried Line, crossing the Rhine on a wide front and seizing the Ruhr and the Saar: the call from London to mitigate the V2 menace by roping off areas near Amsterdam and Rotterdam: Eisenhower's allocation to Montgomery of the whole of the Allied Airborne Army with its two American divisions: the further postponement due to lack of supplies and, finally the undertaking by SHAEF to provide supplies – an undertaking which was never fully implemented. Thus, with many handicaps, the battle of Arnhem would be launched with apparent optimism by Montgomery on 17th September.

However, the records show that he had been a worried man: worried that priority for his Ruhr thrust, no sooner decided by Eisenhower, had been overturned by the actions of subordinate commanders: worried that communications with Eisenhower were difficult and ineffective: and worried that there was no masterhand actively controlling the strategy over the whole Allied front.

He had also been worried about his Chief of Staff and, coming to the conclusion that Freddie was again moving towards a breakdown, had sent him back to the UK from Brussels for medical treatment and rest. By 9th September he was gone, and Belchem, the Operations Brigadier, was deputising for him. In England, hearing of the plan, Freddie telephoned Montgomery from his sick bed and disclosed his fears that the proposed operation was too late, and that bad weather was likely and that the Germans might reinforce the target area. Montgomery told him with some justification that he was too far from the scene of action and was out of touch, although he had been provided with direct telephone communication with the headquarters of 21st Army Group.

In a statement written for posterity many years after the war with the benefit of hindsight Freddie would declare:

Personally, I was never keen on this operation as I considered that we had left it too late and would probably encounter bad weather and by the launching date the Germans would probably have reinforced this area. In any case we knew that some German formations were refitting there. Finally the frontage of the attack that was to join up with the airborne forces was too narrow. However, in spite of these factors Monty would not hear of a cancellation. . . . The three main reasons for failure were first the lack of sufficient aircraft to enable the whole force to be carried in one lift; the extremely bad weather which we experienced during the vital period; and lastly the strength of the enemy's reaction. As regards the weather, we were undoubtedly taking a risk, but were justified in expecting something very much better. I think we had perhaps under-estimated the enemy's powers of recuperation. We were, no doubt, influenced too much by the devastating defeat we had witnessed. Just as the enemy managed to produce forces to organise a defence at Arnhem, so do I believe he would have produced an answer to a single thrust into Westphalia as favoured by Montgomery. On the other hand, I consider that we might have held our bridgehead over the Neder Rijn if we had experienced really good weather . . .[8]

Freddie, the realist, soon after his return from a short convalescence was able, better than his chief, to recognise that the battle of Arnhem was in jeopardy. Later he would also appreciate that although Eisenhower and taken personal responsibility for the outcome, the result at SHAEF headquarters would be a further diminution of Montgomery's stock, which had much declined since the Normandy victory because of his high-handed and ceaseless controversy with the Supreme Commander.

Hardly was he back, than once again he was plunged into the maelstrom of Montgomery's controversial strategy. On 21st September, Montgomery had once again pressed the Supreme Commander to give him operational control of First US Army so that, as overall commander of the northern flank, he might direct the battle to capture the Ruhr. Eisenhower then called a conference at Versailles of his senior commanders on 22nd September. But Montgomery, disinclined as always to attend conferences which could degenerate into debates, and legitimately preoccupied over two hundred miles away with his critical Arnhem battle, declined to attend, sending Freddie to represent him, with a brief in note form.

Simpson, Director of Military Operations at the War Office, who had been invited by Montgomery to visit him, also attended the conference to back Montgomery's arguments on behalf of the CIGS.

Freddie, aware of a sympathetic response from Bedell Smith, opened with a convincing presentation of his C-in-C's plan, and a request that Bradley's 12th Army Group should sidestep northwards to relieve the British 8 Corps and so strengthen Montgomery's thrust. This was agreed by Eisenhower: moreover in the minutes of the conference, the wording of a paragraph designed to curb Bradley's thrust towards Cologne, necessary in order to release logistic resources for the main effort towards the Ruhr, was further strengthened by Freddie in agreement with Bedell Smith. Freddie was delighted with his acheivement and sent a triumphant signal to Montgomery.

However the success was short-lived. Disaster had already struck at Arnhem, and Montgomery's expectations of seizing a crossing over the Rhine, capturing the Ruhr and finishing the war in 1944 vanished into the winter's fog. For the Commander-in-Chief and his Chief of Staff it was a time of great mental and emotional stress. Freddie, always uncertain of the wisdom of Montgomery's argumentative campaign, had stuck loyally to his brief and, in the presence of twenty-one senior Army and Air Force commanders, had deployed to the full his exceptional powers of persuasion and had won the day.

Now, all was in vain.

Throughout October and November there was a disastrous lack of coordination over the Allied front, which depressed the Chief of Staff as much as it caused frustration and despair to his master. Freddie confided his worries to Ramsay who had gone to see him:

[I] Went to see Freddie de Guingand; he was rather depressed at the state of the war in the west, saying that the SHAEF plan had achieved nothing beyond killing and capturing a lot of Germans and that we were no nearer to knocking out Germany. He said in fact that the higher direction of the war had been bad in the last 2 months, that Ike's policy was only skin deep and anyone could deflect it . . . He said that the American leadership had been bad, the Generals being too inexperienced. They did not know how to combine artillery with infantry, put all divisions in line and had no supports to leap-frog and make headway, that they were everywhere too weak to break through and that they had utterly failed to reach their objectives – the Rhine. This was all very depressing but no surprise to me . . .[9]

Simpson, Freddie's rival, now much in evidence as Montgomery's confidential link with the CIGS, would after the war describe this wretched period of indecision in the Alliance in these terms:[10]

> . . . there was a certain pattern in his (Monty's) dealings with Supreme HQ. He would go and talk to Eisenhower, or at least get Eisenhower to talk to him, or perhaps even get de Guingand to talk to Bedell Smith; or sometimes I went over on a visit or was needed as an intermediary. As a result of these talks Monty always got a bit optimistic and thought that he had received agreement with Ike as to what he, Monty, wanted to do: namely concentration of resources behind one single thrust and some amelioration of the somewht chaotic Command system.
>
> Then Ike used to go and talk to some of the American generals, and perhaps without even realising it go back on what he had agreed earlier with Monty.
>
> It seemed that the cycle of this sort of change around took place over a month: agreement, say in the middle of October, which got watered down; Monty did not realise it until the end of October; he realised early in November that things seemed to be going very wrong from his point of view, and he was in a state of despair until all the forces to help him – the CIGS in London, sometimes even the Prime Minister, lesser people like his Chief of Staff and myself – had to be mobilised again to try to get another agreement, which in due course was got by the middle of November, and then the whole cycle used to start up again.

So great was the controversy over the question of dispersal of effort that Eisenhower made an attempt to enlist the support of Churchill despite the opposition of Brooke, who meanwhile warned Montgomery to keep silent. When Eisenhower's attempt failed, he proposed that his plan of attack should be referred to a committee of staff officers drawn from his headquarters, from Whitehall and from the three Allied Army Groups. Montgomery's reaction could have been foreseen: he wrote to Simpson:

> My Chief of Staff has been approached by SHAEF as to whether I will send my complete planning staff down to Versailles to help work out a plan for the campaign of 1945. The matter was referred to me and I have

refused, *absolutely and definitely*, to do this.

I have had it made clear to SHAEF that I will not on any account be drawn away from first principles; that it is for the commanders to make plans and give decisions, and staffs then to work out the details *of those plans*; on no account will I have a plan forced on me by a planning staff; when the Supreme Commander has made his plan and issued his orders, the detailed planning for my part of that plan will be done at my HQ *and nowhere else*. I will send a staff officer to SHAEF, at any time, to give the SHAEF planners any information they may want about my front, or situation, which will help them to decide on their plan. I have told them that I will do all I can to help them; but I refuse to be involved in unsound procedure.[11]

Montgomery, now temporarily muzzled by the CIGS, wrote to Simpson; 'If we go on as we are at present it will be a remarkable thing if I don't go mad.'[12] He then started to plan a quiet Christmas holiday in England with his son. However, Hitler now played his hand, launching von Rundstedt's offensive in the Ardennes over a sixty mile front on 16th December 1944. Once again Freddie was absent in England and his return was delayed by fog, but Belchem responded with great efficiency to Montgomery's masterly handling of the emergency, which soon restored stability to the Allied front.

On 28th December Montgomery once more returned to the subject of command, which by now was an obsession; he had a meeting with Eisenhower in the Supreme Commander's train at Hasselt. It had been only two months before, in October that, disgusted by the lack of decision following the failure of his Arnhem operation, he had raised the subject forcibly wth Eisenhower.

Faced then with the Supreme Commander's threat to refer the command controversy to a higher level, he had abjectly climbed down, assuring him that the matter was closed. However, in the Ardennes emergency he had of necessity been given command of 12th US Army Group, and had by his personal leadership stabilised a highly critical situation. Thus it was not surprising that he returned to the charge in a mood of arrogance.

Eisenhower's train, in which the meeting was to be held, arrived at Hasselt station in the early afternoon. The Supreme Commander was not accompanied by Bedell Smith his Chief of Staff, so

Montgomery told Freddie, who by then was present, that he was not
required for the discussion. Thus there is no independent record of
what took place. But, according to a report sent by Montgomery to
Simpson in the War Office, Eisenhower agreed that the Ruhr thrust
should have priority, and that Montgomery should have full powers
of operational control and coordination over the two Army Groups
used for the northern thrust. Eisenhower had been primarily
interested in the starting date for a counter-attack against the
northern face of the enemy salient: Montgomery's eye was fixed on
his previously planned operation to take place after the Ardennes
battle, with the Ruhr as his objective.

Montgomery then asked Freddie to get himself invited to
SHAEF, there to work on Bedell Smith in order to reinforce
Eisenhower's decision on command, which had wavered so often
before. However by the time that Freddie reached Versailles in
atrocious weather on 30th December to stay with Bedell Smith, he
found that his master's detractors had already got to work. He found
there a strange situation: senior members of the SHAEF staff who
had been highly apprehensive at the beginning of von Rundstedt's
attack were now calling for an instant counter-offensive. Freddie
ridiculed the idea, endeavouring to teach them some of
Montgomery's battlefield lessons, of which he had had much
personal experience. Eisenhower was incensed, and Bedell Smith
claimed that Montgomery at Hasselt had promised to attack on 1st
January, but Freddie refused to commit his commander to a
premature operation.

Meanwhile a very forceful letter from Montgomery dated 29th
December which Freddie had brought with him had been read by
Eisenhower: in it Montgomery had emphasised the 'failures' of
recent months [of which Arnhem and the Ardennes were prime
examples][13] and then advised his superior commander 'to be very
firm on the subject [of command] of the northern thrust – any
loosely worded statement would be quite useless . . .'[14] It was then
that Eisenhower received from Marshall, the Chairman of the
Combined Chiefs of Staff in the United States, a telegram strongly
endorsing his negative reaction to Montgomery's demands and
instructing him not to make any concessions. Marshall concluded by
assuring Eisenhower of 'our complete confidence'. The Chairman

of the Combined Chiefs of Staff had intervened after seeing articles in London newspapers proposing a Deputy Land Force commander; inevitably these articles had boosted Montgomery's reputation, as the saviour in the Ardennes emergency, at the expense of Bradley's.

Armed with this assurance, Eisenhower had drafted a reply to Montgomery's letter, contained a polite ultimatum by which he had suggested that if Montgomery persisted in his demands, an unbridgeable gap between them would be created and there would be no alternative but to present their differences to the Combined Chiefs of Staff for decision, despite the damage to the Allied cause that might follow. This signal was to be copied to the Combined Chiefs of Staff.

Freddie having seen the draft was aghast; if Montgomery's persistence over his obsession were to become a resignation issue it would be Montgomery not Eisenhower who would have to go. He prevailed on Eisenhower not to send the signal until he might have an opportunity to speak to his master. Returning on 31st December to Montgomery's headquarters, Freddie had a session *à deux*. Montgomery at first could not believe that the situation was so serious. Who could succeed him? Freddie replied: 'Alex'. For Montgomery this was the last straw: to have to give way to someone as ineffective in his eyes as Alexander would be outrageous. Much distressed, he asked Freddie what he should do, and thereupon the Chief of Staff produced a draft of an apologetic signal to Eisenhower.[15]

Dear IKE,
    Have seen Freddie and understand you are greatly worried by many considerations in these difficult days. I have given you my frank views because I have felt you like this. I am sure there are many factors which may have a bearing quite beyond anything I realise. Whatever your decision may be you can rely on me one hundred percent to make it work and I know BRAD will do the same. Very distressed that my letter may have upset you and I would ask you to tear it up.
                    Your very devoted subordinate,
                            Monty.

Freddie claimed after the war that he had rescued his commander from a dangerous situation, which was indeed true. We can but speculate on what would have happened if the Combined Chiefs of Staff had been called upon to decide the issue. Brooke, who had supported Montgomery's proposition throughout, would have fought mightily in his defence, particularly as he had never regarded Alexander as in the same class as a battlefield commander; Churchill, however, greatly admired Alexander, and the United States was in every sense the major partner and could have called the tune. Montgomery was on a losing wicket. There is no doubt that the admiration of both Eisenhower and Bedell Smith for Freddie, and their appreciation of his personal influence over Montgomery, played a critical part in resolving an issue which might have gravely damaged the Allied cause. Strategy had to give way to political demands in the Alliance, and the command issue was fudged once again.

It was perhaps the strain of these events combined with the effect of a harsh winter that once again caused problems over Freddie's health. Montgomery in his nightly signal to Brooke, dated 7th January, wrote: – 'I am afraid my Chief of Staff is not very well these days, and the doctors tell me that he must go into the Cambridge Hospital for treatment, and then really needs three or four weeks rest . . .' The staff officers close to Freddie were appalled at his condition, and had introduced into his office a 'remembrancer' Bill Bovill, so as to keep track of decisions given by Freddie to those senior officers who came to see him.

A few days later Freddie was despatched to hospital. Due to illness, he played no part in the ill-starred Press conference which Montgomery in his 'cock on a dunghill mood' gave at the conclusion of the Ardennes battle. The conference created further dissension in Anglo-American relations and greatly embittered Bradley, who was licking his wounds after a battle which had been very damaging to his reputation.

On his return from another short convalescence in England, Freddie resumed his place as the chief executive of 21st Army Group and confidential advisor to his master. Together with Bedell Smith he handled the problem of getting food to the Dutch population while still under German occupation. As Montgomery's representative and advocate he would continue to attend Eisenhower's major conferences to which Commanders-in-Chief were summoned, but to which Montgomery seldom went, maintaining his principle that, in battle conditions, a senior commander should go forward to confer with his subordinates. Freddie was then heavily involved in the intricate planning for the crossing of the Rhine, and on Montgomery's instructions, he continued to try to persuade Eisenhower through Bedell Smith to adopt his master's strategy for the final phase of the war. Despite strong support from Brooke and Churchill persuasion failed, with the strategic consequences that are all too well-known.

These tasks of attempted negotiation when Freddie often believed that he had succeeded, only to find that the Supreme Commander after listening to other counsellors had changed his mind, were mentally very exhausting, and Freddie suffered the consequences. Once again the Army's medical specialist reported to Montgomery that his Chief of Staff was ill and should have a rest. After the war Freddie recalled being summoned by an ADC to Montgomery's caravan where Brigadier Bulmer the specialist was sitting beside the Commander-in-Chief. As was his habit, Montgomery came straight to the point.[16]

'Bulmer tells me you are unfit and should go and have a rest.'

'What do you say about it?'

I was naturally a bit shaken; I didn't think things had reached this point. Bulmer was a top class specialist and had helped me from time to time. Five years of continuous strain had undoubtedly left their mark and like thousands of others I suppose I was badly in need of a rest. However with the war reaching its final phase, this was the last thing I wanted to happen. So I turned to Bulmer and made some such remark as, 'Oh you can't do that to me.' He then briefly summarised his conclusions, which were no doubt the arguments he had been using when speaking to Montgomery before I arrived.

Being a very human person the doctor asked the Army Group Commander how long he thought the war would last. He received the following reply:

'You'd better ask my Chief of Staff, he's supposed to work out those kinds of answers.'

So I stuck out my neck and said that I thought about three months would see it through; which wasn't a bad guess . . .

After some discussion and a certain amount of pressure and persuasion from Montgomery and myself, Bulmer eventually offered to compromise. He agreed to treat me with sedatives and drugs to help me to sleep and in addition he said that I would have to visit a hospital in Brussels, once every two or three weeks, where they would put me out for the most of twenty-four hours. But he made all this conditional on the war ending in three months and if this did not happen, then I would have to be relieved of my appointment. Much to my relief this solution was agreed on by the three of us, and the meeting broke up. I left the caravan with a slight sense of shock. To me it was unthinkable that I should 'desert the ship' at such an historic and exciting time.

I was immediately put on certain pills which I found most helpful and that same evening I was very touched by my Chief coming into my caravan, when I was preparing to go to bed, with a tin of ovaltine, saying that I should have a hot drink made with milk, before I went to sleep.

The proposed twenty-four hour 'black-out' in the Brussels hospital however turned out to be a complete failure. To be honest I was rather looking foward to this treatment, and my personal staff thought it an excellent idea, as it would give them a night out in that cheerful city. On the appointed day we all flew to Brussels in my personal aircraft and I was driven to the hospital, arriving there somewhere around 5 pm. I was received by a very nice doctor who took me to a large private ward, which was staffed by an attractive blond sister. The doctor then described the procedure. However in spite of pills and injection I woke up during the night, and so the treatment was a failure and we returned the next morning to our HQs . . .

And so I continued with my job as Chief of Staff of the 21st Army Group, watching the progress of the war, with an eye on the calendar.

This was the third time that Montgomery, recognising the indispensability of Freddie, had intervened, although with the victim's consent, to overrule the doctors and retain his services.

Freddie's estimate was correct, and all German armed forces in Holland, in NW Germany including the Frisian Islands and Heligoland and all other islands, in Schleswig-Holstein and in Denmark surrendered to his Chief on 4th May 1945. Montgomery took the surrender at his Tactical Headquarters attended only by pressmen, photographers and a senior Intelligence staff officer who acted as interpreter. Freddie, the Chief of Staff, was not invited.

At the end of May it became imperative that Freddie should have a long period of sick leave. A few weeks before, Churchill had proposed that he be appointed as Deputy Military Governor in

Germany and had commented that 'de Guingand was a very good man, personally agreeable to Montgomery and would have many of the qualities for this task which, in the first six months would involve the active and immediate phase of disarming the Germans and destroying their material'.[17] But because of Freddie's poor health this proposal was inevitably vetoed by the War Office, and after an emotional farewell to his faithful staff at 21st Army Group headquarters he went off on six months' sick leave. He wrote to many of those, high and low, who had served with him. One letter very characteristic of Freddie may be quoted: it was to his close friend Bedell Smith:[18]

39 Yeomans Row
Off Brompton Rd
London S.W.

25/5/45

My dear Bedell,

This is not a good-bye letter for I feel we will see each other many times again. It is sincerely an attempt to say 'thank-you' for all you have done.

I shall never forget turning up at Norfolk House in early January last year – very frightened and weighed down with the thought of my new responsibilities. Then I met you, and after so short a talk, everything changed & I knew that I could do it, with your support from above. Since that day until now you have gone out of your way to help me in every possible direction. During good times and bad your support has never wavered. Myself and all of us at 21 Army Group have always known that any of our problem & difficulties would receive from you the fairest of attention and the wisest of counsel. I, probably before all others, know what our HQs and our Armies owe to you.

As to our personal relationship – I could never express what I feel. I shall remember all those kindnesses – big and small – long after memories of great battles have faded away.

My last two days at my HQ were very hard to bear – saying goodbye to so many who had worked with me for over three years was not easy. To think I have reached the point when I shall not be seeing you often is a very sad thought indeed.

It's hopeless to try to say what I really feel Bedell; but perhaps what I have written will help you to guess the rest.

As always,

Freddie

Many of those who had served with Freddie wrote expressing admiration for his leadership gratitude for his friendship and sorrow at his departure.

Montgomery wrote him the following letter:[19]

TAC HEADQUARTERS
31.5.45   21 Army Group

My dear Freddie,

I feel I would like to send you a short note of personal thanks for all you have done for me during the time we served together. No commander can ever have had, or will ever have, a better Chief of Staff than you were; you never spared yourself, in fact you wore yourself out completely for the good of the show.

Together we achieved much; and together we saw the thing through to the end. You must now have a good rest, and then later on, together we will conquer fresh fields.

Thank you very much.

Yrs ever,
B. L. Montgomery

Forty years later the verdict of history still confirms everything he wrote that day, except that the 'fresh fields' to conquer never materialised. The tragic circumstances of Freddie's eclipse have been told many times, but must be recalled here as they affected the remaining thirty-four years of his life.

He replied to Montgomery's letter on 2nd June 1945. If today the emotions expressed seem extravagant, it must be remembered that Freddie, in a state of mental as well as physical exhaustion, was also feeling the anti-climax inevitable after VE Day.

My dear Field-Marshal

Thank you so very much for your charming letter. It had done a lot to help dispel a very natural feeling of melancholy and depression which has set in since leaving you. Parting from you and the Army Group was the most difficult thing that has happened to me since I joined the Army.

It is no good my trying to say all I feel, or to thank you adequately for all you have done for me. Being Chief of Staff to you was not difficult for two main reasons. First, you gave us such clear direction, and secondly you showed me your confidence by letting me get on with the

In 1944 the strain of the war was beginning to tell on Freddie but he could relax in a game of cards with Bill Bovill.

Freddie with Monty, Horrocks and Coningham at the Alamein Reunion in Brussels, 1944.

Monty, Crocker and Freddie before the battle of the Rhine.

Freddie's farewell to HQ 21 Army Group, *L to R*: 'Joe' Ewart, Author, Freddie, David Strangeways, Bill Williams, Gen Sir Drummond Inglis (Chief Engineer).

Business without petty interference. For these two Blessings I thank you most deeply.

It has been a most wonderful experience for me. I was a very raw and untried Chief of Staff when you arrived to command 8th Army. But under you I have learnt a lot. I owe you a debt for this alone.

The past makes the future look pretty drab, and it will be hard for me to settle down. At the moment I feel rather like a deserter. I hope that feeling will pass.

And so ends a colourful and unforgettable chapter of my life, which would never have been written without your confidence and your kindness. Perhaps there is another of a similar nature, just around the corner – who knows.

Yours ever
Freddie.

Montgomery, who had remained in Germany as C-in-C and Military Governor of the British Zone, continued to keep in touch by letter with his old Chief of Staff for whom it is evident he had great admiration and some affection. In June he had sent to Freddie's wife the photograph which she had asked for, had commiserated with her about her illness and had enquired after Marylou, his goddaughter. A fortnight later he had sent Freddie a copy of his pamphlet on 'High Command in War' and a bound copy of his Personal Messages. He hoped Freddie now on extended sick leave, was having a good rest and not bothering about "WAR". In July Montgomery had been anxious again about Freddie's health and had advised him once more to see Bulmer, his erstwhile doctor, now demobilised in Birmingham. In the same letter from Berlin he had given Freddie an interesting insight into the Potsdam Conference.

In July 1945, half way through his six months' convalescence, when he was fishing in Scotland, Freddie received a telephone call from Montgomery. He enquired about Freddie's health and was told he was feeling much better and expected to be fit at the end of his period of sick leave. Montgomery then asked him to come to Claridges Hotel in London for a talk in a few days' time. No reason was given and Montgomery rang off. Freddie's reaction during the next few days was first to wonder whether Montgomery was going to interfere once again with his convalescence, as he had done so often before: if so he would resist it. 'How wrong I was proved to be' he wrote in 1964; '*having been separated from him for over three months had made me forget the influence he had over me.*'[20] At Claridges, Montgomery told him that the Prime Minister and Alanbrooke had offered him the appointment of CIGS in five months' time as from the 1st January 1946, and he had accepted. He went on to say that he wanted Freddie to be his Vice-Chief, provided he was fit enough. Freddie replied that he was flattered by the invitation, and thought he would be ready to start work again at the end of his convalescence in three months' time. But Montgomery then said he could not wait, and that Alanbrooke had agreed that Freddie should take over the job of Director of Military Intelligence on a temporary basis to gain experience in the War Office. He was to start in a few days' time and Montgomery would once again 'square' the doctors.

In the War Office hierarchy, the role of VCIGS is of great importance. Taking his broad guidance from the CIGS, the Vice-Chief must be in complete accord with him and relieve him as much as possible of all detailed work. He must be *persona grata* with the other members of the Army Board, some of whom will be senior to him, and must cooperate closely with the other two Services while maintaining the position of his own Service. Inasmuch as some decisions can be pre-empted by a word between friends in the corridors of power, he must understand how the establishment works, informally as well as formally. Freddie was highly qualified for all these tasks except for the last: the War Office had greatly changed since Hore-Belisha's days; there were many new faces and Freddie's experience had been elsewhere.

It was for this reason that on 19th September 1945 Freddie for a temporary period became Director of Military Intelligence, the important post for which Montgomery had previously recommended him to Brooke three years before in 1942, because he then needed a rest and had been in the Middle East for 'far too long'. In the War Office Simpson, the rival, had been promoted to assistant CIGS, and Freddie was subordinated to him – an unfortunate juxtaposition.

Although those around Freddie in his new job for years afterwards spoke of his thoughtful treatment of his War Office subordinates and the way he inspired affection in all types of people, he was not at his best in that environment, despite the laughter that was often heard from his room. By those who feared or disparaged Montgomery he was regarded as a forerunner of that ruthless 'new broom': ponderous asides were heard about the advent of St John the Baptist. He was far from fit, and was still suffering from depression and insomnia, and to many he appeared to be living on his nerves. Nor did this assignment really suit him intellectually. There was a marked difference between on the one hand absorbing the immediate intelligence relevant in the short term to a current campaign, and on the other chairing a large committee of intelligence experts composing reports of a long-term significance applicable in peace-time to the world-wide threat. His enthusiastic pursuit of immediate, and constructive action sometimes led him to blur the necessary distinction between hard evidence and his own opinions. Moreover as the recent beneficiary of a select entourage with cars and a private aeroplane, (called Marylou), at call, he found it difficult to submit happily to the cheese-paring economies of a Government Department adjusting to peace conditions after a long and expensive war.

During the next three months Freddie, working hard whilst nursing his health, was uncertain about his future, as was Arlie his wife. She was not too keen on living in England, but thought that after a proposed visit to Australia to see her parents she would be reconciled to the prospect for another year or two.

Freddie, as DMI, met Montgomery again in August, September and November 1945. By December, Montgomery was less certain about his choice of Vice, and Freddie himself was aware of this. On 28th December he wrote to Montgomery to clarify the question of their 'future re-association': two factors might become stumbling blocks: his health and his domestic life. After saying that he would love to work again directly under Montgomery, if he wanted him, and thought he was up to the job professionally, he described his wife's mixed reactions to the prospect, but commented 'she says she knows I would be happier working for you than anyone else'. Then he reported on his health not very reassuringly, but 'the more interesting the job the easier it is to carry the load'. He concluded:

Providing Arlie thinks she will be happy if we stay in England, I feel there is a good chance of my health standing the pace as long as I live a quiet life.

All this of course apart from;

(a) Whether you want me

(b) Whether you think I am up to the job professionally

If you do in fact want me, I suggest when the time comes we get Bulmer to come to see me with the Millbank [Army Medical] specialist to see what opinion they arrive at.

This letter shows clearly that the post of VCIGS had only been suggested, not guaranteed, by Montgomery, and that for Freddie a return to health was an essential pre-requisite.[21]

Montgomery, not yet publicly proclaimed as CIGS designate, replied that the situation was quite clear and that the important point for Freddie was to get an agreed verdict on his fitness. Something might emerge in early January.

Events then moved faster than expected. Nye, who had been VCIGS during the war, was selected as Governor of Madras, and a new VCIGS was needed quickly. Montgomery had two discussions about future appointments with Viscount Alanbrooke (as Brooke had become on 1st January 1946) and hearing that McCreery was the CIGS's choice flatly declined to have him. Alanbrooke then asked Montgomery: 'Whom do you intend to get in?' 'De Guingand,' said Montgomery. 'I won't have him' Alanbrooke replied, 'I don't trust him. He is an unbalanced chap. [Alanbrooke must have meant 'I don't trust his judgement'] I won't have him as VCIGS.'[22] For Montgomery that answer was final. Simpson was then selected, commenting sardonically that he was the lowest common dominator. It was an excellent choice.

Alanbrooke had of course observed his Director of Military intelligence at close quarters, and due to Freddie's curtailed convalescence and his continuing nervous prostration and insomnia, his performance had not been impressive. The DMI was indeed living on his nerves, and it was not surprising that his judgements were not as uniformly reliable as the exacting job demanded. A further point in Alanbrooke's mind was that by taking Freddie as his Vice, Montgomery would weaken his position in relation to the post-war Army by appearing in peace to be favouring 'the Monty

gang', as he had done in the war. But the war had not been won by
Eighth Army and 21st Army Group alone, and there were many
good officers from other theatres who at that time were already
hostile to Montgomery under the misapprehension that there might
be little future for them in the peacetime Army.

Freddie would have instantly appreciated this point, had
Montgomery immediately explained it to him. Instead, in Freddie's
own words recorded long afterwards, the following scene
occurred:[23]

> One day in January 1946, Monty arrived at the War Office, flung the
> door of my office open . . . He called me outside and in great haste he
> said, 'Oh Freddie, I've decided not to have you for my Vice.'
> I naturally asked, 'Why not?'
> His reply was, 'Because it would not do me any good'. He then
> rushed off.

To all those who knew Montgomery and his wartime relationship
with his Chief of Staff, his discarding of Freddie like yesterday's
shirt would forever beggar belief. Granted that Montgomery was
beset by the immense problems of leading the Army through a
period of great difficulty and change: granted that he had to inform
Freddie quickly before the news could reach him through other
channels: but knowing Freddie's temperament so intimately and his
depressed condition, why did he not explain the situation fully and
patiently that evening in congenial surroundings? Perhaps it is only
the psychiatrist who can attempt an answer. Was this performance
typical? There were others who had served Montgomery well and
found that he could dispense with them instantly when they ceased
to be useful – but not with such callousness and total lack of
sympathy. He was dealing still with the insomniac whom he had
sought tenderly to lull with Ovaltine only a year before.

Now, forty years after the dust has settled, some of the
considerations which must have entered Montgomery's mind can be
identified. Alanbrooke's veto on an appointment which the CIGS
designate might reasonably have regarded as within his own gift was
an unexpected rebuff, but the two reasons for it, Freddie's poor
health and favouritism for the 'Monty Gang', were indisputable.
However, Montgomery could not have disclosed to Freddie

Alanbrooke's opinion of his unimpressive performance as DMI: to have done so would have been to contravene the military convention under which the assessment of an officer by his immediate employer is made known, but not the confidential opinions of superior officers further up the hierarchy. He may also have felt that to have disclosed to the stricken Freddie Alanbrooke's opinion of his unfitness for the job would have been to inflict an avoidable wound. Furthermore Montgomery would not have relished admitting that his personal opinion of his Chief of Staff was not shared by the head man of the Army, whom he revered. To have fully disclosed the second objection – favouritism for 'Monty men' – would also have involved loss of face, because Alanbrooke's unwelcome criticism should have been evident when, five months before, he had first suggested the VCIGS appointment to Freddie.

So Montgomery took refuge in the cryptic statement: 'It wouldn't do me any good.' To Freddie this reply was open to many interpretations, and in his depression he tormented himself in seeking complex explanations. In his distress at the cruel reverse, he broke down in tears before his wife, and then poured out the bitter searchings of his heart in draft after draft, prepared as an appeal to his old chief for elucidation. Page after page was written, exhuming incidents of ingratitude and shabby treatment long past. Some are disclosed here only because they reflect the extent of Freddie's ailing condition, and the degree to which his pride was wounded by the unaccountable behaviour of his chief. In the years ahead they would not be easily expunged from his memory.

'Delving into past history', in one of his drafts he complained that in North Africa and Sicily he had been granted the 'local' rank of major-general, (which excluded any increase in pay) whereas General Leese, on taking over command of Eighth Army had secured 'temporary' rank, much more beneficial, for his Chief of Staff. Moreover for NW Europe, as Chief of Staff of an Army Group Freddie, at Montgomery's express wish, had agreed to remain in the rank of temporary major-general, although the appropriate rank was lieutenant-general. Both these decisions of Montgomery's now appear irregular and unwise: perhaps they can be explained as a symptom of his subconscious desire always to keep in subordination anyone too near the 'throne'. During the latter period of their association Freddie wrote in another draft, 'I was often treated in front of other people not as a Chief of Staff but as a G III [the most junior grade of the General Staff]. Stated thus, the complaint is difficult to accept, but it is a sad fact that there was a period when Montgomery was less susceptible to the influence of his Chief of Staff, and this without doubt was unfortunate both for him and for the Alliance.

There were other incidents which appeared to Freddie as slights; his exclusion from the signing of the Treaty of Surrender at Tac HQ at Luneberg Heath although, knowing his man, he surely could not have expected that any portion of the limelight would have been permitted to fall other than on the Commander-in-Chief. He was disappointed by the absence of any British award after VE Day following his KBE in June 1944; he had received five foreign decorations initiated by Montgomery, and it is difficult now to see what British award could have been appropriate for a temporary major-general aged forty-five, already knighted and with another ten to fifteen years of further service ahead of him. Finally no special provision was made for him and his wife to view the Victory Parade, although in fact seats were reserved for senior members of the War Office of which Freddie was a member, in the balconies overlooking Whitehall. None of the great commanders had their Chiefs of Staff with them in the procession.

Notwithstanding the triviality of some of these complaints, it was a tragedy for the British Army that at the end of the war no place was found for Freddie. After a long uninterrupted convalescence could he not have accepted some other appropriate appointment? Many officers who had been rapidly promoted in war-time, accepted demotion in rank in order to gain wider experience, and many of these eventually reached high positions. It seems that the possibility was discussed with Montgomery, but to no avail.

Finally Freddie was greatly upset because, he claimed, Montgomery had told him that Alanbrooke had *agreed to his appointment*. That seems highly unlikely; Alanbrooke must have agreed to Freddie's appointment as DMI with the *possibility* of becoming thereafter Montgomery's VCIGS; but the CIGS like Freddie himself knew that a return to fitness and a demonstration of full competence would be essential.

Further discussion with Montgomery took place but Freddie's final letter, which would have been typewritten, has not come to light. However, it was almost certainly from a manuscript draft on which Freddie scribbled 'To FM Mon'.

This is not a bellyache because I have been turned down for VCIGS. I naturally accept the position, and would hate it to be raised again. I am sufficiently a realist to know that either age, seniority, efficiency or health were factors which could have been put forward to support such a decision. I am however, to say the least of it, hurt at the particular reason given by the CIGS i.e. that such an appointment would be damaging to you personally. To start with, he might have thought of that one before, instead of, as you told me at Claridges in August, that he agreed with the proposal. It infers that our three years association in war was not a successful one, and for that the Army generally would be put out by such a natural reunion. It certainly suggests that your position and prestige are not very firm.

As regards the first point events speak for themselves. As to the second I'm sure you will agree that I subordinated entirely my interests to yours, and never attempted to claim any kudos – and there were occasions when I might have done. This I know the Army realise.

When yesterday I said I saw the point – that was correct, but I did not agree with the arguments used. So I wish some other reason had been given.

You also said that it would look bad if I left the War office in the near future. I find it difficult to see that any damage would be done. It's certainly a rather flattering suggestion from my point of view.

I tried to explain my feelings at Hindhead the other day. I would be only human if I found it difficult to serve you in a minor capacity at the War Office after our past association, particularly when the other plot had been on the tapis.

In war we can and must subordinate all personal feelings, but in peace these to some extent must be taken into account.

Again I was put into DMI – a job I did not like – for a special purpose.

I hope therefore, if I stay in the Army that you will remember our talks in Germany as regards something *outside* the War Office.

It was most unlike Freddie to raise the subject of his Chief's prestige, particularly as it had little relevance. Montgomery replied two days later in a letter which showed no regret but some restraint and, in the last sentence an attempt at sympathy for his ailing friend:[24]

Tac Headquarters

7.1.46   British Army of the Rhine

Mr dear Freddie,

I have your letter of 4 Jan. I am quite unable to agree with the inferences you draw: i.e.

A. That our 3 years association in war was not a successful one

B. That my position and prestige are not very firm,

As regards 'A'

Our association would be quoted for years to come as an example of complete trust and confidence. Of that there is no doubt.

As regards 'B'

I am not in the least interested in my own position. I have reached the top and can go no higher. I can at any time withdraw to the House of Lords and give tongue as I like. I do not want to be CIGS and have told everyone so. Only a strong sense of duty makes me say that, if I am wanted for the job, then I will take it on.

I really want a good rest.

If I become CIGS, my family will be the whole Army.

If I take you on as Vice, the Army will say that I am collecting in the old gang again and that no one will have any future unless he is one of my chaps. That will never do. I have already put in Kirkie [Kirkman] and Lyne, [Maj-Gen L. O. Lyne], and all my old Corps Cdrs are now in the Home Commands. Future appointments will be watched and criticized.

If it were war, I would not care what anyone said. But it is peace, and there is a herculean job ahead.

I can have only one yardstick: the best interests of the Army.

If I consider only my own interests, I would pull you straight in as Vice. But I have decided that I must not do so.

Do not make it harder for me by 'bellyaching'.

No one has ever had, or will ever have, a more loyal and devoted Chief of Staff than you were. If we go to War again in my time, I would pull you straight in as Chief of Staff.

I hope above is clear.

Yours ever

B. L. Montgomery.

Even if Montgomery had at the outset patiently explained Alanbrooke's argument, Freddie in his uncertain mood could see himself serving only as Vice to his old Chief. The tragedy could hardly have been avoided: the Army was going to lose a brilliant officer whose intellectual power, versatility and dynamism could have been of incalculable value to post-war Britain.

CHAPTER THIRTEEN

Author and Tycoon

For Freddie this was his darkest hour. Montgomery's letter had virtually shut the door on any peace-time military career. The statement 'if we go to war again in my time I would pull you straight in as Chief of Staff', although intended as balm to Freddie's wounded pride, in practical terms was valueless: in the next two years of Montgomery's stewardship there would be no war. Shattered by disappointment and bitterly wounded, he brooded over the treatment he had received from his wartime chief. As a professional soldier he had demonstrated exceptional abilities in war, which had been fully recognised not only by Montgomery but to an even greater extent by Eisenhower, Bradley and Bedell Smith. But having been barred from the appointment of VCIGS, did he now have any future in the Army? Should he resign, and if so when? Should he, with Arlie his wife and Marylou, try his luck in England or go abroad?

If he were to resign his commission, how could he make sufficient income to sustain himself and his family in the life-style which he had always sought and which even under the exigencies of war he had often attempted to maintain? By agreeing in 1943 to remain in the temporary rank of major-general instead of lieutenant-general, his substantive rank which would govern his retirement pension had risen only to full colonel in March 1945, and a colonel's pension was inadequate. These were the rules; but was such a decision equitable for an officer who had served in war for eighteen months as the Chief of Staff of an Army Group? Montgomery, to whom Freddie appealed for help in remedying the anomaly, had brushed the question aside. In Master's philosophy this was one of those 'details', in which great commanders should not get entangled. Fortunately for Freddie, but to the shame of Whitehall officials, the remedy was achieved by pressure from Eisenhower. Bedell Smith had written to him about it on 13th June 1945, and Freddie eventually was promoted in September 1946 to the substantive rank of major-general, having worn the insignia of that rank in war of close on three years. 'God knows you have earned it a dozen times,' was Bedell Smith's comment. He also sent him the ribbon of the United States' Distinguished Service Medal to wear as a stop-gap until presented By Eisenhower. It had been 'approved by both sides', so was perfectly legal.

Freddie's private income was small. What were his other assets? A first class, versatile brain which after a period of recuperation could be expected to function once again with its usual brilliance: some experience of the corridors of power, and a host of loyal and important friends. Freddie had always had the capacity to make friends easily and to value and, when appropriate, use their friendship thereafter. He was known to Churchill, Eisenhower, Bedell Smith, Smuts and others. He had nurtured his close friendship with Eisenhower by exchanging Christmas greetings, and by sending him congratulations following the announcement in November 1945 of Eisenhower's appointment as Chief of Staff of the US Army. Freddie wrote: 'It is a great thing not only for America but also for this country; you understand us so well. I do hope I may have the opportunity of seeing you again one of these days.' To which Eisenhower replied, referring to a possible visit to the United Kingdom in 1946, 'If I do, you will be one of the first I will get in touch with.[1]

But Freddie was desperately tired and in need of medical attention. On 26th February 1946 he sought an interview with Alanbrooke, the CIGS, and told him that his state of health was no longer good enough for the job of DMI. The CIGS agreed that he must go on sick leave. Montgomery was still C-in-C BAOR so there was no need for any emotional farewell in that quarter.

But was their relationship now to be severed for good? Unquestionably they were fond of each other, and shared many nostalgic memories of triumphant days in battle. Freddie had always tolerated his master's idiosyncrasies: that was a small price to pay alongside Montgomery's outstanding virtues as a battlefield commander. Montgomery for his part, by his reactions to Freddie's breakdowns, had shown conclusively the value that he had placed upon retaining him as his Chief of Staff. At any time he could have replaced him with any brilliant officer in the entire officer corps, but he had never done so. 'Freddie knows my ways'; but more than that, Freddie's intellect, more subtle and more wide-ranging than his master's, acted as an essential complement, even if his master may not have perceived it.

Montgomery himself, still C-in-C BAOR, having written in his own round hand his explanatory letter of 7th January, would have instantly put the matter of Freddie's future out of his mind. He had given the reason for his decision, which was incontrovertible, and he had emphasised again the debt he owed to Freddie for his services in war. The matter was closed and there was no need for resentment or 'bellyaching'.

Surprisingly, the cooling-off period was very short – seventeen days. Montgomery, also needing a rest, had caught flu and a touch of pneumonia but was 'taking M and B – a bit drastic. I am now recovering from the treatment . . .' He continued: 'I would much value your views on the organisation of the Military Operations/Military Intelligence set up in the War Office. Send me a paper on it (privately of course).'[2]

This letter may have been sent just to keep in touch with his stricken friend and test his response. Happily by 16th February 1946, the old amicable correspondence was reopened, and Montgomery who had heard from Freddie about his illnesses, commiserated with him: 'It is probably a good thing to let the doctors have a really good go at the business. It is bound to be a longish business to get you really cured 100%.'

He then referred to the book *Normandy to the Baltic*, which had been 'ghosted' on his behalf by Belchem.

I have instructed David Belchem to keep entirely off all political and international background, interservice arguments, and so on. It is to be a plain tale of the facts unembellished by any controversial or unsavoury details . . . It is possible that later on, in my evening of life, I may give the true facts to the world; but not yet and not until I have retired from Active Army Life. Butcher [author of *Three Years with Eisenhower*] is doing enough harm; and I tremble to think what may not [sic] emerge when he gets on to the campaign in NW Europe. Tedder seems to have said some very indiscreet things to him in Normandy, and very probably was even more indiscreet later on: and it will all come out. Ike is very much upset at the whole affair and he has written me a letter about it – which he says I can publish if I like.

I have told him I shall treat the whole thing with silent contempt . . .

Montgomery's letter, now seen to be full of sound advice to those, including Freddie, who on both sides of the Atlantic were reaching for their typewriters, defines the beginning of a new phase in their relationship. It was to last nearly thirty years and to be marked by a continuous exchange of cordial letters leading to confidential discussions at felicitous meetings, and several commemorative dinners at which Montgomery was to be Freddie's guest. It almost seemed that Freddie's wound was to be healed.

It was on 27th February 1946 that Freddie, now seriously contemplating retirement on a major-general's pension of £900 per annum, equivalent in 1986 to £11,250 pa, left London with his wife, daughter and nanny bound for France on sick leave. He had attempted unavailingly to secure other sources of income – an appointment with the Federation of British Industry as Public Relations Officer, a Conservative seat at Blackpool North, and more enthusiastically the governorship of Southern Rhodesia, adjacent to his old hunting ground in Nyasaland. Despite Montgomery's very strong personal recommendation to the Secretary of State for the Colonies, this appointment went to Sir John Kennedy, the retired Director of Military Operations in the War Office, who was also in indifferent health, but whose wife's experience appeared particularly suitable for her future role. In the light of Freddie's multifarious activities over the next few years there is little doubt that he would have felt intolerably restricted in that appointment.

In Cannes where Aly Khan, a friend from Cairo days, had lent the de Guingands a villa adjacent to the Casino, complete with 'couple' to look after them, Freddie now settled down to get his health restored. On the way there, he had had a bad fall in the darkness of the Gare du Nord and had severely damaged his nose and face. But after a few days of sitting in the sun, his restless creative mind sought relief in writing a book of memoirs, *Operation Victory*. It was completed very quickly, largely without research, and was to cause a considerable public stir when published in 1947.

In April he had to return to London for a hernia operation, and he finally decided to resign his commission. Not without some difficulty, as active service conditions still applied, his resignation was approved, with Montgomery's consent. In deciding where to seek his fortune, Australia, the birthplace of his wife, was considered; but finally Southern Rhodesia was chosen. Freddie had been attracted to that country by the recommendation of Robert Long, a staff officer of Freddie's in Eighth Army days. Bob Long, now a senior officer in the Army of the Federation had assured Freddie that Sir Godfrey Huggins the Governor would welcome his intention to immigrate. In November 1946, with his wife Arlie and his two-year old daughter Marylou, he arrived at Cape Town, and alone went north to find a home in Southern Rhodesia, where he was welcomed and helped by the Governor Sir John Kennedy and by Ellis Robins of the British South Africa Company, and Roy Welensky and Bob Long.

Almost immediately he became involved in his first venture into industry. David Stirling, the renowned SAS leader, whom Freddie had known in Egypt, asked him to become chairman of a company called Gemsbok, which had been set up by Stirling and his brother and was now in an early stage of development. Freddie took on the chairmanship, and was able to contribute in a small way to the company's progress; but he had always been dubious of the prospects of future development and, by agreement resigned from Gemsbok a year later. Although his first venture into industry had not succeeded, and his reputation had to some extent been damaged, he had gained valuable experience; many attractive offers were to follow.

In January 1947 *Operation Victory* was published by Hodder and Stoughton. Freddie, in a mood of despondency some months before, had decided to accept from his publisher a lump sum in lieu of royalties. This was unfortunate, as the book became an instant success. It was serialised in *The Times* and reviewed in the leader column, and went to seven editions with a paper-back followed by two further impressions. All this was well-deserved, as the book had a topical freshness, was modest and devoid of bitterness, and was well written in a lively informal style.

Freddie sent inscribed copies to many of his wartime friends and to Churchill, Eisenhower and Montgomery. As an eye-witness account of the campaigns in North Africa and NW Europe, although beaten to the post by Butcher's controversial volume *Three Years with Eisenhower* published in May 1946, it received enthusiastic reviews throughout the English-speaking world.

Because of the agreed lump-sum payment it did not immediately produce riches for Freddie, and that had not been his aim. It did however give him immense publicity in Britain, Southern Rhodesia, South Africa, United States and eventually still further afield. Freddie was not slow to exploit his good fortune by following this up with supplementary reminiscences of his wartime experiences, and soon he was to be quoted in the *Rand Daily Mail* as the expert on defence and international affairs. From 1947 onwards he produced a steady flow of newspaper articles, topical reports, and published speeches covering the World War, Mongomery and other wartime personalities, defence of the African Continent, the communist threat, internal security and the racial problem. All this was good for Africa and for Freddie. But there were repercussions arising from the reactions of Montgomery and Eisenhower, the principal actors in the drama now being unfolded, who by this time were the professional heads of the armies of Britain and the United States.

Montgomery's first reaction was generously enthusiastic. On 21st February 1947, some months after despatching a letter saying he had recommended Freddie for the governorship of S. Rhodesia, he wrote from Switzerland:

> Thank you for your letter of 8 Feb which I was delighted to get, it is ages since I last heard news of you. I am reading with great interest the *Times* articles of extracts from your book; I have written for a copy of the book itself as it is difficult to get a clear idea of what you have written when things are taken out of their context. So far I have read the first three articles and I think they are excellent; there was a very good leading article in *The Times* of 17th February. The book should have a tremendous sale, you are a rising market as just at present I seem to be what is called 'news'. The first edition of Moorehead's book is sold out. *Normandy to the Baltic* is being published on 27 Feb and the first edition of 30,000 was all taken up two weeks ago: so I was told by Hutchinson, the publisher . . .

Right: Happy days in South Africa: Monty visits Freddie

Below: Freddie, Arlie and their daughter Marylou in Johannesburg.

Monty visits the Hercules Bicycle depot in Cape Town.

Monty at one of the Rupert cigarette factories in South Africa.

It is difficult to tell you in a letter like this, which may go astray, what I really think about things. I am going to visit Southern Rhodesia in December next; I understand I am to stay with the Governor and I will arrange to see you and have a good talk.

As regards the Army, I am quite happy. I am getting what I want . . . I have introduced the Chief of Staff system into the whole Army, including Home Commands . . .

As regards our strategic position in the world, I am far from happy. I got the government to agree that a firm hold on the Middle East area was an essential part of our defence problem; we must hold it in peace and fight for it in war. But the handling of the Palestine situation has been so weak and spineless that we may well lose our position there: if the UNO decides against us. . . .

Thirdly, the Chiefs of Staff are a useless body. We never initiate anything; we meet and deal with whatever the Secretariat put on the agenda; we resemble a Board of Directors. I would say we are a completely spineless outfit. Tedder is utterly useless as Chairman; he sits on the fence and never gives a definite opinion on any matter . . .

The time is coming when the Chiefs of Staff must line up to the Government with an ultimatum. United in a firm body, we would be unbeatable. I got them to agree to do this once before, but the mere threat that this might happen was enough and I won my point. Palestine and India have gone west since I have been here on leave; when I left UK on 4 Feb I thought I had left things in a safe state.

It is all very distressing.

My Moscow trip was a terrific success. I had 1½ hours alone with Stalin and did a lot of good business; it has left the way clear for Bevin to get on with a Military alliance: which Stalin is most anxious to have. I cannot safely write more about it in this letter. No more news. My love to you both and my Goddaughter.

Yrs ever

Montgomery of Alamein.

I would be grateful if you would ACK this letter: by air letter card.

This letter may perhaps be read today as a peace-offering; but Montgomery, a lonely man in his high office, was also seeking solace by confiding to his old friend and *alter ego* the major defence problems that he was facing, almost as if Freddie was his Vice. In a regular flow of similar letter sent over the next twenty years he continued to do so, and to arrange meetings where he and his old Chief of Staff could 'have a good talk'. Although there exist only a very few of Freddie's letters to reply, it is clear that Montgomery still greatly valued his advice on world problems, and Freddie, reciprocally, was happy to use the aura of his old master to support his own public activities in his newly adopted homeland. Much later as book succeeded book from each author, a friendly competitive interchange took place. The presentation copies sent by Montgomery to Freddie all contained most glowing references to his superb services as chief of staff.

However, Freddie in publishing *Operation Victory* had strayed, wittingly or not, from the caution implied in Montgomery's letter sent to him almost exactly a year before about his own book *Normandy to the Baltic*. 'It is to be a plain tale of facts unembellished by any controversial and unsavoury details'. Although not the first to do so he had commented on one of the two major strategic controversies, and inevitably this was seized upon by the world press. Trouble was on the way; the controversial ripple now created would eventually spread through the deep waters of the Atlantic and finally destroy the relationship between Eisenhower and Montgomery, the two great leaders in the Allies' victory.

Montgomery, only five days after his 'olive branch' letter, wrote again from Gstaad, Switzerland:

> I have now read the whole of *Operation Victory* and I think it is quite first class. I congratulate you on it. There is one point of very great interest to me and that is where you state that you always disagreed with me over the development of Allied strategy after crossing the Seine, when I wanted to halt the right and put everything into a hard left north of the Ruhr: you apparently always agreed with the broad front strategy adopted by Ike.
>
> The point of interest to me is that I cannot remember that you ever told me that you disagreed; I cannot remember that you ever argued the matter with me.
>
> I of course agree entirely with the letter in *The Times* of Monday 24 Feb, written by Miles Graham;[3] which I have just seen today. I am delighted he wrote it. It has always been my view that administratively it could have been done. The real reason that Ike wouldn't do it was that it meant halting the right i.e. the bulk of the Americans. He said that public opinion in America wouldn't stand for it; I told him that victories won wars not public opinion; the whole discussion took place between

us two alone, in my caravan, as we were moving up to the Seine after the Falaise battle.

The broad front strategy finally led us into the most frightful mess, involved a great waste of life, and meant that the war had to go on to the summer of 1945. My plan involved a bold move; but the prize was terrific. Ike wouldn't face adverse American opinion, and told me so; admin reasons were brought up afterwards.

Good luck to you.

This letter written only thirteen months after the 'VCIGS crisis' discloses some points of interest in the fascinating relationship between the two men. Although very friendly in tone, there is a hint of censure that Freddie should have publicly raised the northern front strategy in his book without having previously argued the matter with his Chief; this implied that such important matters had always been 'argued' between them. Montgomery's memory may have misled him, but certainly up to August 1944 he had encouraged such salutary argumentation by his Chief of Staff, and many disasters might have been avoided had the system continued in full force till VE Day. Montgomery's comment was both a recongition of the value of his Chief of Staff's advice, and a mild rebuke that he should now have publicly disclosed his disagreement with his old chief. Hand-written, with no benefit of a secretary (like all his correspondence with Freddie) the CIGS's letter shows unusual restraint. Unfortunately there is no record of Freddie's immediate reaction, but he maintained his criticism of Montgomery's 'northern thrust strategy' and corresponded with Eisenhower about it to the end of his life. He did, however, drop the logistic argument.

While this interchange had been going on with Freddie, now a retired officer, many crucial problems affecting the security of the Western World and the future of Britain's defence forces were being thrashed out in Whitehall. Montgomery's role as CIGS was not easy; his relationship with Tedder was abrasive and he found his colleagues reluctant to support him in persuading the Government to adopt a more realistic defence policy despite the rigorous economy drive which inevitably had followed the end of the war. He personally had no doubt that the USSR was now the enemy, and that given a few years in which to recover from the immense damage inflicted on them, they might well launch some aggressive action against the Western democracies, which obviously were in a state of considerable disarray. For the CIGS to have to read in *The Times* in 1947 a studied criticism of his strategic decisions of 1944, written by his then Chief of Staff and blazoned world-wide, could not have been welcome; in the hands of Montgomery's many detractors, such publicity could serve only to undermine his standing with the other Services and the British Government and with Eisenhower in the Pentagon, whose support and assistance in the defence of Western Europe he would soon be seeking; Montgomery's tolerant reaction can be read as some measure of his friendship with his erstwhile Chief of Staff.

It may not have occurred to Freddie, the year before, while pouring his reminiscences into his book in Aly Khan's garden in Cannes that there might be some impropriety in a Chief of Staff, not yet retired, criticising publicly his Commander's strategy only a year after the successful termination of the war, by which time the Commander had become the professional head of the British Army. Nevertheless, it could scarcely have come as a surprise to receive from the CIGS in April a letter asking him, still in a friendly fashion, to remain silent on the issue.

Montgomery, like many of the great commanders and indeed Freddie himself, was a keen guardian of his own reputation; he had entered the lists at a very early date by publishing *Normandy to the Baltic*, although ironically in that account he had diminished the reality of his reputation by insisting that all his plans were pursued with no divergencies due to enemy action.

It is clear that at this time in the spring of 1947 he had a sincere intention to steer clear of public recriminations by the war leaders, which had already started, and he realised that Freddie's published opinions carried considerable weight, not only in South Africa and the United Kingdom but also in the United States. Freddie for his part was in a quandary. As the anonymous, invisible 'brain behind Monty' in the war years, he had now emerged as the great chief's *alter ego* and, while loyally supporting his master in public, he was not averse to some strengthening of his own reputation. Nevertheless he heeded Master's words. Montgomery's letter read as follows:

War Office
Whitehall
London S.W.1.

8 – 4 – 47

My dear Freddie

I was delighted to get your letter of 31 March from New York. Also to know that you are well, and are to become a £6000 a year man. [1986 equivalent: £54,000 p.a]

As regards the controversy of the broad front V. the hard left punch, I do hope you will not go into print again on the issue.

You have seen what I say in Chapter Eleven of *Normandy to the Baltic*; I gave my view of what were the two possible courses open; said which one I favoured and why; said what conditions were essential if my proposition was agreed, gave the Supreme Commander's decision; and then passed on. I indulged in no controversy. You opened the controversy in your book; Miles replied; I remain silent and always will.

What is the good of my Chief of Staff and my CAO having an argument in the Press over a matter which was the sole concern of Ike and myself? It is no good and can only make things awkward for Ike and me, who must remain silent.

Actually, if I were to disclose what took place between Ike and myself in my caravan at my Tac HQ at GACE, when I forced from Ike the real reasons for the broad front, I could shoot everyone sky high. We were alone, and no one else can ever know the true story of our talk.

I sincerely hope you will chuck the whole thing and remain silent. There is trouble enough in the world without stirring up any more.

Then, giving the dates for his visit, he concluded:

I am the guest of the Rhodesian Govt and must stay with the Governor. I have told Kennedy that I want to have a good talk with you. Will you take this up with him. Just to meet at some official dinner is quite useless. I would like to have a complete afternoon with you: alone.

I hope Arlie is well. And my Goddaughter.

Yours ever
Montgomery of Alamein

The controversy, 'Montgomery's Northern Thrust versus Eisenhower's Broad Front', which first emerged as a hypothetical problem for the experts in military history, in after years developed into a question more dangerous and highly charged with emotion:

did Eisenhower needlessly prolong the war by six months? It was the posing of that question that eventually destroyed the relationship between Montgomery and the man who by then had become the President of the United States of America.

Meanwhile across the Atlantic the reaction to *Operation Victory*, which was published later in an American edition by Charles Scribner, was even more enthusiastic than in Britain. Freddie had visited Eisenhower in Washington early in 1947 and had asked him for a letter with a few quotable passages which the publisher could use. Eisenhower responded splendidly, referring to Freddie's standing among all his associates as one of the truly brilliant officers of the Allied Armies, and commended the book for its great interest and authenticity. General Omar Bradley also provided a testimonial referring to Freddie's 'patience, modesty and understanding, which helped to forge the Allied Armies into a single fighting machine. Somewhere in almost every critical Allied decision of the war in Europe, you will find the anonymous but masterful handwork of this British soldier.' Both testimonials were printed on the dust covers of the American edition.

Freddie in his book made little reference to the second controversy which had arisen, namely Montgomery's insistence that an overall land force commander under Eisenhower was essential. But the point caused great public interest when in 1948 Eisenhower's *Crusade in Europe* was published. Montgomery deplored the publication of that book at such an early stage, and was quick to send Freddie two letters in December 1948, seeking his opinion:

11th Dec 1948

There is certain criticism going on about Ike's book; I have also seen press cuttings from America and Canada. You may I imagine be asked to write articles in the Press about it. My view is that IKE has opened up certain very controversial issues; he should not have done so *at the present time*. Many of his statements will be hotly contested by historians in due course; if I were to publish some of my private correspondence with him I could twist some of his statements inside out; but I have *no* intention of doing so, as it would not be right.

Then again he has analysed the characters of some of his British colleagues, applying a harder yardstick than to their American counterparts. I get very rough treatment in some passages. I cannot understand why he should have done this.

The crux of the matter is that he is the first great war leader who has written a personal story, opening up controversial issues and giving his views on the characters of his subordinates.

Such action is bound to unloose a spate of comment across the Atlantic.

Why then do it, *just now?* The book is, naturally written for American consumption and has brought in to IKE a lot of money. Was that the object? I cannot believe it.

We know he employed a ghost writer (a Press man), as he came over to London and saw some of my staff about certain points.

If you write about it, I do hope you will bring out clearly the points that:

1. He should not have opened up on issues which are very controversial
2. He should not have analysed the characters of other war leaders.
3. Having done so, he had only himself to blame for the hoo-haa that is going on.

I hope you are in good health. When next you come this way I could give you some very good dope about my present job.

Only three days later a second letter followed:

4 – 12 – 48

I hear there is a growing volume of Press comment in America pointing out that Ike's book is highly inaccurate and that he would have been better advised to have postponed it until he had checked up on his facts. My own view is that he has been very foolish to open up on controversial issues many of which are bound to be hotly contested. The war leaders had far better remain silent for some years to come . . .

Montgomery continued:

It think the real point is that we all love Ike and we all realise his immense contribution to winning the war. And we have all said so. And no British war leader has ever publically criticised him or anything he did. No one has raised any controversial issues, except of course the war correspondents and professional military writers. All the war leaders on our side of the Atlantic have remained silent, though there is much we could say.

Ike's book conveys the impression that America won the war; all British ideas were 'shot down' by Marshall and Ike.

Why has he done this? it is not good taste.

Apart from this aspect, the book is of great interest and is a real contribution to the story of the war.

What do you think?

Freddie reviewed Eisenhower's book in the *Sunday Graphic* of 2nd January 1949. Although in such matters Freddie took his own line, it is obvious that he had now taken to heart some of Montgomery's advice. He referred to the book as 'most readable, modest and reasonably accurate'. But Montgomery did not come off too well. No useful purpose was served in arguing about 'might have beens', especially when Anglo-American relations were thereby endangered. Montgomery was not ranked by Eisenhower as highly as by the British: was it necessary to be so outspoken, when Montgomery in his present appointment could not reply? He would have liked to have seen references to the part played by Montgomery in preparing the final plan for Tunisia, his insistence on a change of plan for Sicily and his modification of 'Overlord'. Freddie then emphasised the extent of the much greater American contribution compared with the British. He supported Montgomery's style of personal command but thought it was a pity that he did not occasionally visit Eisenhower's headquarters, as did his colleagues. On the land force commander controversy, Freddie now wrote that the best answer would have been to appoint a land force commander from the start; by the end of 1944 this would have been difficult. After various other points, he concluded by deprecating any writings 'which tended to throw grit into the Anglo-American relationship, which was so important to the world'.

Read today, Freddie's view was a case of trying to shut the stable door after his own horse 'northern thrust' had bolted. However Montgomery liked the review, and in a letter dated 10th January wrote to Eisenhower saying he agreed with de Guingand: 'I think it is a pity that you should have thought it necessary to criticise me and my ways, just at this time in the history of the Western Union when things are not too easy for any of us.'

Freddie now attempted to play the honest broker between Montgomery and Eisenhower but placed himself in a difficult position. On 12th January he wrote to Eisenhower thanking him for sending a personal copy of *Crusade in Europe* (with a charming inscription) and mentioned that he had arranged for a copy of his review to be sent to Washington. He referred also to another article in which Montgomery's old 'war cries' had been reiterated, and he concluded: 'I'm afraid Monty, in his endeavour to justify his *every* action forgot that some of us could tell a very damaging story. It is a pity he is so sensitive – and I have inferred this in my review'.[4] The review when read by Eisenhower in Washington, drew from him a three-page letter containing a well-argued defence of his decision on the land force commander issue, and a criticism of Montgomery's personal style of command of an Army Group – alien to American practice. Freddie in reply had some difficulty in justifying the mediating position which he had adopted in his review. He wrote to Eisenhower from Johannesburg on 20th January as follows:[5]

> . . . Just as I had written a draft I received a long letter from Monty who claimed that you had attacked him etc. and asking me, if I wrote any review, to bring out certain points. I was then faced with a very difficult situation. There was a conflict between loyalty to my old chief and loyalty to my conscience. It was important that I did not say anything that would make more difficult his position as Chairman of Western Union Defense.
>
> In the end I modified my article a bit and tried to water down anything which might be taken as an attack on him. I then wrote him a very frank letter saying that I thought your book most fair and accurate and I agreed with you on all controversial matters. I accused him of being too sensitive and warned him about 'flogging dead horses' and also again trying to justify might-have-beens later on by producing signals between you and him. I reminded him how difficult he had been at times and his employment of little intrigues . . . I referred to certain letters which I had seen . . . which might well remove him from his present pedestal, if published. It is interesting to note that I have since received a letter from Monty on another subject and he never even referred to my long one about your book. So like Monty, he is inclined to forget a difficult situation if it goes against him.
>
> Now to the point which you raised.
>
> I hope you did not think my comment of 'within my knowledge, reasonably accurate account of great events' sounded patronising – it wasn't meant as such.

I think you have been most fair and generous to Monty, but that does not mean that one is not left with the impression that he was difficult and that you ranked other generals higher. To Monty himself and to a lot of Englishmen Montgomery was considered supreme in every field. It is difficult to see how you could have dealt differently with this subject, and you and I know that you could in all fairness have said a lot more. I tried to say in my review that you were very generous in recognising difficulties which we came up against, eg. the Catanian plain business. As to Monty's method of command, I was careful to infer that as Monty commanded an Army Group as he did an Army, his method was well suited. But I never did agree that it was the right method for an Army Group Commander. As I think I said in my book, he would never have allowed Alex to have commanded him in Sicily and Italy as he commanded Dempsey. It certainly made my job and that of the staff much more difficult. Now the question of the Land Force Commander from the start. Re-reading my review I don't think I have made it very clear what I was getting at. I agreed that it was not *necessary* to have a Land Force Commander between the Supreme Commander and the Army Groups, c.f., the Red Army 'fronts' and Stalin. But in view of the initial need for one – you appointed Monty at first – I still believe it might have served you well to have had a Deputy Supreme Commander who looked over the land forces, planning, coordinating, visiting fronts, etc. etc. . . . . You as the Supreme Commander would of course have had to make the final decisions in strategy and big plans. But your Land Force Deputy would help you. He would have dealt with Tedder re any special air support, and *if* there arose a conflict you would have had to settle it. You would have been freer and had an easier time. I did however say in the review that I did not see how you could have made such an appointment owing to the difficulty of selection. So there we are – not a very satisfactory explanation I fear. Let me say once again, I thought Crusade in Europe really excellent and all whom I have met who have read it feel the same way.

As ever,
Yours,
Freddie

Freddie's analysis of this complex problem was not very convincing.

The next phase in the battle of reputations opened in 1958 when Montgomery's *Memoirs* were published. He had retired from Supreme Headquarters Allied Powers in Europe, and thus was able to give his version of the controversy, which inevitably drew very strong criticism from President Eisenhower and the Americans, particularly when Montgomery elaborated his arguments in a CBS broadcast. The early part of the book also caused violent antagonism between Montgomery and Auchinleck. Freddie offered to act as mediator between them, but his services were declined by Montgomery in a tart letter explaining his reasons for warning off Freddie from 'The Monty/Auk contest', and ending 'So pipe down – please'.

Freddie still attempting to bridge the chasm between Montgomery and Eisenhower wrote to the President on 8th May 1959 to say how distressed he had been over the recent outbursts by Montgomery:

> I just don't think he realises what he writes or says – neither do I understand the motive. It's a pity he has no Chief of Staff at hand now that he has retired.
>
> Naturally I still retain an affection for him (I don't know whether that is the right word), but these attacks against you try my loyalty very hard. All I can say is that I believe, in his heart of hearts he is now sorry for what has happened . . .[6]

The President's secretary replied expressing Eisenhower's gratitude and indicating that he very much wanted to see Freddie on his proposed visit to Washington in June 1959. After that visit, at which Montgomery's attitude was discussed, Freddie wrote to Eisenhower from London on 14th June:

> My dear Mr President,
> . . . On my return here I had occasion to drop Monty a note and as a p.s. I told him I had seen you in Washington. Within two minutes of receiving my letter he was on the telephone saying he must see me at once and so I went had had tea with him at the House of Lords. It was an interesting experience!
>
> He naturally asked how you felt about him and I did not mince my words. I reiterated my previous views regarding what he had written and said. I also told him that I understood that Al G [General 'Al' Gruenther, SACEUR, to whom Montgomery had been Deputy] and others were incensed with how he had behaved towards you. For the second time in my life – (the first was that occasion which you know about during the Ardennes Battle) I saw Monty completely at a loss and

really humble. He admitted that he had gone too far and had 'overstated the case' etc. etc.; and obviously sincerely wished that the past could be undone.

He asked me what he could do and in fact indicated that he would be prepared to do almost anything to undo the harm already done for the 'Good of the Cause' (Anglo-American relations) – 'the most important factor in the world today.' I naturally took the opportunity to point out that it was a pity that he had not kept this great objective in front of him during the last 12 months.

Monty even asked whether he should write to you; or fly over for 24 hours to see you. I advised him against this for the time being, and said I would think things over and let him have my advice later.

I really think Monty is sincere in his desire to make amends and I had one of those rare opportunities of seeing his better side.

Perhaps you might let me have your thoughts as to whether anything of value could be done, for as you must know if it were possible I would like to see this wound healed – between two men I so much admire.

With deep affection,

Yours,

Freddie

P.S. I could put forward some suggestions if you wish.

Three weeks later, Freddie received the President's reply,[7] covering three carefully drafted pages. Eisenhower began: 'Your letter is truly interesting. I am sorry that so many people seem to get a little wisdom only with hindsight.' He went on to claim that he 'had said not a word publicly in criticism of any officer of World War II, including Monty'. He continued: 'Following the policy of ignoring such criticism publicly *I have also, except in such circumstances as when you and I have met, avoided conversations of this type even in private'*. But many others, especially old military friends, had voiced considerable resentment. He went on to say that the telecasting of Montgomery's interview (following publication of the *Memoirs*), had seemed to many Americans as a deliberate affront. As to 'might have beens' the war in Western Europe had been conducted under his programme, and victory had been achieved much more rapidly than official prophets had foreseen.

Because of the probable resentment of some of his old friends any attempt by Montgomery to visit him 'would likely be bad judgment'. He felt disappointment not rancor. Similarly any exchange of letters, after Montgomery's public utterances would not generate better 'allied' feeling. Time would have to be relied on as the healer. Eisenhower's statement about avoiding public criticism overlooked that it was his *Crusade to Europe* published in 1948 that had first antagonised Montgomery. Freddie, while exchanging criticisms of his old Chief with Eisenhower, would have known this.

This letter marked the final rupture between Eisenhower and Montgomery. Freddie's courageous attempt at mediation had failed. Inevitably the President had bitterly resented Montgomery's accusation that by failing to concentrate the Allied armies after the victory in Normandy he had prolonged the war, leading to the loss of thousands of American lives.

Freddie returned to these controversies in 1964 in his book *Generals at War*. His aim once again was to effect a reconciliation, but he did not succeed in damping down the fire to which unsuspectingly he had contributed in Aly Khan's garden in Cannes nearly twenty years before.

On the publicising of strategic controversies, Montgomery had always drawn a clear and valid distinction between the views of a staff officer and those of his commander. 'It is one thing to say what you think should be done when you are a staff officer and have no responsiblity for the outcome. It is quite another thing to decide on the action to be taken when you are the boss and are directly responsible for success or failure'.[8] No soldier would disagree. However, Montgomery congratulated Freddie on this latest book saying he was fascinated by it: 'It brought back vividly many memories of those days we spent together. Among other things I learnt quite a lot about myself which I did not know before.' This showed generosity, since Freddie had devoted several pages describing how he had intervened to save his chief from being sacked in December 1944, and subsequently the Press had made much of this.

In 1969, in his obituary of Eisenhower, published in *The Times* on 31st March, Freddie would finally contribute a mature, well-balanced summing-up of the strategic controversy. He commented that Montgomery's policy of concentration was attractive in theory and that Eisenhower, possibly, lost a great opportunity; however factors such as the coming winter, American public opinion and the effect of a failure on Allied cooperation had to be considered.

However, Freddie's literary work and public speaking were but an accompaniment to his main purpose: to carve out a new career in business, make money to support his family in the style that he aspired to, and show princely generosity to his friends.

Throughout those early years in South Africa, Freddie had been endeavouring to establish himself. After the disappointing start with Gemsbok, he had been invited by Field-Marshal Smuts to carry out an official visit to the Union, and to lecture on his war experiences. Freddie had met Smuts during the war, and his arrival in Africa had been drawn to the South African Prime Minister's attention by a letter from Bedell Smith, written from the United States Embassy in Moscow, where Eisenhower's Chief of Staff was Ambassador:[9]

November 20th 1946

My dear Field Marshal:

When we last talked in Paris, I spoke to you about Freddie de Guingand, and you were good enough to say that you would keep him in mind. I believe he has already left England for Southern Rhodesia having missed an appointment to a governorship by a matter of days.

General de Guingand is the best staff officer I have ever seen regardless of nationality; and if our American military theories are correct, he would have been equally good as a commander. He would fill with great ability any position under government which the Union of South African might see fit to place him, and I do not know of any man in whom I have more confidence and for whom I have greater affection. Since I know he will never approach you or anyone else on his own behalf, I am taking the liberty of reminding you of his availability.

Faithfully your friend

Bedell Smith.

The tour of the Union that followed gave Freddie a comprehensive introduction into the political, racial and industrial problems of the country in which he was to spend the next twenty-five years of his life. On these subjects he would form definite and constructive views which would be publicised widely in speeches and newspaper articles, and soon he would appreciate that his future as an industrialist and as a man of affairs would lie in the Union rather than in Southern Rhodesia. Passing through Johannesberg on his tour, he called on the Chairman of the Anglo-Transvaal Group and also met the man who shortly was to succeed him. Freddie's visit was intended to sort out a problem over Gemsbok, but after a late-night discussion they asked him to join the Anglo-Transvaal Board. As he was still involved with Gemsbok he did not immediately accept, but that meeting led to an assignment for which his talents were particularly suited: to bear-lead a team of Anglo-Vaals' experts to America to investigate the feasibility of an oil-from-coal scheme which it was intended to establish in the Transvaal with the backing of the South African Government. Freddie's friendship with Eisenhower, now Chief of Staff of the Army, was an advantage, and he grasped the opportunity of staying with him, and also had many meetings with high officials, military and industrial. Freddie's ambassadorial talents combined with his charismatic personality and negotiating ability, supported as always by a meticulous study of his brief, achieved success, and in due course, after approaching Smuts himself in Cape Town, a government licence was granted. This event marked him out as a versatile 'fixer' who could be of great use to many top industrialists; in a comparatively short time he found himself heavily involved in many industrial concerns.

Despite frequent warnings from Montgomery to safeguard his health, it was not in Freddie's temperament to ease off. His home at Rosebank in Johannesberg, where for some months they had lived out of suitcases, now became a centre of hospitality and entertainment. With his two servants Willie and Sam, wearing kummerbunds in the West Yorkshire's colours, he often enjoyed presiding as 'chef' concocting sophisticated French dishes with great *panache*. He was gambling as always: his friend 'Bob' Long who stayed with him commented that the scene resembled the old 'Operations Room' in the Desert in the middle of a battle, with three telephones ringing at once. Freddie was taking a great interest in horse-racing and in four years time would become Chairman of the Jockey Club of South Africa. But most important of all he was well-launched on a rewarding career in business.

His first successful venture was as Chairman of the Ace Cycle Company in which Anglo-Transvaal and General Mining Industries held a controlling interest. Freddie had been invited to become a director of each of these companies after resigning from Gemsbok. Finding that the Ace Cycle Company was in poor shape, he sought technical help from the United Kingdom and through the kind offices of his old friend Sir Geoffrey Burton, who in 1933 had invited him to leave the Army and enter industry, he was introduced to Ivan Stedeford, Chairman of Tube Investments, the biggest manufacturer of cycles in Britain.

Freddie, through his executive ability and his happy knack in handling people, made a success of the cycle business in South Africa which was bought out later by Tube Investments. The Ace Cycle Company which had shown a loss of £19,200 in 1950 declared in 1969 a profit of about £400,000. He became Resident Director of T.I. South Africa in 1949, and in 1959 a director of the main corporation in the United Kingdom, as well as director of the British Aluminium Company and, in 1960, of Raleigh Industries.

In 1956 he was invited by Stedeford to come to the UK to study the structure of the TI group which, after rapid expansion under Stedeford as Chairman and Managing Director, had become unwieldy. Freddie produced sensible proposals, many of which after Stedeford's retirement were adopted; but he was not invited, as many expected, to become managing director of the group, as Stedeford was not persuaded to change his style of management and delegate his personal authority. So Freddie returned to South Africa, and was to retire finally from TI in 1970.

But before that came about he was to become involved in yet another commercial enterprise, this time concerned with tobacco, the raw material to which the de Guingand family's fortunes had been linked at the time of Freddie's birth in 1900. He was asked in 1960 by Dr Anton Rupert to join his Rembrandt/Rothmans group which had recently acquired 50% of the voting shares of Carreras Ltd based in London. Freddie accepted, first on a part-time basis, and soon became Rupert's deputy chairman of Carreras and shortly afterwards chairman. This venture, which again was successful, resulted in a move of the de Guingand family to the United Kingdom.

In this varied career in industry he had played many parts: after the misfortune of Gemsbok he had revived the Ace Cycle Company by hard work, enlightened management and skilful use of experts:

Freddie, as author, tycoon and sportsman, returning to Johannesburg from Chicago.

Monty's 'First Eleven' fifteen years later: *Back row*: Harry Llewellyn, Oliver Poole, David Belchem, Sidney Kirkman, Brian Horrocks, Geoffrey Keating, Sandy Galloway, Gerald Templer, Johnny Henderson, Bill Williams, Author; *Front row*: Oliver Leese, Bobby Erskine, Monty, Harry Broadhurst, Freddie, Slap White, Brian Robertson.

Freddie, principal speaker at Bloemfontein Memorial.

in Anglo-Vaal's commission to the United States he had displayed his exceptional talents in diplomacy and negotiation while skilfully exploiting his war-time contacts with prominent Americans: with Tube Investments and Rothman's International he had frequently been used in other capacities as 'trouble shooter' or as a top-level 'fixer' in a quasi-diplomatic role in the numerous countries to which he was so happy to travel. He had always had a powerful urge to make a fortune, and he enjoyed the glitter of tycoonery. It was not uncommon to see him engaged in talking to a friend while holding a telephone to each ear, linking Johannesberg with New York.

As a reaction to the callous treatment he had received in 1946 Freddie in South Africa was determined to demonstrate that he was not just Montgomery's creature, the wayward officer into whom 'Master' had breathed life, but a man in his own right, to be seen on the world's stage demonstrating talents which extended far beyond those of a mere soldier.

Yet paradoxically he never ceased to hope for some military role. In November 1950, when Eisenhower's appointment as Supreme Commander in Europe was announced, Freddie wrote to him enquiring whether Bedell Smith would be joining him again: 'Now that I am fit once more, it makes me rather hanker after playing a part with the old team once again.' On 29th December he telegraphed Eisenhower saying that he did not know whether his old master would remain in the new organisation, but in any case he himself might play a useful part at some stage. He followed this up on 2nd January 1951, explaining to Eisenhower that he was not an out-of-work soldier looking for an assignment, but merely wanted to help if he thought fit. He indicated that, if Montgomery were to hold some post, his own services would be available or, if Montgomery retired, there might be an appointment for which his experience would fit him. Presumably Freddie was hinting here at an appointment as Deputy to Eisenhower. Late in 1952 he put himself forward as a contender for the job of Secretary General of NATO. Although Eisenhower sent courteous non-committal replies to all these suggestions, nothing came of them.

However with the help of his wealthy influential friends who admired his qualities he prospered in his role as tycoon. Only in one aspect of his life, success was absent: his marriage. For some years past relations between Freddie and Arlie had been difficult, and in 1957 a divorce was granted in Pretoria; Freddie obtained custody of his teenage daughter, Marylou, to whom he was deeply attached. In his busy life he had always shown a devoted interest in her, and had even found time to write and print at Marylou's request a children's book of 143 pages. The story, from a keen racehorse owner, was inevitably packed with equine adventures as well as romance.

In South Africa before very long he became a well-known personality, while in the United Kingdom and in the United States his opinions, particularly about Africa, were valued and respected. The large income derived from his many directorships enabled him to develop and enjoy his sporting interests, and to treat his friends and family with great generosity. But behind all this intense activity he was impelled by an idealistic motive; that the peoples of the African continent, black, coloured and white, might be reconciled and live in harmony and prosperity. The future of Africa was always placed high on his personal agenda. Freddie now a public figure, established author and successful tycoon, simultaneously devoted great efforts to the solution of that problem.

CHAPTER FOURTEEN

The Future of Africa

In his search for a constructive policy for the development of the continent of Africa, Freddie was fortunate in finding that Montgomery had a shared interest, although focused in his case primarily on defence. Freddie's own motivation, amounting almost to a passion, went back to those early years in Nyasaland where he had kept the peace under the primitive colonial conditions of that time. Apart from shooting every form of game from partridge to elephant, at which to the delight of his *askaris* he had become highly adept, he had gained some insight into the mind of the tribal African, whose life in the KAR in those days had been dominated by tough training, sympathetic administration, the paternal vigilance of young British officers and a regime of strict discipline. This was buttressed by an occasional sentence of twenty lashes awarded without benefit of trial by court martial. On Freddie those far-off days in Nyasaland had had a lasting effect; he had developed a genuine affection for the Bantu and a respect of his simple loyalty and latent ability.

The story, which started then, moves twenty-one years later to 1947, when Montgomery as CIGS wrote to Freddie before leaving on a world tour which was to finish at Southern Rhodesia and Kenya: 'I was delighted to get your letter on 26th May. It was a long time since I had heard any news of you. I hope you will keep me in touch with your doings; we have been through so much together that we do not now want to drift apart: just because our ways lie in different directions.' He then went on to tell Freddie of his War Office problems and continued: 'There are a vast number of things I want to tell you. But not in a letter. We must have a good talk when I come Salisbury (S. Rhodesia) in December; several hours will be necessary; fix it with Kennedy; we must be alone.'[1]

Montgomery was never a man to solicit favours; yet here he was

virtually pleading to patch up their differences and get back to the
old relationship. The letter shows the value he still placed on those
talks *à deux*, with their nostalgic associations all the way from
Alamein to Luneberg Heath.

In anticipation of the visit, Freddie sent Montgomery a copy of
a speech on 'British Commonwealth Planning' which he had made
to the 1820 Memorial Settlers Association. Taking as background
the desperate economic situation of Britain, he had argued that the
development of the Empire on a gigantic scale should be brought
about by the movement of capital and manpower to Commonwealth
countries. The Dominions and Colonies, he said, must cooperate in
such a plan; defence must be coordinated, and assistance from the
USA should be encouraged and welcomed. The relationship
between the Union and Southern Rhodesia should be strengthened,
and the Afrikaans and English-speaking peoples of the Union should
cooperate in much greater harmony.

These ideas of Freddie's, utopian as they seem, were acknow-
ledged by Montgomery in a letter in October:

7 Westminster Gardens
Marsham Street SW1

4 – 10 – 47

My dear Freddie

Thank you for your letter of 25 Sept which I was delighted to get. I
was very interested in your paper on 'Commonwealth Planning' and it
seems to me there is a great deal in what you say. One of the main
objects of my tour which begins on 15 Nov is to study all that problem;
as things are moving in the world today it is clear to me that Africa is
a highly important continent to the British Empire and one in which we
should consolidate our position. I will expand more on that subject when
we meet and will explain my ideas on what should be our overall world
strategy.

Meanwhile in Britain we are moving rapidly towards a crisis, the
potentialities of which we can but dimly discern. Europe is in deep
distress.

The CIGS went on to criticise Mountbatten's role in the recent
partition of India, and warned that in Britain he expected 'a Row'

in the spring. He then lambasted the Trade Unions for their unrealistic attitude to work. 'A showdown is needed and if the thing goes sky high I may have to play a part: and would do so.' 'I think you are needed in Africa' and, indeed, he prophesied, 'You are destined for great things in that Continent. You must safeguard your health; you will need it in the next few years and one cannot handle a big crisis if one is unfit.'

The visit, meticulously planned not only by Freddie but also by his old chief in his World War I role as a staff officer making lists of items to be packed, was a great success; and Freddie, a generous and accomplished host, was happy to bask in reflected glory, while Montgomery much enjoyed meeting some of Freddie's important business friends. He and Freddie discussed together the future of S. Rhodesia and of the Union, and the part that the African Continent should play in the defence of the Western world. Although problems of economics and defence were always uppermost in their talks, no discussion could have been complete without considering the problem of internal security and hence of racial policy both in Southern Rhodesia and the Union, viewed against the ever-present threat of Communist infiltration, of which the CIGS was well aware.

After his departure Montgomery wrote to Freddie from Government House, Kenya: 'I enjoyed our talks greatly and gained much good from them. I shall make things hum when I get home, on the subject of African Development.' He warned him again to be careful of his health (Freddie was to have a relapse only weeks later) and he concluded, 'We need you in South Africa if we are to get things moving along the lines we all want. So please do not over do it.'

During the next few years, Freddie and Montgomery kept up an exchange of views on these and kindred problems by correspondence and meetings. Freddie, already well known as the author of *Operation Victory*, was very active in making speeches and publishing articles on African race relations. In an important speech reported in the press, he condemned as defeatist the prevailing attitude taken in the Union that the progress of the African should be retarded for fear that he might catch up with the white man, and hence that he should be segregated. Though he did not use the word apartheid, he declared that unnatural restrictions on any large community were against the laws of nature. He recommended that a solution should be found by tackling the matter by stages, keeping a flexible mind in order to ring the changes as experience might point the way.

Montgomery, after his return to London, informed Freddie that he had sent the Prime Minister a copy of his report on his African tour ('very hot stuff'), which had been considerably influenced by Freddie. The Colonial Secretary had hated it, but Bevin and Cripps had agreed with it. He would show Freddie a copy in London ('too explosive for the post'). Then, keeping Freddie posted on his Whitehall problems he went on to comment on the ineffectiveness of the Chiefs of Staff Committee, and the need for an independent Chairman. He felt that Britain was moving towards a crisis – political or financial – and he would remain on hand in case he might have a part to play. It was vitally important to get the land forces of France and the Benelux countries built up on a proper basis and, in the line-up, it was important that Germany should 'march with the West'. In all these musings, Montgomery was already anticipating his future appointment as the military leader of Western European Union to which he would go after retiring from CIGS. Later, in 1949, Freddie would back up his old chief by publishing an article emphasising the importance of Western European Union, the need for harmony (Montgomery had written to him about his confrontation with General de Lattre) and the unique qualifications to Montgomery to lead WEU successfully. Montgomery wrote on 2nd September 1949 that he thought the article was 'very good'. 'He had been told that the general reaction in Allied staff circles in Fontainebleau was very favourable. He had no idea what de Lattre might think of it . . . the set-up for the Atlantic Pact (the genesis of NATO) was to be on the lines he had sketched during a visit Freddie had paid to Montgomery's chateau at Courance in France.

In January 1951 Montgomery, after a successful visit to Eisenhower, wrote to Freddie that they had discussed the shape of the command set-up in Western Europe . . . and that he (Montgomery) was 'wanted in the party' and that he had agreed. As regards Freddie's future he wrote:

In my view you should stay where you are and build up financial strength for your family. There will be no war in Western Europe in 1951; in my view the dangerous time will be 1952 . . . PS I will rope you in quickly enough if there is going to be any dirty work.

Freddie was still keen to march once more to the sound of the drums, but the dirty work did not appear.

Their previous cordial relationship appeared on the surface to have been restored by their shared interest in the future of Africa, and in little ways they helped each other. Montgomery, naive in financial affairs, had observed Freddie's business acumen, and had asked him to invest some money in South African shares to make a capital gain which would enable him to pay his income tax, a source of worry to the Field-Marshal. Freddie duly obliged. Later he arranged that Montgomery, once retired, should be retained as a consultant by Tube Investments Ltd at an appropriate fee. Freddie gave private dinners in London for Montgomery and his surviving comrades and he was a special guest at Alamein Reunions in London; they also played in double harness at various public events.

During the next few years, Freddie's position of influence in the Union was further strengthened by his increasing successes in business, by further visits by Montgomery and by the many newspaper articles he wrote, including expert commentaries on the Korean war, the probable duration of the Cold War and the chance of Russian agression, the part to be played by the Union in African defence, the need for German cooperation in the defence of Europe, and an analysis of the problem of Egypt, culminating in the Suez operation, of the conduct of which he was highly critical.

His virulent contempt for Eden, derived from his experiences in the expedition to Greece in 1941, was once again aroused, so much so that in London at the height of the Suez crisis on 5th September 1956 he obtained an interview with Hugh Gaitskell. Previously he had written him a letter of congratulation on his election as leader of the Labour Party, in which he had said that in his opinion the Tories ought either to get a new leader (in place of Eden) or give way to a new Government altogether. In Gaitskell's office he immediately launched into a bitter attack on Eden: reverting to the expedition to Greece, he stated that 'all the military evidence was absolutely against the campaign, and it was clearly going to be a disaster from the start. Eden had obviously made up his mind that we had to do it, was quite unscrupulous, and tried to make him fudge the figures, counting rifles as guns and things like that.' [ie, in the lists of available British military support to the Greek Government][2]

In much of Freddie's South African output it is possible to trace the confidential comments written to him by his old Chief covering the resurgence of Germany, the intentions of the Soviet Union, French fears that war with the Soviet Union would break out in 1952, and other topics. Freddie delighted in these verbal activities which gave free rein to his intellect and his quick analytical grasp of world affairs.

But the future of the African continent was never far from his thoughts, and in 1952 he published his second book of memoirs, *African Assignment*, and sent copies to Montgomery and other friends. The early chapters contained a spirited account, infused with humour, of Freddie's service with the King's African Rifles, based on his diaries and letters. In the foreword he wrote: 'Beyond all else I hope that this book will act as a small tribute to that fine corps the King's African Rifles. We were a happy band of brothers in every sense of the world, irrespective of colour.'[3] The last chapter 'South Africa revisited' was on a different theme. In sixty-six closely argued pages he put forward his views on 'South Africa's Great Problem'. Having stated that he refused to look forward to future relations with the African in terms of a rearguard, he defined his objective: to evolve a way whereby the various races in South Africa might live in harmony and the country prosper. He commented that no party in South Africa had put forward a really practical and constructive approach to the great problem of race relations, and this fact had been largely responsible for the avalanche of adverse criticism from overseas. He then described the complex diversity of the various races in South Africa, together with a short history of each. After a summary of recent industrial progress, he criticised the industrial colour-bar created by the Trade Unions which he attributed to a sense of fear, and then recited the aims of the various political parties. He ruled out a policy of suppression, as such a course was out of date and would lead to ultimate disaster. Equally he discarded an extreme liberal policy because no existing political party would ever obtain support for it. (At the time of writing the new Liberal party had not been formed). He then considered 'Apartheid' and identified the following features as viewed by him in the year 1953:

(1) Social segregation.
(2) No mixing of the races.
(3) The African to be helped and encouraged to develop in his own areas – to the highest levels.
(4) The non-European to have full political rights in his own areas and even to sit as members of the senate
(5) No European to have political rights in the 'native' areas.
(6) No non-European to have the vote in the European areas, but he could if he chose find employment and live there.
(7) The European to hold all the power in the European areas.

He commented that although that plan looked attractive, in practice it would be faced with insuperable difficulties, and concluded that only a compromise solution, a middle course brought into operation by stages, could provide a long-term solution. The immediate steps were not defined with any precision, but he visualised that improvement in food, housing, health and education should take first priority. The two races, white and black, must not be split into two camps, nor must the position of the Europeans be jeopardised, as they had contributed so much to the advancement of the Union and would continue to do so. The industrial colour-bar should gradually be modified, and the non-Europeans must eventually have some political representation, provided the Europeans' position was safeguarded.

He visualised that an American loan (under Point 4) would be needed to supplement the finance from the South African tax-payer, and he encapsulated his proposals in an illuminating diagram (see page 218).

African Assignment received much publicity in the Press of South Africa and in the principal London newspapers. Many reviews were

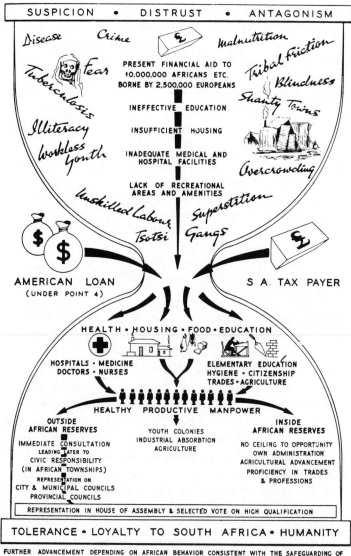

Diagram illustrating Freddie's proposals for African advancement, published by Hodder & Stoughton in 1953 in African Assignment.

complimentary; but from a minority there were comments such as 'a naive political commentator with a negative line, sitting on the fence.' Laurens van der Post, after praising the early part of the book took issue, with Freddie's last chapter, writing that he had 'failed to grasp the extreme gravity of the internal problem which had seized South Africa.'

Nevertheless Freddie, aware from his travels on business of the world-wide criticism of the Unions's racial policy, was not to be deterred and, in 1958 with some friends including 'that fine citizen' Eric Gallo, he initiated the South Africa Foundation. The concept of a South African group to combat 'the cold war' waged by the western world against the Union had first been discussed by Gallo with the Head of the South African Information Office, which as an official propaganda agency was inevitably suspect. It was agreed that to achieve any success the group must be a voluntary non-political body composed of both English-speaking and Afrikaans-speaking citizens of varying political persuasions, but all dedicated to presenting the Union's case honestly both at home and overseas.

Gallo reported this discussion to Freddie, who as the author of *African Assignment* found it constructive and attractive; the past-master of planning then put down his thoughts in a paper which accurately forecast the Foundation's development over the next twelve years. Soon the two founders mobilised moral and financial support from friends and business acquaintances. The first Annual General Meeting of the Foundation was fixed from 14 December 1959 and an announcement was made in the Johannesburg Press as follows:[4]

SOUTH AFRICA FOUNDATION TO BE LAUNCHED THIS WEEK

Most Important event in Union for many years. Leading citizens in bid to present positive picture.

A group of 24 well known English and Afrikaans speaking South Africans will meet this week to launch the South Africa Foundation.

Because of the status, prestige and influence of the sponsors, the formation of the South Africa Foundation is regarded as one of the most important and worthwhile steps taken in South Africa for many years . . .

Sir Francis de Guingand is quoted as saying: 'While true things are being said about us which we do not like, a lot of untrue things are also being said. It is these untruths we propose to fight. In addition a lot of good things about South Africa are never said. We propose to say them. Our purpose is to show the world that South Africa has made a massive contribution to the development of Africa and to the welfare of its peoples. And what many people do not understand is that South Africa had done more for these people than has been done in any other territory in Africa. The South Africa Foundation is non-political and its sponsors are drawn from all groups. The calibre and quality of these men are a complete guarantee of its independence and goodwill.

'The South Africa Foundation's work will consist primarily of disseminating information abroad about South Africa with the emphasis on the soundness of South Africa's economy, its attractiveness as a field for investment, its efforts to improve the welfare of the people of Africa, and the part that it is playing and should play in the Western Community of Nations.'

Freddie took the chair at a management meeting which followed; it included many men who controlled much of the private wealth of South Africa. He re-stated the objects of the Foundation and ended by saying that people in South Africa had been living together for over 200 years in a multiracial society: they would have to continue to do so and it was therefore absolutely essential that they find the right solution. He was then unanimously elected President, thereafter Vice-Presidents, Trustees and members of the Executive Committee were duty appointed. It was decided to work out a plan to raise an initial £50,000 to cover primarily two professional fact-finding surveys.

Press reaction to the announcement was, in general, very favourable. The cogent point was made that, although the primary concern of the Foundation's members was to enlighten foreigners, they could not act in a vacuum, and part of their duty would be to warn the Union Government against measures and statements likely to cause 'avoidable misunderstandings'. The Afrikaans Press welcomed the Foundation and wished it success though regretting the necessity for it. One writer commented on the absence amongst the twenty-five founders of any woman, professor, artist, philosopher or farmer, and of the slender representation of men from the Orange Free State, Natal and South-West Africa. Only the left-wing view was hostile: under a headline entitled 'Foundation Cream', the writer referred to the Foundation as 'pathetic and frightening like a worn-out whore decked by the House of Dior'.[5]

In 1959 and again in 1961 and 1962 Montgomery, released from the position of Deputy Supreme Commander Europe, visited South Africa at Freddie's invitation. He had written to him with glee that the first edition of 140,000 of his *Memoirs* had been sold out and that a further 60,000 copies were being printed. Full of confidence as a best-selling author, he decided to write articles for the *Sunday Times* on the defence of Africa and the racial problem. His first article, 'A Plain View of Apartheid', showed Freddie's influence at work, but he was immediately attacked in the London Press for supporting apartheid.

In the year following its inauguration the infant Foundation also had to face great difficulties. Prime Minister Macmillan en route to South Africa on a goodwill visit made his 'wind of change' speech. The Pan-African Congress, a break-away group from the African Nationalist Congress, started its anti-pass campaign, leading to rioting and the death of many blacks at Sharpeville. Then in Cape Town a bill was passed banning the Pan-African Congress and the African National Congress: this led to panic on the Johannesburg Stock Exchange. Early in that year a mad farmer attempted to assassinate the Prime Minister. In October, after a referendum, a Republic was declared; and a year later at Lancaster House in London, Prime Minister Verwoerd withdrew the Republic's application for continued membership of the Commonwealth, thus breaking the link with Britain, which had been forged by Smuts and well-tempered in war and peace.

Against such an adverse background it was surprising that the Foundation survived. Much criticism was levelled against it for its inadequate response to these critical events, but it was heavily occupied in establishing a sound financial position and with attempting to introduce a broader non-white membership into its councils.

Freddie, as Founder President, took the chair at the AGM of 1960, which was attended by sixty-six trustees. He said that the events of the past year had only accentuated the need for concerted action, and spoke of the need for faith to create an atmosphere at home and abroad which would ensure the understanding and cooperation needed to work out solutions, which must be just and acceptable to all peoples. Charles Engelhard, who came from the United States, emphasised that South Africans must convince the world that they shared in the task of building up the dignity of man. The implication was clear: Government policies would have to change if the image of South Africa abroad was to improve.

The staff of the Foundation, as well as Freddie the President, had from early days maintained close contact with the Government. As far back as 1955, Freddie had approached Dr Verwoerd, then the Minister for Native Affairs with a proposal that a fund, to be raised by private companies, should be used to assist the living conditions of the Bantu population by improving their local transport facilities and their housing. In 1960 after the formation of the Foundation in the previous year he had an interview with the Prime Minister, at which the plans of the Foundation were discussed, and in December of the following year Freddie sent him an advance copy of his Presidential speech. In it he spoke of a change of heart overseas about South Africa's racial problems; there was no liking for them, but there was an improved understanding.

In July of that year the Foundation had launched an ambitious project to foster international goodwill, the so-called 'Man to Man' programme designed to expand personal contacts throughout the world in order to promote greater understanding of South Africa. Leif Egeland, a former South African High Commissioner in London, master-minded this project and Freddie, using his ambassadorial talents, made a great contribution to it. Following a personal approach by Freddie in London, Sir Alec Douglas-Home visited the Union as guest of the Foundation, and he was followed by Selwyn Lloyd, and Reginald Maudling and many other distinguished people. Through the contacts of the Foundation's trustees and of the members of branches established in the major capitals of the world a stream of journalists, politicians and business men arrived on fact-finding tours of the Union. Meanwhile Freddie on his frequent business trips exploited every opportunity to put South Africa's case to world political leaders in the USA and elsewhere.

He appreciated that the attitude of the United States to the problems of South Africa was crucial, and through his enduring friendship with Eisenhower he was able to generate sympathic understanding; but concrete support could not be expected from such a heterogeneous country. However he maintained contact with his friend and admirer, first in the Pentagon, later in the White House, and finally at Gettysburg, Eisenhower's retirement home; his friendship was sustained by visits and a lively correspondence extending from 1945 to 1968. The books which they published were exchanged with complimentary inscriptions, and Freddie repeatedly invited Eisenhower to South Africa, but without success. In 1954 an excellent article on 'Understanding America' written by Freddie and published in London was very well received by the President; in it Freddie proposed the establishment of a Trust to promote annually a two-months' visit by a thousand selected citizens from Britain and the USA – MPs, Trade Unionists, teachers, scholars, factory workers, the Press etc, and indicated that financial help from powerful Foundations such as the Ford would be needed. This scheme, with the object of promoting better mutual understanding between the two nations found favour with President Eisenhower, but never came to fruition due to lack of financial support.

When, two years later, Anglo-American relations became severely strained after the Suez debacle, he was in correspondence again with the President, spelling out his severe criticism of Eden. Eisenhower's attitude was that as a true friend he could not have encouraged action that he had believed to be unwise and even inexpedient, but he hoped that relations would now improve.

In an attempt three years later to restore mutual understanding and amicable relations, Freddie and the President started to plan a reunion at Camp David of some dozen notable guests from each country, drawn from those who had fought shoulder to shoulder in the war; one of the objectives was to produce an agreed document on the strategic controversy of 1944. But this again foundered because of financial problems, notwithstanding that those invited were to be the personal guests of the President, and their transportation in the United States provided. There was however a reunion dinner held for the President by the US Ambassador in

London on 1st September 1959, attended by Churchill and the war
leaders and their principal staff officers. Freddie was there, and
Montgomery was included despite the rift in his personal relations
with Eisenhower, which was now final. The Field-Marshal,
somewhat embarrassed, arranged for Freddie to escort him, while
Eisenhower thought it best to demonstrate to the British public his
unconcern with Montgomery's charges.

Freddie in his attempts to create a more enlightened appreciation
in the United States of the problem of South Africa wrote at length
to his friend in 1962 and received encouragement; Eisenhower, now
a private citizen, sent copies immediately to the Secretary of State
and to leaders of the Republican Party. He appreciated 'receiving
the convictions of a thoughtful, patriotic and Western-oriented man
who lived in South Africa, and he urged his compatriots towards
study and moderation, as time would be necessary to find a
solution'.[6]

But Freddie was facing revolutionary forces of a strength which
he may not have fully appreciated. The wind of change had not
abated the time was marching on. The Foundation's policy was
cautious and certainly not revolutionary. It was still intent on
supporting the principle of separate development, accompanied by
great improvements in the living and working conditions of non-
whites and in their education, and the removal of existing petty
restrictions imposed on racial grounds. The Foundation continued
to rule out both universal suffrage and a qualified vote, the first
because in their view the whites would never accept it, and the
second because the non-whites would never be satisfied with it. Yet
there were moments when the National Party Government showed
signs of anxiety that the Foundation might turn into a pressure
group; this was refuted by a semantic reference to its constitution.
It was evident, nevertheless, that the Foundation's objective of
advancing the prosperity of *all* the races of the Union could not be
achieved without major changes in Government policy, and that the
publicising of South Africa's case round the world must contribute
to that demand for change.

In his Presidential address of 1963 Freddie referred to the
sophisticated well-financed campaign against South Africa
conducted on a world scale. The origins of this attack and the

Freddie entertains his old chief at a London restaurant, where the chef was a wartime comrade.

Meeting of the South Africa Foundation: the Founder President speaks.

Monty's Eightieth Birthday Party at the Royal Hospital Chelsea: *Back row*: Kit Dawnay, Hugh Mainwaring, Simbo Simpson, Johnny Henderson, Bill Williams, Author, Llewellyn Wansborough-Jones, Dixie Redman, George Cole, Richard Sharples; *Front row*: Freddie, Monty, Brian Robertson, Miles Graham, John Harding, Oliver Leese.

Monty's funeral: Freddie (*bottom right*), pepped up with 'a king-sized injection' and with guardsman escort, marches up Windsor hill as a pall-bearer to his old chief.

finances to support it were not readily identifiable, he said, but it was obviously helping the East in its cold war against the West. South Africans were ready to admit errors in their attempts to solve one of the most challenging and complex problems facing the modern world – coexistence in a multi-racial society. But they were not prepared to let their enemies, under a cloak of so-called humanity, destroy what they had achieved . . .

In the same year he sent to General Eisenhower, now retired in Gettysburg, a comprehensive paper on the South African situation, in which he commented on the 'double standard' applied by the Great Powers at the United Nations, the justification as he saw it of the Ninety Days Detention Law, the true meaning of apartheid, the reason for rejecting any qualified vote, and the negative effect if sanctions were applied.

Eisenhower, without committing himself, had shown a great interest in the views which Freddie frequently expressed to him by letter and verbally on his visits, and this continued even after the President had retired. Typically, in a letter to Freddie dated 29 November 1966, Eisenhower wrote: 'Scarcely a week passes that I am not writing to some friend of mine urging more study of the South African situation before he makes some pronouncement about the problems and situation of that country as they now exist.'[7]

Meanwhile in South Africa Freddie had continued to publicise his themes at every opportunity such as the unveiling of war memorials, opening of exhibitions, presentation of school prizes, or as guest of honour at various dinners. He had also visited England frequently on business, combining this with dinners for Montgomery, Alamein reunions and, notably, the farewell Army Council dinner to Montgomery on his final retirement as Deputy Supreme Commander, Europe in 1958. Montgomery had insisted Freddie should attend, writing to the Council Secretary: 'Anything I have been able to achieve during the late war could not have been done if he had not been at my side.'

Nevertheless as a public figure from South Africa, Freddie was strongly attacked by the Anti-apartheid movement in Britain with a pamphlet 'The Collaborators', issued with a foreword by Barbara Castle. However he was in good company, as the other so-called collaborators accused of 'building and defending apartheid' included Engelhard, Anton Rupert, Lord Fraser of Lonsdale, Lord Brabazon of Tara and many other notabilities.

At the Foundation's 1964 Annual General Meeting he made a plea for the relaxation of petty apartheid while maintaining the policy of separate development, and one newspaper urged Dr Verwoerd to 'heed Sir Francis' words'. Again, as a guest of honour at the South Africa Club's dinner at the Savoy Hotel in London 1964, attended by a distinguished company including Montgomery, Robertson of Oakridge, Stedeford and Cayzer, Freddie said that there were things going on in the Republic which were difficult or impossible to defend, but that the conditions enjoyed by all races were nothing like as bad as many people in England believed. Their country was not a police state and they found the attitude of the United States bordering on the hypercritical. The chairman of the dinner, the South African Ambassador in London, Carol de Wet, greatly appreciated his speech, and a South African newspaper reported it in full under the headline 'De Guingand explains South Africa in London'. Eisenhower, to whom Freddie had sent a copy of his speech wrote to say how impressed he was by it, and he agreed that 'people are always prone to take a 'holier than thou' attitude when they look at someone else's problems and deficiencies'. Montgomery also delivered a short speech 'fired off like a runaway sten gun' declaring that if Britain took part in sanctions against South Africa it would be a calamity of the first magnitude. Fortunately Freddie in previous talks with British politicians of both parties had already been reassured on that point.

During the next seven years until his retirement from the Presidency of the Foundation on 9th December 1971, Freddie made further speeches at Annual General Meetings, and at Graduation Ceremonies at various universities; all showed a remarkable grasp of the world scene. He continued to preface these with cogent reviews of topical developments as they affected South Africa, commenting on the break-up of British power in the Middle East and the Persian Gulf, Russian activity in the Indian Ocean, the enduring strategic importance of the Cape Route and the lack by the Western Powers of a global policy in the military and political spheres. He fulminated against the unpredictability and irrelevance of the United Nations Organisation, and the fickleness of American policy towards South Africa, which in his view was over-influenced by their negro vote and their desire to appease the Afro-Asian bloc. He criticised the imposition of the arms embargo, but concluded that attempts to isolate South Africa were proving fruitless.

On the racial problem, which in his view was the most explosive problem confronting the whole world, he moved slowly, claiming that the living conditions of the non-whites in South Africa were better than those of their brothers in the African countries which had recently gained their independence. He pointed to the lawlessness, bloodshed and economic disaster, which appeared to be the normal accompaniments of majority rule elsewhere in Africa.

By 1971 the Foundation after seven years had become a respected organisation, well-supported financially by important citizens of both language groups, and active in presenting the Republic's case in the Foundation's well-established publications and through their international committees in the principal capital cities of the world. At the Annual General Meeting of that year, Freddie now aged 71 decided to hand over to a younger man. He seized the opportunity to speak out more boldly, as was manifestly necessary in view of the deteriorating political situation, evidenced by a newspaper article in Canada where Freddie was well known. It stated that South Africa in the eyes of much of the world community, was a pariah; it was a nation ruled by wicked, frightened men who had woven a network of despicable laws that offended against every concept of justice and were framed to deny the basic equality of all mankind.

By contrast the *Rand Daily Mail* which, over the last twenty-three years had published so much of Freddie's immense output, reported on his courageous speech as follows:

CRACK IN THE FOUNDATION

It is a measure of the extent to which the Government has fallen out of step with the times that even such a pillar of the Establishment as the South Africa Foundation should feel constrained to criticise it on some pretty fundamental issues. Never before has the Foundation raised its voice in criticism of the Government on a policy matter. Its declared purpose when it was launched 12 years ago was to 'present the positive South African story to the world', and it has always interpreted that to mean criticism was negative and therefore to be eschewed.

Yet now, out of the true blue as it were, it has upbraided the Government quite sharply. In Durban on Wednesday night the president, Major-General Sir Francis de Guingand, called for free social contact between the races at the highest possible level; he attacked job reservation and influx control; and he urged a review of all discriminatory legislation to see whether much of it could not be scrapped or modified . . .

One can see what has happened to the men who run this organisation. They are business men, and they are also propagandists for South Africa, and apartheid is making life pretty well impossible for both these days. Job reservation has become a nightmare to the business man while, as Sir Francis says, it is becoming more and more difficult to defend overseas. Likewise with influx control. Thus have these exasperated gentlemen finally been driven to dropping a little gravel into their white-wash bucket.

But the real significance of Sir Francis's speech lies in the change of attitude among the business community that it reflects. A few years ago the business community was prepared, broadly speaking, to stand by the Goverment – even if only in a professedly 'non-political' way. At least the Government was efficient, and apartheid appeared to be providing stability in an otherwise turbulent continent.

How all that has changed. Now the business men are standing up one after another, day after day, to strike out against apartheid. Building men, motor men, radio men; organised industry, organised commerce . . .

Et tu, Francis.

Freddie, with his trustees certainly pointed the way, but successive governments if they heeded his cautious words moved too slowly. The political development of Africa in the period 1960 to 1986 has had, as Freddie feared in 1953, the nature of a rearguard action. Time was not on his side, and five years after his death the mounting crisis was all too evident. From the comprehensive Annual Report of the Foundation for 1984 two paragraphs may be taken: the first from the Director General's report, shows the undoubted success of one aspect of the organisation founded by Freddie:

After a bitter struggle for at least the first 15 years of its existence to gain acceptance and credibility in our target areas abroad, to convince them of our independence and our non-partisan role, the breakthrough finally came. In the last few years we have built up an impressive record of personal contact and private discussion at the top levels of business and government round the world. Much of the credit for these satisfactory developments must go to our National MM Committees and also to foreign diplomats who have served in South Africa over the years. They have been able to assess the Foundation for themselves at first hand and their reports back to their home countries have helped to open many vital doors for us . . .[8]

However, the second paragraph taken from the President's address of 1984 struck a sombre note:[9]

. . . South Africa has seldom if ever found itself in a more unenviable situation than at present. International condemnation of our policies has reached new peaks. Anti-South African campaigns are increasing and have undoubtedly and more significant successes than ever before. Our economy is ragged and to cap it all we have simmering unrest in our black townships and unpredictable instability in our labour force.

Worse was to follow. It is too early to give the verdict of history on that courageous and optimistic initiative made in 1959 by Freddie and his friends, and pursued by him with such energy and selfless devotion for the following eleven years. Some mitigation of the 'rearguard disaster' can perhaps be claimed: a gallant failure would be too harsh an epithet. Let us call it a noble attempt: the harvest came too slowly, and was overtaken by the first wind of change which brought tempests in its wake.

But the name de Guingand has now found a place in the history of the Republic of South Africa. His services to his adopted country were recognised by the award of 'The Great Star of the Order of Good Hope', the Union's highest decoration; it was a much more meaningful recognition than the Soviet order of Kutuzov 1st class sent in 1945 to Freddie by Marshal Zhukov through Montgomery, who had written across the corner in red ink:[10]

> Dear Freddie,
> Herewith the doings
> Yrs ever
> B.L.M.

CHAPTER FIFTEEN

The Shadows Fall

Death would soon claim the aged Field-Marshal despite his vigorous activities on the world stage in the closing years of his life. Freddie, thirteen years his junior, still immensely active but dogged by ill-health which he faced with great fortitude, was moving towards the same destination: it was doubly tragic therefore that the enigmatic post-war relationship between the idiosyncratic commander and his partner in battle, should yet again founder needlessly, to be salvaged only by the intervention of loyal friends.

The incident that sparked off the rupture was the visit of Montgomery to the Alamein battlefield in 1967, an event sponsored by the *Sunday Times*, the editor of which, Sir Denis Hamilton, was a friend of the Field-Marshal and had helped him with his literary activities. The project was mooted in 1966; early in 1967 Freddie heard of it and, in his capacity as Montgomery's Chief of Staff during the battle, expected to be included. Greatly surprised, he wrote to Montgomery and received the following laconic reply:

8.1.67

My dear Freddie,

Yes, you are quite right. I plan to visit the Alamein battlefield in May next. It is the 25th anniversary of the battle, and it is my 80th year . . .

It is a very small party, and a very 'closed shop'. I shall have a talk with Nasser in Cairo; he has agreed to this. I am very fit. But do not seem to get any younger.

Freddie, much distressed, confided his troubles to his friend Eisenhower who in his reply diagnosed jealousy as the cause of Montgomery's strange behaviour. This verdict was simplistic: there was more to it than that. Montgomery's Alamein event, if Nasser were to act as expected, was to be more than a nostalgic visit to a battlefield: like many of Montgomery's previous sallies it was expected by him to have a political impact. In such a scenario, Montgomery as always would wish to stand alone.

But Freddie, who had been encouraged, motivated and brought to military prominence by Montgomery had, since 1946, radically changed his persona. He was no longer the anonymous Chief of Staff behind the scenes: by now he also was a public figure, though on a different scale.

He was recognised in many capital cities by the Press as a wealthy man of affairs ready with shrewd, urbane comment on world events, including the choice topic of his special relationship with the Field-Marshal. As such might he not upstage the central figure? That would never do.

So instead of his Chief of Staff, Montgomery took Hugh Mainwaring, who had been captured immediately after the Alamein battle. Mainwaring performed his duties admirably as a high-powered ADC, succeeding even in pin-pointing from a helicopter the location of Auchinleck's headquarters in the Desert where Montgomery in 1942 had prematurely assumed command of Eighth Army. By choosing Mainwaring, Montgomery was able also to offer some recompense to him for that fatal error in a moment of post-Alamein euphoria when he was despatched to reconnoitre the next position of Army Headquarters well beyond Rommel's rearguards, leading to the capture of the entire reconnaissance party.

Montgomery with some embarrassment could have explained to Freddie the reasons for his choice. It would however have meant disclosing his innermost thoughts on their changed relationship which, cordial as it was, was nevertheless sustained, as with all others, at arm's length. The coded phrase 'closed shop' was an easier option.

For Freddie, worse was to follow. Barred from the 'closed shop', he wrote a letter of protest which Montgomery, inflated perhaps by his triumphant reception in Egypt by Nasser and the adulation of those who had accompanied him, categorised as 'impudent'. As a punishment, Freddie was to be barred from Montgomery's 80th birthday dinner in November 1967. This was to be an important reunion following the many informal dinners that Freddie had given to his chief in the intervening years. It was to take place at the Royal Hospital, Chelsea, where Simpson, who organised the event, was Governor. Dempsey and Leese, on becoming aware of Freddie's proposed exclusion, threatened not to attend; so Freddie was reprieved and was present having in Montgomery's phrase now become 'penitent'. Dempsey however, whose sensitivity was comparable to Freddie's, maintained his boycott.[1]

Again, this callous wound, which must have reminded Freddie of 1946, remained unhealed. Robertson, a man of great integrity who knew them both well, almost despaired at this petty display of human folly. 'I told both of them,' said Brian Robertson, 'You are old men now; you must not behave like children.'[2]

Happily in the following year 1968, at the marriage at St Margaret's, Westminster of Freddie's sparklingly attractive daughter Marylou to John Henderson, Montgomery, the godfather, now aged eighty behaved well. Although showing some tendency to take command of the proceedings and terminate them too expeditiously, he made an admirably witty speech in proposing the health of the bride and groom.

Four years later at the age of 72 Freddie, having handed over in Johannesburg the presidency of the South Africa Foundation and having resigned from Tube Investments and Carreras, moved his 'base' to a sumptuous flat in Cannes. He still maintained touch with his many friends round the world, and made new ones in Cannes who cherished him in his later years when he was increasingly disabled by serious illness, and a game of bridge was his main relaxation. Montgomery, too, after the strain of two world wars and great activity thereafter was nearing the end of the road. Freddie still visited him. The Field-Mashal lacked other intimate friends but held court at Isington Mill, receiving from time to time chosen wartime comrades, who often were instructed in advance not only on the hour to arrive but also the time to depart.

With his brother and son at his bedside the Field-Marshal died on 24th March 1976. Freddie had written an obituary for the *Sunday Times*, in which he recounted their earlier friendship and the great qualities of his chief as a commander in battle:

I studied the way the Field-Marshal operated with tremendous interest and it is worth recalling some of my impressions. Probably his greatest quality, beside being a real master of his profession, was his supreme self-confidence, and what is more important his ability to project this quality to all who served under him. This of course, helped build up a high morale, so vital in war. He achieved this by frequent visits to his troops and formations, by frequent visits to his commanders and by issuing from time to time his personal messages.

These measured phrases, suitable for an obituary, were less spontaneous and revealing than some paragraphs which had been written by Freddie thirty years before in *Operation Victory*:

> There was often a lot of smoothing out to be done when my Chief had been on the war-path, or explanations in more silky phrases after a 'Montygram' had gone forth. . . .
>
> I very soon learnt how to get what I wanted and even on occasion to make him change his mind. One had to wait for the right mood; it was no good tackling him with someone else there. An audience was not a help. When my great friend Miles Graham, who was the head of 21st Army Group Administration, and I used to go and see the Commander-in-Chief, I had a secret sign to ask him to leave the caravan when I knew that a talk *à deux* would prove more successful.[3]

In 1976 on 1st April at the request of David, Montgomery's son, Freddie took his rightful place as a pall bearer at the Field-Marshal's funeral at St George's Chapel Windsor. In the uniform of a major-general he accompanied five field-marshals, an admiral and an air-marshal. He was in very poor health due to a tumour affecting the pituitary gland which, despite painful treatment, continued to impair many of his functions. His doctor bolstered him up with drugs for the march up Windsor hill, and a sturdy guardsman was provided to shadow him in case the worst should befall.

This generous act of public homage should have brought down the final curtain on the enigmatic relationship between Freddie and his chief, but this was not to be. At the age of seventy-eight, he had decided to publish one more book, *From Brass Hat to Bowler Hat*, concerned primarily with his remarkable second career as author, tycoon and public figure in South Africa. With his mental vigour now in decline, he was assisted in knocking into shape the volumin-ous typescripts covering that story which since 1946 he had repeatedly produced. But like many old men at the end of a full and vigorous life his memory harped back to that ill-starred year, and at the end of his book the ancient grudges, of which two at least were well-founded, were again brought to public notice. Freddie's reputation needed no such bitter embellishment. The incidents of 1946 and 1967 will for ever cast a fierce light on the character of Montgomery, but they were well-known to a limited circle and adequately documented for future biographers. It was not the moment, only three years after the Field-Marshal's death to publish them to the world. Perhaps the long years of his self-imposed domicile in South Africa where he had achieved such great successes and won the admiration of a host of important and wealthy friends had so dimmed his judgement that he could no longer resist the temptation to put the record straight. Perhaps he was also influenced by the opinions of his greater hero Eisenhower, whose assessment of Montgomery had finally turned to utter contempt.

However, Freddie's achievement as the examplar of a Chief of Staff in modern battle remains unaffected by vagaries in the post-war relationship with his old chief. In those August days of 1942 he had faced a formidable challenge when, at the crisis of the North African campaign he had found himself taken over by a new commander to perform as Chief of Staff of an army, a role as yet undefined in British practice, and still lacking official sanction. In many ways he was an outside choice for the job. As a young man, his instincts had not been specifically tuned to a conventional military career: he had always had the urge to make a fortune in order to enjoy the good things of life and to pursue his expensive tastes. With his shrewdness, quick intelligence, and charismatic personality he could have succeeded in many other walks of life.

His experiences on the staff from 1939 to 1942 leading up to the climax of his career were not particularly relevant to the challenge that lay ahead; his best performance however had been sufficiently successful to catch the eye of both Wavell and Auchinleck. Ideally he should have had staff experience at the level of division and corps before finding himself Chief of Staff of an Army; but, lacking this, he had talents which fully compensated: an intuitive grasp of the articulated activities of a group of Allied divisions on a vast battlefield: a remarkable perception of enemy reactions 'over the hill': a brilliantly responsive intellect, a faultless memory and grasp of detail, and finally a deep-seated desire to generate cooperation at all levels by the exercise of humorous, friendly persuasion on a very personal basis.

Freddie was thus a splendid man to serve: accessible, never pompous and with a quick comprehension of all the varied problems presented to him and the authority to give immediate decisions. All of us, his devoted subordinates, followed him with admiration and affection.

Later as Chief of Staff of an Army Group, he demonstrated his great abilities as the head of an international team, planning and exploiting the greatest amphibious operation in military history. In that capacity, working with great urgency he coordinated a vast range of detailed preparations in a period of time that was dangerously short, relieving his chief completely of that burden, and thus releasing him for the duty which he alone could perform – the motivation of the commanders and soldiers he was to lead into battle.

In his contacts with American allies and to a lesser extent with Canadians and subsequently French, Belgians and Dutch, he was remarkably effective in translating Montgomery's decisive commands into a diplomatic form which was immediately acceptable. He was particularly successful with Eisenhower, Bedell Smith and Bradley who all had great confidence in him, and admired the way in which he smoothed out the rough edges created by Montgomery's single-minded pursuit of purely military policies regardless of their political implications.

In their memoirs written after the war, Eisenhower and Bradley paid tributes – glowing and accurate – to Freddie's personality and achievments. Commenting on Montgomery's behaviour in separating himself from his staff, Eisenhower wrote:

The harm was minimised by the presence in 21 Army Group of a Chief of Staff who had an enviable reputation and standing in the entire Allied force. . . . He lived the code of the Allies, and his tremendous capacity, ability and energy were devoted to the coordination of the plan and detail that was absolutely essential to victory.[4]

Bradley painted the same picture:

> Like Bedell Smith he was a dedicated staff officer, dedicated to
> anonymity and his job. De Guingand went one further by
> complementing the personality of his chief. In Freddie, as he was
> affectionately known to the American Command, we found a ready
> intermediary and peacemaker. For whenever the distant attitude of
> Montgomery ruffled a US staff, it was good old cheerful Freddie who
> came down to smooth things over . . . Although Freddie's popularity
> with the American Command stemmed partly from the adeptness with
> which he bridged our good relations, he was uncompromisingly devoted
> and loyal to his chief. De Guingand earned our affection not because he
> toadied to us but because he helped to compose our differences with
> justice and discretion.[5]

Some of Freddie's successes could have been achieved by other
brilliant staff officers of his standing. But few if any could have
matched him in one particular area of his mastery: his influence on
Montgomery. Only in war could the paradox have occurred that a
man like Freddie could establish with a man as unique as
Montgomery a partnership which, formed from two disparate
personalities, would create a duo which was greater and more
effective than the sum of its two parts. On the one hand was
Montgomery, once the awkward boy from an uneasy home who had
prepared himself exclusively for professional leadership in war: on
the other, was Freddie, raised from the happy home of an anglicised
French businessman, financially well-found to permit enjoyment of
the good things of life – yachting, fishing, shooting, horse-racing,
gambling and girls, rejected by the Navy and sent to Sandhurst as
second best, where the prize-cadet, achieving little distinction except
as the life and soul of any party, had remained quietly confident that
if he stuck to the Army his chance would come in war.

Montgomery, in the subject that he had made his own – the art
of war – showed an acute analytical mind reinforced by vast
experience and deep study, but outside that subject was untutored
and naive. Freddie, born in 1900, had missed World War I, and had
had no battle experience when he became Chief of Staff;
nevertheless his Gallic flair was combined with a most fertile mind
and an immensely quick grasp of military problems. Outside his

profession he was an urbane man of affairs who had mixed with other communities and, with that trace of foreign sophistication observed in his schooldays, was by nature a friendly extrovert. He was also a sensitive soul, and perhaps with his chief over-sensitive.

Montgomery, confident and secure in his military professionalism, and with a remarkable ability to sift the wheat of decision-making from the chaff of battlefield chaos was single-minded, didactic and ruthless. Freddie, by contrast, usually discerned more than one solution, and would often be happy that a commander-in-chief or indeed the chairman of a corporation would be at hand to make the final decision.

In their personal relationships also the contrast was maintained. Montgomery regarded by many as hardly a 'nice chap', yet capable of inspiring immense loyalty and even affection from those whom he used, as well as from young people like the Freddie of 1922 whom he could help and motivate, displayed on occasion a mean lack of consideration that defied belief. Freddie, a charismatic personality in any society, made friends so easily not only because he was by temperament tactful and diplomatic, but because under the carapace of military professionalism that he had to adopt in war everyone knew there lay a generous and warm-hearted spirit, eager always to inspire cooperation and build bridges.

Freddie defined the professional relationship thus:

> Between the C-in-C and his staff there must be complete mutual confidence and trust. In their discussions no subject should be banned, and the Chief of Staff must at all times be open and frank. Unpleasant facts must never be hidden from the Chief – although there are the right and wrong times to present them. The Chief of Staff must be able to adjust himself to his commander's habits, his likes and dislikes. He should watch out for even little things that irritate his commander. The C-in-C shoulders great responsibility and is the man who matters in the eyes of the fighting troops. The Chief of Staff therefore must be careful to do nothing which will detract from his Chief's position.[6]

Freddie went on to summarise the techniques which had enabled him not only to execute so faultlessly Montgomery's battle decisions throughout the long campaigns from Alamein to the Baltic, to which Montgomery repeatedly paid glowing tributes, but also to influence his master in a constructive way. Montgomery would on occasion give way to euphoria, but Freddie's judgement was often more realistic.

It was fortunate indeed that Montgomery's proposal in December 1942 at Benghazi that Freddie should be sent home to recuperate was not pursued; but there can be no doubt that Mongomery's subsequent exploitation of him, with his repeated interference with medical advice, contributed to Freddie's breakdown in health in 1945. However this was war, and Montgomery's phrase 'Freddie knows my ways' brought a penalty, which Freddie like any good soldier was only too willing to pay.

With such a debt owed to Freddie, how was it that Montgomery, despite a genuine mutual affection, could wound his pride so callously on at least two occasions? Possible answers can only be found in Montgomery's insecure personality. On the first occasion loss of face was involved if he were to disclose that Alanbrooke had vetoed a decision that he, Montgomery, felt should have been his. He had unwittingly entangled himself in a potentially awkward situation by offering Freddie an appointment which in peace-time was no longer in his gift. Then by truncating Freddie's convalescence he had diminished the chances of his regaining the fitness which was essential to the job. Finally when faced with Alanbrooke's unexpected veto, Montgomery did not seize the chance of withdrawing from the impasse with some grace by offering a patient and sympathetic apology, but chose instead to deliver a brusque and cryptic dictum. So far as the ailing Freddie was concerned the matter, having misfired, would have to be settled for the good of the patient with a clean cut of the surgeon's knife: no bellyaching to follow.

On the second occasion, in 1967, of the Alamein visit followed later by the birthday dinner, Freddie's changed stature and his intimate links with Eisenhower, both casting doubts in Montgomery's mind whether he could keep 'his creation' on a leash, may have led to the further wounds, inflicted so childishly twenty-one years after the first.

After Montgomery's Alamein visit, Eisenhower had replied to a letter from Freddie:

The final paragraph of your letter of January thirteenth (1967) relates a shocking example of bad manners and arrogance. I think you suffer from the fact that too many people have recognised your incalculable value to the Allied Forces during W W II; this recognition has lowered your standing with one who ought to be exceedingly proud of it.[7]

Again in July of that year Eisenhower wrote to him:

I share you sadness over the abominable treatment you have received from a man who has every reason to feel deeply obliged to you for long years of service. Indeed I have often wondered how you found it possible to be so tolerant towards the whole affair. I suggest the best thing to do is to put it out of your mind.[8]

Ever since 1946 Freddie had been able to seek solace from the sympathetic Eisenhower and, increasingly, he had found in him a patron more congenial than Montgomery: inevitably this had affected their relationship. The former President died in 1969 but Freddie, invited to the funeral, was not fit enough to travel. In that same year, Montgomery's letters to Freddie ceased, and the Field-Marshal began to cut short his travels, withdrawing more and more into his peaceful home, where he died in 1976.

Deep in Freddie's heart Montgomery's wound never healed, but in the public eye, they were reconciled as the Field-Marshal's coffin was escorted up the hill to Windsor Castle.

Freddie will live in history as the perfect foil to Montgomery. After the war, in the battle of reputations in which so many great men joined, his fluency as an author led him to make statements which historians may yet dispute. But he remained, in public, despite Montgomery's savage pinpricks, a loyal supporter of his chief.

Montgomery himself searched for his place in history, and writers have compared him to Nelson and Wellington. Tedder once commented acidly: 'Monty thinks of himself as Napoleon.' But when Freddie heard that his own name had been linked with Berthier, Napoleon's Chief of Staff, he laughingly deprecated the idea: nevertheless Montgomery saw relevance in the analogy.[9] The contrast in historical context needs no emphasis, but a comparison was drawn by Montgomery between his meeting with Brigadier de Guingand on the road from Alexandria on 13th August 1942 and that of Lieutenant-Colonel Napoleon Bonaparte with Général de

As a staff officer he was superb, in my opinion. As a Chief of Staff he had no equal, again in my opinion.

It is difficult to compare him with other Chiefs of Staff, because there were none. I introduced the system when I made him Chief of Staff of the Eighth Army at 6.30 p.m. on the 13th August 1942. All others were merely Chief of the General Staff.

You would have to go back to Napoleon and Berthier, to get the comparison. Berthier was Chief of Staff, as is the continental custom.

When Napoleon left Paris, by carriage, to take command of the Army of Italy, in which army Berthier was Chief of Staff, he sent orders for Berthier to meet him at a rendezvous some miles from his H.Q. so that they could travel the last miles together and the C-in-C would get an idea of the situation before he took over.

I did the same with Freddie. I ordered him to meet me outside Alexandria, as you know. And when we arrived at Eighth Army H.Q. I knew pretty well what I was in for.

Freddie was, in fact, the first proper Chief of Staff in the British Army — and right well did he carry it through.

Extract from a letter sent by Field-Marshal Montgomery to Sir Edgar Williams, dated 7th March 1962.

Brigade Berthier, at Antibes on 25th March 1796. Both commanders were on the point of achieving military fame, and thereafter both were served with superb efficiency and exemplary loyalty by their Chiefs of Staff.

Subsequently, Montgomery's strange treatment of his Chief of Staff, which was compounded of public recognition of his services, high-handed exploitation and displays of affection punctuated by incidents of callous behaviour, appears exemplary compared to the Emperor's shameful treatment of Berthier, who was repeatedly cursed, and reviled in public.

But when disaster struck in the retreat from Moscow, Berthier, sorely wounded by his Emperor's unfounded criticisms and sour ingratitude, recalled a comment made to his staff: 'Remember that one day it will be a fine thing to be second to that man'. Later, Napoleon desperate with fatigue, sent a note to his Chief of Staff: 'Old friend, I believe I have not forgotten anything . . . If by any chance I should have forgotten anything and left any divisions or battalions behind, send me a list of them again.'[10]

This letter, like Montgomery's to Freddie after their rupture in 1946, was the signal for reconciliation, which even great men sooner or later are wont to seek. Amicable relations with Napoleon were restored, and Berthier and his staff continued to serve the Emperor with devoted efficiency. It was only at Waterloo, after Berthier's tragic death, wrongly suspected as suicide, that the staff no longer responded effectively to its commander's driving force, and Napoleon was moved to exclaim in sad frustration: 'If only my poor Berthier were here.'[11]

At Mareth, which for Eighth Army could have been a minor Waterloo, Montgomery, bereft of his habitual poise after the failure of his frontal assault, was heard that night to say: 'Send for Freddie.'

Those who marched with Montgomery from Alamein to the Baltic, and witnessed Freddie's contribution to those victories, will remember that phrase, a simple but significant tribute: it remains a fitting epitaph for a man who rendered great services to his chief and to his country, and earned the admiration and affection of all who served with him.

He died at Cannes on 29th June 1979.

NOTES AND SOURCES

A number of sources are referred to in abbreviated form as follows:

Alanbrooke   Archive: at Liddell Hart Centre, King's College
                  London
Bradley   *A Soldier's Story*. (New York 1951)
De Guingand   *Operation Victory*. (Hodder and Stoughton, 1947)
                  African Assignment. (Hodder and Stoughton, 1953)
                  Generals at War. (Hodder and Stoughton, 1964)
                  From Brass Hat to Bowler Hat. (Hamish Hamilton,
                  1979)
                  De Guingand Papers, now with Montgomery
                  Papers in the Imperial War Museum.
                  Typescript: autobiographical account, unpub-
                  lished.
                  Arnhem: note for posterity, unpublished.
Eisenhower   Dwight D. Eisenhower Library: de Guingand
                  letters, Bedell Smith letters *Crusade in Europe*.
                  (1948).
Ellis   *The Battle of Normandy* (HMSO 1962 and 1968)
Frankland   *Decisive Battles of the 20th Century* Noble Frankland
                  and Christopher Dowling: *Normandy 1944* (Ed)
                  Chapter by Martin Blumenson (19XX)
Gaitskell   *The Diary of Hugh Gaitskell. 1945–1946*, edited by
                  Philip M.Williams (Jonathan Cape)
Gerber   *The Diplomacy of Private Enterprise*, Louis Gerber
                  (Purnell 1973)
Grigg   *Prejudice and Judgement*, P. J. Grigg (London 1948)
Guedalla   *Middle East 1940–42. A Study in Air Power*.
                  (Hodder and Stoughton, 1944)
Hamilton   *Monty*, Vol I, *The Making of a General*. Nigel
                  Hamilton (Hamish Hamilton 1981): Vol II *The
                  Master of the Battlefield*. (1983): Vol III *The Field-
                  Marshal*. (1986)
Hinsley   *British Intelligence in the Second World War*, F. H.
                  Hinsley & others Vol I (HMSO 1979)
                  Vol II (HMSO 1981)
Lewin   *Ultra Goes to War*. Ronald Lewin (Hutchinson 1979)

Mainwaring	*Three Score Years and Ten*, H. S. K. Mainwaring. Privately published
Molony	*History of the Second World War*, Vol V, *The Mediterranean and the Middle East*, C. J. C. Molony (HMSO 1973)
Montgomery	Papers: Imperial War Museum
	Memoirs: B. L. Montgomery (London 1958)
Playfair	*The History of the Second World War*, Vol IV *The Mediterranean and the Middle East*. Playfair & Molony (HMSO 1966)
Regimental Journal	*Ca Ira*, Journal of the Prince of Wales' Own Regiment of Yorkshire
Richardson	*Flashback, A Soldier's Story*, Gen Sir Charles Richardson (Wm Kimber 1985)
Simpson	Letters: F. M. Montgomery to Gen Sir Frank Simpson. (Imperial War Museum)
Terraine	*The Right of the Line*, John Terraine (Hodder and Stoughton, 1985)
Watson	*By Command of the Emperor*, S. J. Watson
Williams	Address at Requiem Mass for Maj-Gen Sir Francis de Guingand 1979 Letter from Montgomery 1962 to Sir Edgar Williams

Chapter 1. Le Comte de Guingand
Pages 15 to 23

This chapter is based on information obtained from correspondence and interviews with members of the de Guingand family, the headmasters of St Benedict's School, Ampleforth College and Wellington College, Mr Brian Maples of the Royal Corinthian Yacht Club, de Guingand's contemporaries in the Prince of Wales' Own Regiment of Yorkshire, Archives of the Royal Military Academy Sandhurst, contemporaries at the Staff College Camberley, the Regimental Colonel of the Prince of Wales's Own Regiment of Yorkshire, the *Dictionnaire Historique et Geographique de la Haute-Vienne*, and Oppenheimer and Co Ltd.

1 De Guingand *Operation Victory* pp 165, 166
2 Montgomery: Letter to Sir Edgar Williams 1962
3 Ibid
4 Ibid
5 Regimental Journal

Chapter 2. Whiz-Bang in Africa
Pages 24 to 33

1 Regimental Journal
2 De Guingand typescript
3 Regimental Journal
4 Ibid
5 Montgomery: Letter to Sir Edgar Williams 1962
6 Montgomery Papers

Chapter 3. Playboy Student
Pages 34 to 42

1 The 'order of battle' is the detail of the organisation of the enemy's Armies, Corps, Divisions and Regiments.
2 De Guingand: *Operation Victory* p 19
3 De Guingand: Typescript p 28
4 De Guingand: *Operation Victory* p 38
5 Grigg: *Prejudice and Judgement* p 336

Chapter 4. Peerless Planner
Pages 43 to 56

1 Richardson: *Flashback* p 75
2 Letter from Lavinia Greacen re Maj-Gen E. E. Dorman-Smith
3 Field-Marshal Sir Geoffrey Baker and Field-Marshal Lord Carver
4 De Guingand: typescript p 89
5 *Operation Victory*, published in 1947
6 *Generals at War*, published in 1964
7 De Guingand: Typescript pp 83–88
8 Hinsley: Vol I p 398
9 Ibid p 399
10 De Guingand: *Generals at War* p 54
11 Ibid
12 De Guingand: *Operation Victory* p 102

Chapter 5. Intelligence Chief
Pages 57 to 65

1 Lewin: *Ultra Goes to War* p 161
2 De Guingand: *Generals at War* p 179
3 Sir Edgar Williams, who after the war became Warden of Rhodes

House Oxford, and Colonel 'Joe' Ewart who was killed in a car crash
on 1.7.45
4 Williams: Address
5 Ibid
6 De Guingand: *Operation Victory* p 122
7 Mrs Lavinia Greacen: letter to author

Chapter 6. Desert Warrior
Pages 66 to 72

1 De Guingand: *Generals at War* p 190

Chapter 7. Chief of Staff
Pages 73 to 83

1 Montgomery: *Memoirs* p 97
2 De Guingand: *Operation Victory* p 136
3 The late General Sir Frank Simpson, who had been Brigade-Major to
   Montgomery in 1939, and Chief of Staff of Montgomery's Corps in
   1940
4 Hinsley: Vol II p 410
5 De Guingand: *Operation Victory* p 189

Chapter 8. Partner in Triumph
Pages 84 to 101

1 De Guingand: *Operation Victory* p 151
2 Ibid p. 199
3 De Guingand: *From Brass Hat to Bowler Hat* p 10

Chapter 9. The Willing Horse
Pages 102 to 123

1 Hamilton: *Monty* Vol II p 15
2 Guedalla: p 207: quoted in Terraine p 380
3 De Guingand: *From Brass Hat to Bowler Hat* p 13
4 De Guingand: *Generals at War* p 71
5 Montgomery Papers: quoted in *Generals at War* p 70
6 Alanbrooke: Archive
7 Montgomery Papers: quoted in *Generals at War* p 81
8 De Guingand: *Generals at War* p 82

9 De Guingand: *Operation Victory* p 241
10 Ibid p 258
11 For morale purposes, Montgomery chose to use the same codeword as the final attack at Alamein
12 More accurately this should have been stated as 'Kittybomber and Warhawk'
13 Montgomery: *Memoirs* p 162

Chapter 10. Invasion Expert
Pages 124 to 140

1 Montgomery Papers: quoted in *Generals at War* p 88
2 Ibid
3 Montgomery Papers: quoted in Hamilton Vol II p 386
4 Molony p 236
5 Montgomery: *Memoirs* p 201
6 Mainwaring: *Three Score Years and Ten*, privately published 1976
7 Montgomery: *Memoirs* p 205

Chapter 11. Serving the Alliance
Pages 141 to 159

1 Montgomery: *Memoirs* p 207
2 Ibid p 222
3 Montgomery Papers: quoted in Hamilton *Monty* Vol II p 502
4 Ibid p 503
5 Williams: Letter from Montgomery 1962
6 Montgomery Papers
7 Ibid
8 Ibid
9 Ibid
10 Dwight D. Eisenhower Library
11 Frankland p 273
12 De Guingand: *Operation Victory* p 399
13 Ellis: *The Battle of Normandy* pp 265 353–5
14 De Guingand: *Generals at War* p 200
15 Hamilton: *Monty* Vol II p 739

Chapter 12. Victory and Eclipse
Pages 160 to 186

1 Lewin: p 341
2 The adjective actually used was one heard in the barrack room

3 Montgomery: *Memoirs* p 269
4 Richardson: *Flashback* p 186
5 Montgomery: *Memoirs* p 297
6 Author's italics
7 See Hamilton: *Monty* Vol III chs 5–7
8 De Guingand: Arnhem, note for posterity
9 PRO CAB 106/1124: Diary of Naval C in C 28.11.44
10 Hamilton: *Monty* Vol III pp 149 and 150
11 Montgomery Papers: quoted in *Monty* Vol III p 174
12 Simpson: letters from Montgomery
13 Author's comment
14 Montgomery: *Memoirs* p 318
15 Montgomery Papers: quoted in *Monty* Vol III p 279
16 De Guingand: Typescript pp 162–164
17 Alanbrooke Archive
18 Dwight D. Eisenhower Library. De Guingand letters
19 Montgomery Papers: quoted in *Generals at War* p 165
20 Author's italics
21 De Guingand Papers: Quoted in *Monty* Vol III p 593
22 The late General Sir Frank Simpson: interview
23 De Guingand: *From Brass Hat to Bowler Hat* p 114
24 De Guingand Papers: quoted in *Monty* Vol III p 601

Chapter 13. Author and Tycoon
Pages 187 to 210

1 Dwight D. Eisenhower Library: De Guingand letters
2 This and all subsequent letters are from Montgomery Papers
3 Major-General Sir Miles Graham who had been Chief Administrative
  Officer of 21st Army Group. He contended that due to the opening in
  September 1944 of Dieppe, Ostend, Boulogne and Calais, together
  with the establishment of a new advanced base in Belgium and the
  bonus of a further seventeen transport companies, it would have been
  adminstratively possible to support successfully Montgomery's
  proposed operation.
4 Dwight D. Eisenhower Library De Guingand Papers
5 Ibid
6 Ibid
7 Dwight D. Eisenhower Library. Italics are the author's
8 Letter to Sir Denis Hamilton 13.8. 1959
9 De Guingand: *From Brass Hat to Bowler Hat* p 33

Chapter 14. The Future of Africa
Pages 211 to 229

1 Montgomery Papers
2 Gaitskell Diary pp 595, 596
3 De Guingand: *African Assignment*: Foreword
4 Gerber: *Diplomacy of Private Enterprise* p 14
5 Gerber: *Diplomacy of Private Enterprise* pp 20, 21
6 Dwight D. Eisenhower Library. De Guingand letters
7 Ibid
8 South Africa Foundation Annual Report for 1984 p 14
9 South Africa Foundation Annual Report for 1984 p 15
10 Montgomery Papers: quoted in *Generals at War* p 151

Chapter 15. The Shadows Fall
Pages 230 to 241

1 The late General Sir Frank Simpson. Interview
2 Recounted to the author
3 De Guingand: *Operation Victory* p 189
4 Dwight D. Eisenhower: *Crusade in Europe* p 314
5 General Omar Bradley: *A Soldier's Story* p 209
6 Pamphlet: *The Principles of War* by Field-Marshal Montgomery; section on the Chief of Staff written by De Guingand
7 Dwight D. Eisenhower Library: de Guingand letters
8 Ibid
9 Williams. Letter from Montgomery 1962. The same comparison is drawn by Watson
10 Watson: *By Command of the Emperor* pp 50, 195
11 Ibid p 107

INDEX

Index

253

White Brig C.M.F. later Maj-Gen
    69, 155
Whiteley Brig 'Jock' later Gen Sir
    John 63, 64, 68
Whiz-bang 22, 29, 33, 57
Wilder's Gap 115
Williams Maj 'Bill' later Brig Sir
    Edgar 61, 81, 87, 99, 115, 139
Wilson F-M Sir Henry 48

World War I 21, 24, 69
World Wild Life Fund 26

'Y' Service (signals interception)
    81, 87, 92, 98
York 74

Zhukov Marshal 229
Zomba Mount (Malawi) 25